JANE'S
MERCHANT
SHIPPING REVIEW

Edited by A.J. Ambrose

Second year of issue

JANE'S

Copyright © Jane's Publishing Company Limited 1984

First published in the United Kingdom in 1984 by
Jane's Publishing Company Limited
238 City Road, London EC1V 2PU

ISBN 0 7106 0302 9

Distributed in the Philippines and the USA and its
dependencies by
Jane's Publishing Inc
135 West 50th Street
New York, NY 10020

Printed in the United Kingdom by
Biddles Limited, Guildford, Surrey

TITLE PAGE PHOTOGRAPH
Ever Guard. One of a class of 34,000 dwt container
ships completed in 1983 for Taiwanese owners
Evergreen by Japanese builders Ishikawajima
Harima's shipyard at Kure. (*FotoFlite, Ashford*)

Contents

Acknowledgements

The Editor would like to extend his thanks to all those who have contributed to the second edition of *Jane's Merchant Shipping Review*. Wherever possible credit for information, photographs, statistics, etc has been given. However, we would like to particularly thank the following people and organisations without whose help and knowledge of the various spheres of the merchant shipping field this publication would not have been possible:

Phil Neauman and staff of *FotoFlite* of Ashford, Kent; *Skyfotos* of New Romney, Kent for their assistance with photography; Ian Wells and members of the *World Ship Society* for their help with the collation of information, dates and photographs, and The Aims of Industry and the National Strategic Information Center for permission to use Captain Vladil Lysenko's article *From a Soviet Seaman's Eye* taken from the papers *The Challenge of Soviet Shipping*. Likewise, Jim Davis and also Nan de Halfweeg, who found time to make contributions, and the various military establishments within the United Kingdom and the United States.

Introduction: Shipping and Shipbuilding – An overview

by J G Davis MA(Cantab), FCIT

Banker and a director of the merchant bank Kleinwort, Benson Ltd. *Mainly concerned with situations appertaining to all forms of transport, Mr Davis is involved particularly in shipping and shipbuilding matters. He is a director of* Associated British Ports, *an advisory Board member of the Danish shipping major* J. Lauritzen A/S, *and* DFDS Danish Seaways, *and is currently Chairman of the* International Maritime Industries Forum. *He is also Deputy Chairman of a new cruise Company operating the cruise ship* Pearl of Scandinavia, *and Vice-President of the international* World Ship Society.

How nice it would be to write some optimistic and happy words about the prospects for shipping and shipbuilding in 1983. It is becoming wearisome to read – indeed to write – more and more doomladen statements about the present position.

I think the most optimistic feature is that some people – an increasing number – are beginning to realise that the ten year old crisis is not a 'typical cyclical affair' but instead has some chronic features that just will not go away.

The unhappiness of the British owners is well-chronicled. They see a declining fleet enjoying a fast declining share of world trade. It is a complicated state

One of the last stable areas of maritime trade are some of the boxship liner routes. However, with massive new-building programmes such as the Evergreen and United States Lines ordering of the past two years, even these trades do not hold much hope for the future. (*A J Ambrose*)

There is at least 150 million deadweight overcapacity in the tanker trades. But new ships continue to be built. (*FotoFlite, Ashford*)

The bulk trades are in a depressing state of imbalance, yet no less than 243 new bulk carriers are on order in 1983. Among many newly completed this year, are the *Neptune Altair*, *Ocean Prosper* and *Bulk Trader*, relatively minor examples of the flood of new tonnage. (*FotoFlite, Ashford*)

of affairs but I would inject a word of caution into the vehement protestations of the GCBS. Who is to say just how big the United Kingdom fleet *should* be? Despite its decline we still have a fleet whose size far exceeds the requirements for the UK's indigenous trade. We are still – despite an increasing lack of true competitiveness – significant and successful cross-traders. I recall the words of Sir Nicholas (now Lord) Cayzer, the Chairman of British & Commonwealth who wrote a few years ago: 'The high tide of British shipping is in the past. It was in my grandfather's day in the last century. But this is a story of change rather than failure. The high point was probably the Great Exhibition of 1851. Shipping depends on goods and we were the workshop of the world. Since then the terms of trade have gone steadily against us.'

But the UK is not alone in its discomfiture. Other North European countries are having similar problems: Norway mostly in the bulk trades, Germany in bulk and liner alike, Sweden and Holland the same . . . and so on.

The comparative advantage of operating ships (in terms of crew costs) has unmistakably turned towards the countries of the Far East. And further to complicate the situation are the aspirations of the Third World countries as now codified in the Unctad Liner Code, which imposes on the signatory nations a recognition of the 40:40:20 arbitrary allocation of liner cargoes (40 per cent to the flag vessels of the exporting nations: 40 per cent to those of the importing nations: and only 20 per cent to the cross-traders).

The tanker trades have remained for all nations in a state of desperate slump. There is still an overhang of at least 50 million dwt of surplus tonnage, particularly in the ULCC and VLCC categories. There has been a healthy increase in the number of these ships going for scrap – a policy long advocated by IMIF – but the

pace even yet is not sufficient.

The dry bulk trades are similarly in a state of depressing imbalance with too many ships chasing too few cargoes. And to the astonishment of all thinking people owners have in 1983 been tempted by 'Bargain Basement . . . unrepeatable' prices offered for newbuildings particularly by the Far Eastern yards, Japanese and Korean. No fewer than 243 vessels of the 'handy sized' 30–50,000 dwt bulkers have already been ordered in 1983. This includes the eccentric Sanko order estimated at around 120 vessels. I simply cannot understand the mentality of those who have ordered these vessels than that they are indulging in a cynical use (or abuse) of other people's money (the 'safe' government shipbuilding finance) and taking a reckless gambler's chance that the market may have changed enormously by the time the day of reckoning arrives. I would counsel these opportunists with the words of Thomas Jefferson: 'Never buy what you do

not want because it is cheap . . . it will be dear to you.'

But these deals reflect the major problem of the maritime industries in 1983 which is the still lingering over-supply of shipbuilding capacity worldwide. We probably still have more than double the capacity required, and every nation is preoccupied with the need to do something to help their shipbuilding industries, all of which are located in politically sensitive and generally depressed geographical areas.

In an appeal for economic sanity in dealing with shipbuilding problems I have in 1983 led IMIF delegations to such countries as Sweden, Holland, France, Italy, The People's Republic of China, Korea, and Japan, as well, naturally, as talking to our own UK Department of Trade and Industry. I am slightly encouraged by the outcome though there is great

Extremely low tenders in Korea have encouraged owners to acquire ships for which work prospects are bleak. Completed in mid-1983 was the 140,000 dwt *Bencruachan* for Ben Line steamers. (*Drawing: Michael J Ambrose*)

Scale: 1:1200

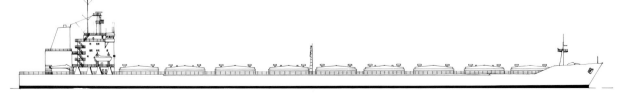

SONG OF AMERICA

difficulty in convincing such dedicated and aggressive shipbuilders as Mr Hong, the President of Daewoo Heavy Industries, Korea, who responded with disarming frankness as he looked at the International Mission: 'Well Mr Davis, you must realise that you come from half-time Europe!' When one considers that the Daewoo workers put in a 6½ day week (10 hours a day) for an average salary of £3,000 one could concede the point he was making. And the 6½ day week did not take into account times of unusual pressure when more overtime was required.

1982–83 has seen pockets of optimistic resilience. Cruising has absorbed an unprecedented number of new deliveries. Although the US market has been sluggish nevertheless the increased number of berths seems to have been absorbed. Evidence there is of extensive rebating (absorption of air-fares in particular) which have diluted earnings and thus the profitability of the various lines. I personally am a Director of Pearl Cruises of Scandinavia whose ship of similar name has started perhaps the most novel new cruising schedule by being permanently based in the Far East and cruising principally to the exotic parts of China. Tientsin (for Peking/Beijing), Tsingtao, Dalian, Shanghai and Whampoa introduce a brand-new experience for the cruising passengers who may be becoming satiated with Caribbean sunsets and rum punches and palms. I certainly found it something

Pockets of optimistic resilience in the cruise markets have inspired the deliveries of many new vessels over the 1982–83 period, with others to follow during 1984–85. Highly placed in this field are the shipbuilders of Europe and Scandinavia, particularly Finland, as they have the experience in this field which the Far East yards lack. A late 1982 delivery which has come 'on stream' during this year, is the Wärtsilä-built *Song of America*. Following her from Wärtsilä's slips will be the world's largest purpose-built cruise ship to date, P&O's *Royal Princess*, which is expected to resemble the former in many ways. (*FotoFlite, Ashford*)

very different to push a Mothercare buggy with my two-year old in it up the Great Wall of China!

Inventiveness may thus save the day despite the forces ranged against recovery in the maritime world. But that recovery will be a long slow process and may never be achieved unless governments, who now hold the whiphand, take decisive action to remove unwanted ships and shipyards (however brutal that action may sound) and refrain from the temptation to build ships simply in order to keep their shipyards busy.

We must be bold and forward-looking. As Charles Hiltzheimer, until recently President of Sealand quoted: 'Perhaps the greatest danger we face is the loss of will to rise to today's challenge. An old proverb states that when courage and reason are lost, ALL is lost'.

A Marine Chronology of 1983

Compiled by R N Ambrose

The opening days of 1983 were largely filled with the residue of business from the previous twelve month period. In (debatably) British waters, the new fishing limits which took effect from midnight on 31 December 1982 were soon to provide their first catch. Further south, the *European Gateway* remained capsized and slowly deteriorating as her salvors raced against the onset of foul weather.

The much troubled CAST shipping group exemplified many aspects of the general shipping trend as it fought to stay in business. Merchant ships continued to be chartered to support the Falklands garrison. The international Greenpeace group continued to make the headlines in their endeavours for environmental enhancement.

Meanwhile, winter storms in the northern hemisphere and summer ones south of the Equator continued to claim ships and lives. South Korean shipbuilders kept finding clients who wanted new ships built while the rest of the free world watched their shipbuilders' losses mount. Iranian oil wells continued to turn the Persio-Arabian Gulf into the 'Black' sea as they pumped their daily 2,000 barrels straight into the water; while the Iraqi military made sure that no one would cap the rogue wells. And all over the world, shipowners of almost all persuasions daily added new hulls to the massive fleet of laid-up tonnage.

While optimistic voices forecast that 1983 would see an upturn from recession-troubled 1982, it would have taken a brave voice to try to convince a shipowner! In short, to the shipping world, the year was all that was new. The entry of 1983 was thus awaited with bated breath and retarded optimism, with a decreased level of trade, and a 3.9 million ton larger world fleet to carry the smaller cargoes in. Thus did 1983 commence.

3 January
Four Danish trawlers enter the disputed fishing grounds off the UK's north-east coast anticipating confrontation with British Fishery Protection vessels over the newly imposed EEC fishing limits.

A collision takes place between the 3,331 dwt Italian tanker *Megara Iblea* (loaded with gas oil) and the nuclear-powered guided missile cruiser *USS Arkansas* in the Strait of Messina between Sicily and the Italian mainland. The agents for the *Megara Iblea* describe the incident as a 'slight collision' and said that their ship was able to proceed with only minor damage. The *USS Arkansas* has a 'slight' ten foot gash in her hull, 15 ft above the waterline, but is able to proceed to Naples under her own power after temporary repairs.

4 January
All major Danish ports are strikebound by stevedores protesting at new daily unemployment pay regulations which took effect from 1 January.

Anti-nuclear demonstrators occupy a crane at the port of Cherbourg to prevent it being used to unload a shipment of nuclear waste from Japan.

6 January
Euro MP and Danish trawler skipper Captain Kent Kirk is arrested as he cast his nets inside Britain's newly imposed 12 mile EEC fishing limit. Boarded by a party from the fisheries protection ship *HMS Dumbarton Castle*, his trawler, *Sand Kirk* (150 tons), is taken to a British port.

More problems at Cherbourg, when the Greenpeace trawler *Sirius* is fired on and towed away by the French authorities while attempting to block the way of *Pacific Crane* expected later this week with a cargo of nuclear waste from Japan.

7 January
Kent Kirk fined £30,000 and £400 costs by a British court for illegal fishing.

8 January
The 8,820 grt Panama flag cargo ship *Bamboo Root*, carrying 12,600 tons of manganese ore, sinks off Sri Lanka. The British OBO carrier *Cast Puffin* responds to SOS call and in rough seas manages to rescue all 27 crew from their lifeboats.

11 January
Omani police and naval units are joined by experts in a bid to prevent 53,500 tons of crude oil pouring into the sea from the blazing Greek tanker *Assimi*. The fire which started in the engine room four days ago has now spread to all eight oil tanks.

12 January
The tanker *Assimi* is towed out into the Indian Ocean

to be sunk following the Dutch tug *Solano*'s successful attempt to get a line aboard her.

More than 100 persons are feared drowned after the 21 metre ferry *Almalyn* carrying 220 passengers and crew sinks off the east Malaysian state of Sabah.

14 January
Extended industrial inaction by Danish dock workers spreads and forces a halt to all DFDS Danish Seaways sailings between Esbjerg and Harwich.

16 January
P&O's *Uganda* is withdrawn from commercial service in readiness for its transfer to the British MoD for a two year charter as a troopship serving the Falkland Islands. She is to be replaced in commercial service by the 5,078 grt ex-ferry *Orpheus* which is to be acquired by P&O from her present owners Epirotiki Line, who have been operating her with Messrs Swan Hellenic on a series of educational cruises not unsimilar to those formerly operated by *Uganda*. The *Orpheus* is now 35 years old however, and it is therefore not clear whether P&O intend to continue this style of cruising in the future.

17 January
The tanker *Assimi* splits into two sections and subsequently sinks while only 200 miles east of the coast of Oman.

British Petroleum's products tanker *BP Battler* which collided with the Limerick Harbour Commissioner's launch *St Munchin*. (*FotoFlite*)

18 January
Following an agreement of Lloyd's Open Form between the owners of the bulk carrier *Kimoliaki Pistis* and the salvage team aboard the tug *Vernicos Dimitrios*, efforts begin to contain a raging fire and salvage the bulker which had been abandoned off Malta by her 25 crew members.

19 January
While the British tug *Lady Debbie* and the US tug *Dr Jack* wait for bad weather to abate before commencing to tow the rig *Penrod 80* to a new position in the North Sea, *Dr Jack* develops mechanical trouble finally causing her to break down completely, and is taken in tow by the *Lady Debbie* which delivers her safely to the Dutch port of Den Helder.

20 January
The Polish cargo vessel *Kudowa Zdroj* (1,991 grt) bound for Libya with a cargo of iron rods from Spain, sinks in stormy weather about seven miles off the coast of Ibiza. Fifteen of the crew are believed to have died and a further five are still missing. It is thought that the vessel's loss was due to bad stowage of cargo

which subsequently shifted during the storm.

The 138,823 dwt Liberian tanker *Tifoso* runs aground and is badly holed off the Atlantic island of Bermuda. She was in ballast at the time.

Following a collision off the estuary of Ireland's River Shannon between a service vessel and the 1,529 grt/2,228 dwt BP tanker *BP Battler*, a search is still underway for two men who were missing following the accident.

21 January

The Norwegian 128,000 tanker dwt *Jarena* arrives under tow in Haugesund, Norway, for repairs to damage sustained when her stern mooring became entangled with her propeller during offshore oil loading trials on the North Sea Statfjord field.

The British MoD announces the charter of the 1,849 grt/3,302 dwt Norwegian flag *Grey Master* and the 1,566 grt/2,677 dwt UK flag *Lakespan Ontario*, as temporary replacements for the *Sir Galahad* and *Sir Tristram* which were both casualties of the Falklands conflict. They are to be operated as Royal Fleet Auxiliaries.

23 January

An attempt is to be made to right the Greek coaster *Georgios* which is lying in Southampton's East Docks with a 30° list. She was towed in to Southampton after her ballast, the remnants of an old cargo, shifted during a storm in the English Channel while en-route from Antwerp to Casablanca.

25 January

The Turkish cargo ship *Kaptan Hantal*, 500 grt, sinks in storms in the Black Sea while en-route from Istanbul for Hopa with a cargo of iron ore. All 11 members of the crew are missing.

27 January

The 61,519 dwt Liberian tanker *Priamos* strikes two Mississippi steamboats, the *Mississippi Queen* and *Nachez*, while attempting to navigate a bend in the river.

30 January

Seven people are killed when the Panamanian oil rig *Eniwetok* strikes the overhead cables of a cable car system linking Singapore with the holiday island of Sentosa.

31 January

An attempt to right the 4,263 grt/3,949 dwt *European Gateway* fails when a chain snaps in heavy seas.

Strong winds causes the postponement of the launch of two tugs at Ferguson-Ailsa today.

1 February

The 12,988 grt North Sea ferry *Norland* arrives back from the Falklands to her home port of Hull today.

After enduring some of the worst weather that the South Atlantic could offer, she arrives off the Humber river in time to experience a severe easterly storm which prevents her from entering her berth for the first time since she commenced operations.

2 February

The drilling rig *STC Platon*, en-route from the Bay of Biscay to the Netherlands, is adrift off the French coast when towlines from the tugs *Typhoon* and *Seaforth Champion* break. The French Navy makes an unsuccessful attempt to evacuate the crew by helicopter.

The B + I service between Pembroke and Cork ceases operations. It is the fourth Irish Sea service to close in the last two years.

3 February

Salvage experts are preparing to sink the Liberian tanker *Tifoso* after she ran aground off Bermuda a fortnight ago. Although she was successfully refloated she has been declared a constructive total loss by her owners.

One of the largest ships ever to be built on the Clyde is named *Pacific Patriot* by the Queen Mother.

6 February

The ro-ro ferry *Saint Killian II* which operates between Eire and France has to put into Falmouth with her 160 passengers after she experiences steering problems off Lands End.

7 February

Five crew members are rescued from the Greek cargo ship *Protoklitos*, presently in lay-up in the Blackwater Estuary, after fire breaks out in the engine room.

Protoklitos at anchor in the Blackwater Estuary prior to the fire which gutted her engine room. *(A J Ambrose)*

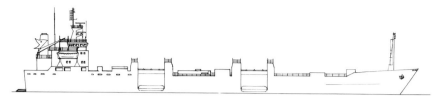

The 1983-built pallet-ship/reefer *Bencomo*. (*Drawing: Michael J Ambrose*)

Scale: 1:1200

8 February

The *Bencomo* (2,280 grt/4,231 dwt), owned by Fred Olsen Lines, sails on her maiden voyage from Tilbury to the Canary Islands. She is the first of a new generation of highly automated reefer ships with low manning and a unique technical specification.

10 February

It is announced that Sealink (UK) Ltd are to charter the 14,378 grt Swedish *Prinsessan Birgitta* to replace the missing *St. Edmund* on the Harwich–Hook of Holland route.

12 February

Twenty-four crew die when the 13,758 grt/25,985 dwt turbo-electric bulk carrier *Marine Electric* sinks in heavy seas about 30 miles off the Virginia coast.

16 February

The British MoD confirms it has bought the Sealink ferry *St. Edmund* for use as a troop ship to operate between Ascension Island and the Falklands. She is to be renamed *Keren*.

17 February

A Dutch motor barge sinks in the Rhine today with her cargo of 887 tonnes of raw phosphates.

18 February

The southern Algarve river, which borders with Spain, is blocked by Portuguese fishermen as a protest against the failure to agree with Spain over fishing rights.

22 February

Three fishermen drown after being trapped in the hull of the French trawler *Petit Fordan* which sinks about 20 miles off Beachy Head, Sussex.

26 February

European Gateway is raised to an angle of 76°.

27 February

A new ro-ro service commences between Barry, South Wales and Cork, Southern Ireland, operated by Welsh Irish Ferries using a chartered Finnish ship.

28 February

The Sealink ferry *St. Edmund* arrives in Wallsend after ten months work as a troopship in the South Atlantic.

1 March

125 out of 200 passengers travelling on the Chinese ferry *Red Star* are missing presumed dead when the vessel capsizes in strong winds while on a trip from Canton to Zhaoqing.

4 March

One man dies when the Panamian cargo ship *Cleo C* catches fire off the Italian coast.

6 March

A total of 67 vessels sail through the Suez Canal netting a record £3.3 million in tolls, the largest amount ever collected in one day.

7 March

DFDS announces the sale of *Dana Sirena* to Saudi Arabian owners.

8 March

The world's first diesel-powered hovercraft goes into passenger service today on the Portsmouth–Isle of Wight route. It is British-built and operated by Sealink.

10 March

Six Iranian vessels are claimed sunk by the Iraqi Navy as they were entering the Khor Moussa creek on the northern tip of the Persian Gulf.

Bencomo, the latest addition to Fred Olsen's fleet, was completed at the yards of Fosen mek Verksteder, Norway. (*FotoFlite*)

Prinsessan Birgitta, now Sealink's *St Nicholas*, is the new 'super-ferry' working the Harwich to Hook of Holland route. (*A J Ambrose*)

11 March

A Spanish fisherman who was fishing in Portuguese waters off the Algarve, is shot and wounded by Portuguese maritime police.

European Gateway is towed to a position one mile off Felixstowe beach.

14 March

The enquiry into the loss of the Penlee lifeboat *Solomon Browne* commences.

The 12 crew members of the 4,099 grt/6,849 dwt Panamanian motor vehicle carrier *Chief Dragon* are rescued by the bulker *Sambow Expert* after she catches fire south-east of Sri Lanka.

It is announced that Mr Graham Day will replace Sir Robert Atkinson as chairman of British Shipbuilders.

15 March

The French Navy are attempting to sink the Panamanian general cargo ship *Niagara* which is ablaze and drifting towards Corsica.

The Danish Polar supply vessel *Nanok S* is reported trapped in pack ice near an Australian base in the Antarctic.

17 March

The British MoD announces the charter of Bibby Line's accommodation barge *Safe Esperia* to house about 1,100 servicemen based on the Falkland Islands.

18 March

Eight Filipino crew are rescued by a Korean Air Force helicopter after their ship *Jasa* (2,992 grt) sinks in high seas with the loss of 11 men off the South Korean coast.

21 March

British Shipbuilders announce their latest design today, a 17,000 dwt multi-purpose vessel designated MP17.

The Panamanian car carrier *Chief Dragon* sinks at anchor five miles off Colombo after being towed there by Safmarine's salvage tug *Wolraad Woltemade* after fire had swept through her engine room causing an explosion in the upper car deck.

23 March

Harland and Wolff announce a new design for a 40,000 dwt products tanker.

29 March

US Coastguards are investigating the collision of the UK-registered ro-ro vessel *Dilkara* which struck a four-lane bascule bridge at Tacoma, near Seattle, Washington today. The same vessel struck this bridge seven years ago but with a different master aboard.

30 March

The tug *Titan* takes *European Gateway* in tow to Amsterdam for drydocking.

The Panamanian vessel *Niagara* was thought to include large amounts of drugs and armaments in her cargo. She finally fetched ashore on a sandbar off Corsica. (*FotoFlite*)

The Pakistani cargo ship *Murree* on which a large amount of drugs were seized, was built in the UK in 1981. (*FotoFlite*)

30 March
Sealink (UK) Ltd confirms that the largest ro-ro ferry ever to work the Isle of Wight route will be entering service this summer. The vessel is the *St. Catherine* which was launched on 29 March 1983 at the Leith shipyard of Henry Robb.

2 April
One passenger is killed following a fire which starts in the forward starboard accommodation on board the Brittany Ferries vessel *Amorique* while en-route from Roscoff to Cork.

The National Union of Seamen is threatening an all-out strike following the Royal Navy's 'collection' of the former Sealink ferry *St. Edmund* due to a dispute over manning. She has been refitted at Wallsend for work as a troopship/ferry to work between Ascension Island and the Falklands under her new name *Keren*.

6 April
Terms are agreed regarded the manning of *Keren*.

10 April
The Salcombe lifeboat *The Baltic Exchange* capsizes in Force 11 winds as she is attempting to make contact with four skin divers in a rubber dingy. She self-righted immediately. One crew member is washed overboard but picked up again.

12 April
Townsend Thoresen's *Baltic Ferry* returns to her home port of Felixstowe after spending 11 months in the South Atlantic serving the Falkland Islands.

13 April
A political storm is brewing after Cunard announces that *Cunard Countess* would have her post-Falklands refit in Malta and not in a British yard.

15 April
Customs officers from Ellesmere Port seize heroin with a street value of approximately £1 million from the Pakistani cargo ship *Murree* (7,923 grt).

20 April
United States Lines are to sign the contract with Daewoo of South Korea for the building of 12 new 4,000 + TEU container ships.

The Port of Tyne Authority announces the building of a new coal handling terminal at Tyne Dock. It is due to be completed in 1985.

22 April
Hurricane strength winds 450 miles off the Azores causes the cargo on board the German container ship *Milhafre* to shift, and the vessel subsequently sinks.

24 April
It is announced that plans to widen and deepen the Suez Canal are to be postponed for two to three years.

25 April
United States Lines finally sign the contract with Daewoo for their 12 new container ships. US Lines would not confirm having placed the order however.

26 April
The French destroyer *Georges Leygues* picks up a lifeboat with 16 crew members from the Panamanian general cargo ship *Gelinda* after she sinks south-east of Palma today.

27 April
The first order for a large sail-assisted merchant ship is placed with a Japanese yard.

The Soviet oceanographic research vessel *Ayu-Dag* is escorted out of Oslo after her master was fined £714 for entering Norwegian waters without permission.

28 April
P&O announce that their new 40,000 grt cruise ship presently building at Wärtsilä in Finland will be named *Royal Princess*.

3 May
An investigation begins into the cause of a fire on board the Norwegian roll-on roll-off ferry *Bolero* which killed one man and caused the 365 passengers to abandon ship. The fire which spread through the car deck was bought under control by crew and six firemen who were airlifted on board.

4 May
Cunard Countess sails into Malta for the commencement of her controversial post-Falklands refit.

6 May
A fire, caused by a welding spark, in Malta Drydock's dry dock causes minor damage to the exterior paint work on the hull of *Cunard Countess* today.

7 May
The Finnish-built Soviet tanker *Auseklis*, 3,568 grt, is detained in Sundsvall harbour by the Swedish Navy.

8 May
The *Lago Lacar* arrives back in Buenos Aires after a week long trip into the South Atlantic with relatives of Argentine servicemen who died in the Falklands.

9 May
Sealink are without a Dover–Dunkirk service today due to a strike by French seamen.

10 May
Holland America Line have refused delivery of the cruise ship *Nieuw Amsterdam* being built for them by France's Chantiers d'Atlantique.

Penlee's new lifeboat *Mabel Alice*, the replacement for *Solomon Browne*, is launched for the first time to tow in the French trawler *Rayon de Soleil*.

11 May
British Rail announce that their subsidiary Sealink(UK) Ltd has reported a trading profit for 1982.

Two additional cruise ships are to join the Cunard fleet in October 1983, it is announced by the company. They are the *Vistafjord* and *Sagafjord*, purchased from Norwegian America Cruises.

Vistafjord, the larger and newer of the two cruise ships which joined the Cunard fleet in 1983. (*SkyFotos*)

13 May

DFDS plan to sell more cargo vessels in an attempt to cut losses.

It is unknown whether a fire on board the Panamanian tanker *Panoceanic Fame* loaded with a full cargo of gas oil off Bandar Khomeini was the result of military action.

18 May

Tugs free the 34,194 dwt Panamanian-registered vessel *Maritime Trader* which ran aground in the River Parana in Argentina on May 17.

Fire breaks out on the 2,095 grt passenger ship *Dona Florentina* in the Central Philippines. There are no casualties.

19 May

Following a boiler room explosion, fire sweeps through the 114,000 bulker *Motilal Nehru*, owned by the Shipping Corporation of India. A large proportion of the cargo of 81,000 tons of grain is destroyed.

Cypriot owners finalise a deal to buy the salvaged *European Gateway*. It is indicated that she may be destined to work between the Aegean Islands.

20 May

The Port of Liverpool's new dredger *Mersey Venture*, built by Appledore Shipbuilders, is officially commissioned after naming.

22 May

Wijsmuller's *Ocean Servant 2* leaves Ijmuiden bound for the North Atlantic to commence salvage operations on the sunken oil rig *Ocean Ranger* (see last year's edition).

23 May

It is announced that Sally the Viking Line are planning a new ferry service operating from London to Zeebrugge.

24 May

300 of the 600 passengers aboard the 883 grt Egyptian vessel *10th of Ramadan* are missing presumed dead after the vessel catches fire and sinks between Aswan and Wadi Halfa.

25 May

The anniversary of the sinking of *Atlantic Conveyor* is marked by a service at Liverpool's merchant navy memorial.

Swedish shipbuilders Kockums plan to produce a new standard roll-on roll-off ship design within the next six months.

A take-over battle begins between two of the UK's major shipping companies following P&Os rejection of a bid from Trafalgar House, owner of Cunard.

The Argentine general cargo ship *Roma* berths at Dover at the end of a voyage in which half of her 1,000

Sub Lt Ian Watson's Sea Harrier landed successfully aboard the Spanish 2,300 grt *Alraigo*, but rolled aft and off its small 'flight deck' as the ship came to a halt. The *Alraigo* is seen here at Tenerife where she attracted wide interest from the world's press. (*FotoFlite & Flag Officer Naval Air Command*)

tonne cargo of timber was destroyed by fire.

31 May
Two merchant ships, the *Apj Priti* and another not disclosed, are attacked and seriously damaged in a rocket attack by Iraqi jets off Bandar Khomeini. The vessels were part of a convoy from Bushire.

2 June
The Hyundai Corporation of South Korea signs a £130 million contract to build eight tankers for the Shipping Corporation of India.

3 June
Cunard announces that *Queen Elizabeth 2* is to have major repairs following problems with one of her turbines. The work will be done by Vosper Shiprepair, a subsidary of British Shipbuilders.

5 June
The former Townsend Thoresen-owned ferry *European Gateway* leaves Amsterdam under tow from the British tug *Point Spencer*, bound for Pireas where her new

The SD-14 *Monte Alto,* which was in collision with the 1959-built 489 grt general cargo ship *Moluno.* (*FotoFlite*)

owners intend to rebuild her.

The Soviet river steamer *Aleksandr Suvorov* is involved in an accident on the River Volga when she collides with a bridge which removes her top deck, causing an undisclosed number of deaths.

6 June
A Royal Navy Sea Harrier from *HMS Illustrious* is forced to land on the Spanish cargo ship *Alraigo* after losing contact with her carrier and running out of fuel.

7 June
The 1982-built French irradiated fuel carrier *Sigyn*, 3,923 grt, is struck by the Liberian-registered 15,576 grt car carrier *European Venture* as she is entering the port of Cherbourg under tow. *Sigyn* breaks away and runs into the roll-on roll-off cargo ferry *Saint Patrick II*. This is the second accident in six months that *Sigyn* has been involved in.

8 June
Preparations are under way to tow the offshore platform *Maureen*, weighing 111,750 tonnes, to Phillips' North Sea Maureen oil field 160 miles off Aberdeen by the most powerful group of tugs that has ever assembled in British waters.

A collision in heavy fog causes the death of four seamen and injuries to four more when the West German vessel *Darion* collides with the Algerian roll-on roll-off vessel *Tenes*. The *Darion* later sinks.

9 June
A collision between the cargo ships *Molund* and *Monte Alto* causes the *Molund* to sink immediately and six seamen to drown in waters off Sweden.

14 June
It is announced that Swedish shipbuilders Kockums have won the contract to build two cruise ships for Miami-based Carnival Cruise Lines.

The heavy-lift cargo ship *Dan Lifter* arrives in the Tees and discharges the Royal Fleet Auxiliary ship *Sir Tristram* which was a victim of an Argentine air attack in the Falklands.

15 June
The Royal Navy Sea Harrier which landed aboard the 2,300 grt Spanish cargo ship *Alraigo* is loaded on board the tanker *British Tay* (15,650 grt/25,000 dwt), which is currently on charter to the British MoD, for transportation from Tenerife back to the UK.

16 June
It is disclosed that the cost of the post-Falklands refit to *Cunard Countess* in Malta will be 30% more than was originally thought, amounting to almost £3 million.

18 June
The World's largest oil tanker *Seawise Giant* (564,783 dwt), which has had no work for the last year, is being chartered to Petroleos Mexicanos (Pemex) as a floating oil terminal.

20 June
It is announced that the *Bonn*, West Germany's largest tanker (392,799 dwt) is to be put into lay-up for three years.

21 June
Cunard Countess is completed on schedule at the Maltese shipyards today. The refit cost £600,000 more than the £2.2 million initially scheduled, but included a significant proportion of extra work. Cunard announce their satisfaction with the work and regret that British yards had been unable to accept the job. British Shipbuilders reasons for refusing the work were based on their lack of confidence in their own ability to complete the refit to Cunard's schedule requirements. The Maltese shipyard was able to offer a competitive price for the work, as their average workers' wage of £140 per week would not have been acceptable to the average British shipyard worker.

Eurocanadian Shipholdings (Cast) suspend all its operations.

22 June
The Royal Bank of Canada announces that they would support the Montreal/Antwerp bulk container service operated by Cast.

26 June
It is announced by Sealink (UK) Ltd that they have withdrawn the ferry *Manx Viking* from her Heysham to Douglas service because of unconfirmed reports of engine troubles.

28 June
The 993 grt West German flag *Ursula Wessels*, with a cargo of chipboard, granulated cork, cork boards for flooring and granite kerb stones, becomes the largest vessel ever to dock at Miştley on the upper reaches of the River Stour on the east coast of Britain. The river has recently been deepened.

29 June
The British standby vessel *Spearfish* is sunk by gunfire from the frigate *HMS Tartar* after she was dragged by strong currents into one of the legs of the jack-up drilling rig *Penrod 85*, 16 miles off the Isle of Wight.

30 June
The British tanker *Ervilia* arrives in Hong Kong after rescuing 25 crew members from the Liberian cargo ship *Kinabalu Lima* 670 miles south of Hong Kong.

1 July
Holland America Line announces a third date for the maiden voyage of their new cruise ship *Nieuw Amsterdam*. She will sail from Le Havre for New York on 10 July, seven weeks behind schedule.

Representatives of West German shipbuilding yards AG Weser, Bremer Vulkan, and Hapag Lloyd meet to draft an agreement on their merger to form the country's largest shipbuilding group.

5 July
The largest boxship to enter Harwich harbour arrives at the Walton terminal due to ABC Container Lines switch from Tilbury. The boxship is the *Ellen Hudig* which is on her maiden voyage.

7 July
It is reported that the *Ypapanti* is in trouble again following an engine fire while she was under tow in Greek waters off Lavrion. She is currently under arrest (see June 1982 in previous edition).

Engineers are attempting to repair the main engines of the six month old BP tanker *British Spirit* adrift in heavy weather 30 miles off the south-west coast of Australia.

8 July
A full investigation is ordered into the engines of three BP tankers following yesterday's breakdown aboard

The 1967 US-built *Adm Wm M Callaghan*. Owned by Sunexport Holdings, she is presently on charter to Military Sealift Command. (*FotoFlite*)

British Spirit to which temporary repairs have now been made.

11 July

The death is announced of Mr Keith Wickendon, chairman of European Ferries, following a crash in a light aircraft at the weekend.

15 July

It is announced that the 1957-built 8,352 grt Panamanian-registered cargo ship *Victory Gleam* with 19 crew members is missing in Indonesian waters.

16 July

The US research ship *Robert D. Conrad* leaves port on her third attempt to locate the *Titanic* which sank in the Atlantic in 1912 with the loss of 1,503 lives. This is the third time Texas oil man Mr Jack Grimm has financed such an expedition, spending about £1.3 million in the process.

It is reported that only hours after the completion of a £3 million refit the Sally Line cross-Channel ferry *Viking* had to return to Bremerhaven with bow thruster and stabiliser faults.

19 July

The world's largest heavy-lift ship, *Ferncarrier* leaves Okpo in South Korea carrying the semi-submersible drilling rib *High Seas Driller* to a location in the North Sea.

The British Airways Sikorsky S-61 helicopter which crashed 2.8 miles off St. Marys in the Scilly Isles on 16 July 1983, is successfully salvaged. Salvage and investigation is co-ordinated from the 1,977 grt *Seaforth Clansman*. HM Ships *Mentor*, *Millbrook*, and *Manley* assist by keeping shipping clear of the area.

A spokesman for Holland America Line announces that they have withdrawn from the Bermuda and Caribbean cruising trade for 1984. The company's new cruise ships *Nieuw Amsterdam* and *Noordam* will be working the US Pacific coast.

Greenpeace announce that six members investigating Soviet whaling activities were arrested when they went ashore in Siberia. A seventh was chased as he fled with film of a whaling expedition.

21 July

The Greenpeace ship *Rainbow Warrior* sails from Nome in Alaska towards a rendezvous in the Bering Sea with a Soviet ship returning the seven men seized on 19 July.

23 July

The Talmadge Bridge in Savannah, Georgia is closed for 90 days after being stuck by the 24,471 grt roll-on roll-off vessel *Adm. Wm. M. Callaghan* presently on charter to Military Sealift Command.

2 August

A Buenos Aires radio station announces that two Argentine fishing boats were intercepted by a British frigate and forced to leave the 150 mile exclusion zone around the Falklands.

Cunard charter two aircraft to fly more than 400 passengers from Cherbourg to Britain after *QE2*'s 11.30 sailing was put back to 22.30 hrs following an emergency ten day refit due to engine troubles. Cunard said the refit had overrun by a couple of hours and the ship had missed the midday tide.

3 August

The South Korean company Hyundai finalise a deal to buy and break up the world's second largest tanker, the 555,051 dwt *Pierre Guillaumat* from the French Compagnie Nationale de Navigation. The tanker has been in the Persian Gulf since February.

The Port of London Authority announces that they are closing the Comclear Terminals on the south side of the Royal Victoria Dock. The closure is due to strikes earlier in the year and the withdrawal of a major customer, Orient Overseas Container Line, to the PLA's new Barking base.

4 August

It is announced that Pan Ocean Storage and Transport owned jointly by P&O and Ocean Transport and Trading, are to sell their entire fleet of seven chemical carriers and will concentrate their efforts on their storage activities which have been built up over the last few years. 130 seafaring jobs will be lost.

A fire breaks out in one of the holds in the Pattje Shipyards newbuilding hull No. 352, the reefer ship *Normandic*, which is due for delivery to her owners Seatrade in September. Fourteen people are taken to hospital but there were no serious casualties.

5 August

South Korean military forces sink a North Korean 'spy ship' off South Korea's east coast.

The Danish-registered freighter *Kraka*, currently on charter to the British MoD, catches fire in Port Stanley harbour. She is carrying a cargo of granite for use in the building of a memorial to British troops. Crew from the destroyer *HMS Birmingham* and other naval units help to fight the blaze.

6 August

The 271,540 dwt Spanish-registered tanker *Castillo de Bellver* explodes and breaks in two off Cape Town leaving an oil slick 20 miles long and three miles wide. The tanker was on its way from Jebel Dhanna to Spain

---

This is all that is now visible of Radio Caroline's former ship *Mi Amigo* which sank in storms in 1980. (*FotoFlite*)

The new base for Radio Caroline is the radio ship *Imagine*, formerly the trawler *Ross Revenge*, which began broadcasting from its anchorage off the Essex coast of England in August 1983. (*FotoFlite*)

One of the most dramatic voyages of 1983, if not one of the most dramatic voyages of the decade, was that of the 11,200 mile journey of the semi-submersible heavy-lift ship *Ferncarrier* with her unusual and outsized load, the 15,500 ton semi-submersible drilling rig *High Seas Driller*. They are seen here en-route to Invergordon in the North Sea when nearing the end of their journey from South Korea. The journey was made at an average speed of 13 knots, which is more than twice the average speed that could have been achieved were the rig to have made the journey with tugs. The most impressive aspect of this journey was that of *High Seas Driller*'s physical size: she extended more than 20 metres either side of *Ferncarrier* and her height from the bottom of her pontoons to the top of her drilling derrick is 107 metres (351 feet). By comparison, when loaded on *Ferncarrier* she was taller, and of course much wider and longer, than London's famous landmark 'Big Ben' which has a height of 361 feet. Were further example necessary, *FotoFlite*'s aircraft taking this picture is flying at an altitude of 150 feet, yet is still flying lower than the rig's main working deck! (*FotoFlite, Ashford*)

when the incident occurred. Safmarine's tug *John Ross* successfully secures a line onto the vessel in order to tow the burning ship away from the coast.

8 August
Safmarine are trying to persuade the Spanish government to allow them to destroy the remainder of the *Castillo de Bellver*.

9 August
The British 58,597 grt container ship *Cardigan Bay* owned by OCL is involved in a collision with the 24,243 dwt tanker *Jamac* while travelling along the southern end of the Suez Canal. *Cardigan Bay* suffers no damage but divers are examining the bottom of *Jamac*.

12 August
The Danish cargo ship *Lonelil* sinks after colliding with the Libyan cargo ship *Ebn Magid* off Cape Silleiro, Spain. Two crew members are missing.

14 August
The fore part of the Spanish tanker *Castillo de Bellver* along with approximately 60,000 tonnes of oil, is successfully sunk using explosives.

16 August
It is reported that the pirate radio station Radio Caroline is to recommence broadcasting from its old anchorage at the Knock Deep off the Essex coast. It will be based on the former Grimsby trawler *Ross Revenge* which has been unofficially renamed *Imagine*.

19 August
The British MoD charters the Cunard tanker *Lucerna* to take over as the fuel oil base ship at Ascension Island.

Safmarine reveals plans to commence a new passenger service operating between South Africa and Europe and islands in the Indian Ocean.

Salvage experts Wijsmuller successfully refloat the semi-submersible drilling rig *Ocean Ranger* which capsized off Newfoundland 18 months ago.

26 August
The drilling rig *High Seas Driller* arrives in Scotland on board the heavy-lift ship *Ferncarrier* after her journey from Okpo in South Korea.

29 August
A Norwegian trawler is rammed twice by a Soviet Coast Guard vessel in the Norwegian sector of the Barents Sea today. The Soviet vessel, which caused substantial damage to the trawler, claims she had been fishing in a disputed area.

1 September

The Liberian jack-up rig *Key Brisbane* breaks free from her tow in huge seas off Australia. She was under tow from Darwin to a new position in Cockburn Sound. All the crew are lifted to safety, and late this evening the rig is sinking approximately 75 miles off Perth.

5 September

The righting of the semi-submersible accommodation platform *Alexander L. Kielland* gets under way in a fjord near Stavanger. The *Alexander L. Kielland* sank in the North Sea in 1980. All previous attempts to right the platform have failed.

6 September

It is announced that the British Government is chartering the Qatari-flag livestock carrier *Dina Khalef* to carry livestock, bought out of donations to the South Atlantic fund, to the Falklands Islands from the United Kingdom.

7 September

It is announced that the largest single contract for the shipment of BNOC's (British National Oil Corp.) liquid petroleum, has been awarded to P&O. The contract will run for twelve months. The vessels used to transport the liquid petroleum from Sullom Voe to northern Europe will be *Gambada* (21,357 grt), *Gazana* (21,357 grt), *Gandara* (15,611 grt) and *Garbeta* (15,480 grt).

The 40,000 dwt Soviet tanker *Jacques Duclos*, fully laden with oil, runs aground on Agersoe Flak in the internationally guaranteed channel passing through Danish territorial waters while on her way from the Baltic to the North Sea. The master of the ship refuses Danish assistance and is waiting for Soviet vessels to arrive and pump some of the oil out to lighten her.

9 September

The *Alexander L. Kielland* is moved to an angle of 90°.

Following the rise in popularity of cruising in recent years, Finnish shipbuilders announce a plan to market a four-masted sail-driven luxury liner/cruise ship designed in concert with the Swedish Saleninvest shipping group.

North Sea Ferries' *Norwave*, which suffered an engine room fire in September. Her crew were highly praised by the passengers for the efficient way they dealt with the crisis. (*SkyFotos/North Sea Ferries*)

Cunard has won a contract worth £8 million to transport construction workers for the building of the new Falklands airport. They will use the ex-DFDS ferry *England* (8,117 grt) which will work between Cape Town and Port Stanley. Originally, it was thought that St. Helena/Curnow Shipping would operate the service using the same vessel, but they were beaten at the last minute for reasons which are not immediately apparent.

A total of 15 ships are swept aground when Typhoon Ellen batters Hong Kong harbour. Faring worst as a result of the storms is the Liberian-registered 5,424 grt *Pacific Coral* which is listing at an angle of 40°. Seven other ships collide, and one strikes the Mobil Oil jetty at the harbour.

10 September
Two South Korean bulk carriers, the 25,057 dwt *Swibon* and the 22,464 dwt *Pan Nova*, collide in fine weather in the Bering Sea. The crew of the *Pan Nova* abandon ship and a coastguard cutter is standing by to see if the vessel remains stable. The *Swibon* only receives minor damage to her bow. The cause of the collision is unknown.

12 September
A fire in the engine room of North Sea Ferries' 3,540 grt ferry *Norwave* occasions her to be towed back to Hull. The fire is believed to have started from a fuel leak, and considerable damage is caused in the engine room. The passengers, forced to disembark from the vessel, later praise the crew for their professional efficiency during the incident, which they said was a directly contributing factor to the lack of any serious injuries.

13 September
Iraq claims to have destroyed two large Iranian vessels at the northern end of the Persian Gulf in an air attack.

A problem with a number of air hoses causes the delay in the final stage of the righting of the *Alexander L. Kielland* which is now almost upright at an angle of 155°.

15 September
The *Alexander L. Kielland* is upright and salvors Stolt Nielsen Seaway are planning to stabilise her before towing her to a deep water anchorage for inspection.

17 September
A fire seriously damages the Saudi Arabian ro-ro *Saudi Tabuk*, almost completed at Kochums Malmo yard in Sweden. The cause of the fire is thought to have been from welding work in the bow section.

20 September
Cunard announces that the *QE 2*'s November refit will be at a West German yard. The British trade unions make much capital of this fact, although

Vosper Shiprepairers were unable to complete the job anyway due to much of their capacity being tied up on gold-plating the interior of the Helsingors-built Arabian luxury yacht *Abdul Aziz*.

23 September
Polish fireman are lowered onto the Finnish bulk carrier *Alppila* (11,503 grt) after fire breaks out in the engine room and causes the stern superstructure to collapse just after the ship had left Gdynia. She is later towed back to port.

27 September
Malta Dry Docks confirm that they have won the contract to 'upgrade' the cruise ship *Vistafjord* which Cunard have bought from Norwegian American Cruises.

28 September
The Iranian tanker *Sivand* (218,587 dwt) collides with an oil berth at Imminghamand sheds approximately 3,000 tonnes of crude oil into the River Humber.

29 September
The Cunard ferry *England* leaves England for the Falkland Islands. She is expected to reach the islands in 21 days time after making a refuelling stop in West Africa. *England* was bought from DFDS for £3 million and has just completed a pre-sale refit in Denmark.

3 October
The Royal Fleet Auxiliary *Sir Lancelot* returns to service after a refit following her service in the Falklands when she was hit by a 454 kg (1,000 lb) bomb. She will be carrying vehicles and supplies into Loch Ryan in Scotland as part of exercise 'Winged Victory'.

5 October
The *Merchant Providence* which left Avonmount ten days ago with the first load of plant and materials for the Falkland Islands airport has to make an unscheduled call at Las Palmas with machinery problems.

11 October
The Soviet Communist Party newspaper *Pravda* reports that 90 Soviet ships, including icebreakers are trapped in thick ice in the Chukhotsk Sea, north of Siberia.

A collision between the 3,774 grt Indonesian registered general cargo vessel *Gunung Klabat* and the Chinese vessel *Kwang Chow* causes the Chinese vessel to sink with the loss of 24 Chinese seaman about 115 miles north east of Hong Kong. The Indonesian vessel which rescued the Chinese crew sustains damage to her bow.

12 October
It is announced that the C.Y. Tung group are buying

the two 25-year old cruise ships *Veendam* and *Volendam*, 23,819 grt and 23,858 grt respectively, from Holland America Line who put them on the market six months ago.

The Soviet government newspaper *Izvestia* announces that the 3,601 grt general cargo vessel *Nina Sagaydak* has sunk due to the pressure of ice cracking her hull in the Sea of Chukhotsk, where she was trapped along with numerous other Soviet merchant vessels. Her 45 crew have all been rescued by helicopter.

16 October

The French tug *Abeille Flandre* is on her way to assist the Bahamas registered 7,697 grt general cargo ship *Turtle* which has reported a fire while rounding Ushant Island outbound from Le Havre. A French trawler and cargo ship are standing by. The cause of the fire is not known.

The Soviet newsagency TASS announces that icebreakers have freed five of the vessels trapped in pack ice off Siberia. A total of 21 vessels are still reported stuck. Before the icebreakers arrived the 3,019 ton *Yevgeniy Chaplanov* and the 10,185 ton *Vladimir Mordvinov* managed to break free without assistance.

17 October

Customs officials using sniffer dogs find 75 kg (165 lb) of cannabis hidden in the air conditioning plant of the 13,004 grt Ghana registered *Keta Lagoon* when she docks in Avonmount. Two fare-paying passengers are arrested.

18 October

The roll-on roll-off ferry *Rangatira* arrived in Devonport yesterday after serving in the Falkland Islands since June 1982. Her future is now uncertain following the completion of a refit at Harland and Wolff, Belfast.

19 October

Following 'premature and inadvertant contact with the shore' near to the Punta Camancho terminal on Lake Maracaibo, Venezuala, the Norwegian 7,418 m³ (261,965 ft³) gas carrier *Hardanger* is refloated following completion of a potentially dangerous operation of lightening the ship through a temporary 200 metre pipeline to the shore.

21 October

Following several threats of strike action at British Shipbuilder's Vosper Shiprepairers yards at Southampton, P&O Cruises managing director is forced to announce the cancellation of *Canberra*'s annual refit and drydocking.

24 October

The Soviet newsagency TASS announce that icebreakers have freed the tankers *Urengoy* (17,200 dwt)

and *Kamensk Uralsky* (17,125 tons) from pack ice off Siberia. Only three cargo vessels remain trapped out of the original total of 90 ships which became icebound earlier this month.

26 October

The River Tyne is closed for 24 hours for the 7,071 dwt heavy-lift ship *Dock Express 20* to load six gas turbine generators. The vessel, which is positioned stern-on to the quay, is jutting 165 metres out into the main channel.

The Danish shipyard of Helsingor closes down after 101 years in existance. The premises have been taken over by a new Company 'Helsingors Reparationsvaerft' which will specialise in shiprepair rather than new construction work. The new Company is a joint venture with Frederikshavn Vaerft and other members of the giant Danish Lauritzen group.

28 October

The cargo ship *Merchant Providence* arrives in the Falklands to take up her duties as base vessel for the airport project. She arrived ten days late due to an unscheduled stop at Las Palmas.

31 October

It is reported that right wing rebels in Nicaragua have attacked the general cargo vessel *Anita* and killed one stevedore at the port of Puerto Sandino. They also made an unsuccessful attempt to blow up her fuel tanks.

1 November

The 3,982 grt *Kampen*, owned by Schulz and Clemmensen of Hamburg, completed earlier this year by Zhonghau shipbuilders, sinks in heavy seas off

---

The ill-fated semi-container ship *Kampen* which tragically sank in November. Built in China for West German owners, she did not even reach her first birthday. (*FotoFlite, Ashford*)

Tor Scandinavia and Dana Futura recently sold to an investment company on a lease back agreement. (*FotoFlite, Ashford*)

Iceland. Seven seamen are lost and six rescued. She was carrying coal from Rotterdam to Iceland.

3 November
Owners of the 10,853 grt cargo ship *Avra* announce that they believe their vessel had been hit by an Exocet missile fired from an Iraqi helicopter near Bandar Khomeini. Part of the superstructure is ripped away and accommodation areas set on fire. The vessel was part of a convoy which was attacked.

4 November
It is reported that 20 Soviet ships are trapped in a new icefield off the Arctic island of Vrangel.

7 November
The inquiry into the collision between Sealink's rail ferry *Speedlink Vanguard* and the freight ferry *European Gateway* starts.

9 November
The 1,190 grt Spanish cargo vessel *Urualar Segundo* sinks in the Humber after colliding with the West German 999 grt cargo ship *Anglia*. *Anglia* is holed above the waterline but manages to berth without assistance.

10 November
British Shipbuilders subsidary Appledore Shipbuilders has won a contract from an Icelandic company to build a 3,000 dwt Pallet-container/bulk carrier. This is the first contract won from Iceland by British Shipbuilders since the mid-1960s.

11 November
DFDS sells two of their ships to Danish investment companies on a lease back agreement. The two ships are the *Tor Scandinavia* (14,893 grt), a passenger/car ferry, and the cargo ship *Dana Futura* (5,991 grt).

14 November
TASS, the official Soviet news agency, reports that the last of the 55 ice-trapped ships off the Northern Siberian coast has now been freed.

A three ship collision between the chemical carrier *Konko Maru No 38*, the Greek bulk carrier *Wismar* (24,198 tonnes) and the South Korean cargo ship *Ilshin Glory* (1,158 grt) takes place in the Kanmon Strait between the Japanese islands of Honshu and Kyushu. The *Konko Maru No 38* is seriously damaged and salvage operations are currently underway.

British shipowner Curnow announce that they are pulling out of a new passenger service to South Africa and would not re-charter the 8,665 grt *World Renaissance* when the present charter expires in April 1984. The decision is due to Safmarine's intention to use their latest acquisition *Astor* on the route commencing in February 1984. However, Curnow will offer an eight-day service to Cape Town from Avonmouth using the 3,150 grt, a 74-passenger ship *St. Helena*.

17 November
Cross Channel hovercraft services resume after a ten day stoppage caused by a pay protest by 40 French engineers.

18 November
The *Alexander L. Kielland* which capsized in 1980 and has recently been righted, is blown up and sunk in a fjord near Stavanger, Norway.

21 November
A cruise to Mexico has been cancelled following Holland America Line booking their newest cruise ship *Nieuw Amsterdam* into America's Triple A shipyards for 12 day engine repairs. This comes only a week after being drydocked for stern gear work.

Two Iranian ships sailing between Kharg Island

and Bandar Khomeini are hit during an Iraqi air attack. The two ships were part of a 40 ship convoy sailing under military escort.

23 November
Up to 200 people are missing after a Philippines inter-island ferry capsizes during a typhoon. The exact number of crew and passengers on board the ferry *Dona Casandra* is not yet known and there are a number of unconfirmed reports of the numbers of bodies found.

25 November
Following the capsizing of the ferry *Dona Casandra* 181 people have been picked up and only 13 dead bodies found.

The container ship *Ever Level* (23,270 grt) and *Itapage* collide in dense fog in the Elbe River. The *Ever Level* burst into flames immediately causing the death of one man. *Itapage* is able to make Hamburg under her own power, but *Ever Level* is reported to be listing badly.

29 November
Nieuw Amsterdam resumes her cruising programme following work on her engines in an American ship repair yard.

30 November
It is revealed that the Norwegian cruise ship *Royal Viking Star* (28,221 grt), bound for Zamboanga in the Southern Philippines, located an Indonesian ferry that had been drifting for almost two weeks after engine failure. All 151 passengers and crew are rescued.

1 December
Two ships belonging to Greece's national carrier Hellenic Lines are arrested, bringing the total number

Sea Containers 'Tackler' class ro-ro *Tollan* capsized three years ago and has recently been salvaged and moved from the Tagus River. (*Skyfotos*)

of their arrested ships to ten. Acceptance of bookings at the company's US offices is suspended.

5 December
The West German salvage company Sealift successfully rights the roll-on roll-off ferry *Tollan* which capsized in the Tagus River, Lisbon. The vessel and her cargo is moved ten miles off the Portuguese coast. *Tollan* capsized three minutes after colliding with the Swedish ro-ro *Barranduna* and a floating crane.

A regular passenger service between Guangzhou and Shanghai, China is reintroduced. The last regular service ceased in 1949. *Ziluolan* makes the first voyage with 300 passengers on board, reported the official Chinese news agency Xinhua.

The passenger ship *Royal Viking Sky* (21,891 grt), owned by the Royal Viking Line of Norway runs aground while entering the port of Puerto Plata in the Dominican Republic while on a cruise from Fort Lauderdale. Attempts are currently underway to refloat her.

Cocaine, estimated to be worth $900,000, is discovered by French customs officials on board the Colombian-registered cargo/container ship *Ciudad de Manizales* in the port of Le Havre.

7 December
The *Uganda* sails from Falmouth for Ascension Island after the completion of a 12 day refit. She will immediately resume her ferry service between Port Stanley and Ascension Island.

9 December
Holland America Lines latest passenger ship *Nieuw Amsterdam* enters dry dock in San Francisco for 24 hour repairs on a propeller shaft stern seal. This comes only two weeks after she was in the same

The 1972 Wärtsilä-built cruise ship *Royal Viking Star*, registered in Norway and owned by the Royal Viking Line. (*Skyfotos*)

American shipyard for some work on her engines and starboard stern tube. The vessel has been plagued with mechanical problems since her completion at French shipyards earlier this year.

Directors of Hellenic Agencies UK Ltd announce that they are going into voluntary liquidation. Hellenic Agencies are wholly owned by Hellenic Lines who continue to face financial problems.

A fire breaks out in the engine room of the Sealink roll-on roll-off ferry *Antrim Princess*, causing a complete engine breakdown 30 minutes after leaving Larne for Stranraer. An air-sea rescue operation is launched as the ferry battles against gale force winds. All passengers are evacuated by helicopter.

10 December

Cunard's new passenger ship *Vistafjord* leaves Malta after a £4.5 million refit. The vessel will commence a series of cruises from Genoa next week.

12 December

QE 2 leaves Bremerhaven half a day earlier than scheduled following extensive modification work at Hapag Lloyds repair yard.

Cunard's latest acquisition *Vistafjord* was purchased earlier in 1983 from Norwegian American Cruises. (*Skyfotos*)

QE 2 following her refit at Hapag Lloyds Bremerhaven ship repair yards. (*FotoFlite, Ashford*)

Seaforth Jarl (1,376 grt), owned by an Aberdeen-based company but currently operating in Canadian waters. (FotoFlite, Ashford)

Mikhail Kalinin of 5,243 grt and built 1958 is one of the Soviet cruise ships operating out of Tilbury that was in the news at the end of 1983 due to passenger complaints. (FotoFlite, Ashford)

The general cargo vessel Aziz Bhatti (built 1966) has been in the news twice this year for bringing drugs into the United Kingdom. (FotoFlite, Ashford)

13 December
QE 2 docks at Southampton six hours late following mechanical problems in one of her boilers. She left Bremerhaven the day before following refit.

16 December
Heroin worth £250,000 is found on board the Pakistani-registered vessel Aziz Bhatti by customs officials in Liverpool. This is the second drugs find on board the same ship this year.

More problems for QE 2 when road tankers fail to deliver enough fuel, resulting in her sailing late.

Transworld Rig 45, the US-owned semi-submersible drilling barge, capsizes off the Texan coast while being towed from Louisiana to Brownsville. The barge had just been purchased by B&B Towing from Transworld. Salvage work is underway.

19 December
The anchor handling tug/supply vessel Seaforth Jarl, owned by Seaforth Maritime of Aberdeen and operated by its Canadian company Seaforth Fednow, sinks off the Newfoundland coast in heavy seas. All 11 crew members are rescued.

22 December
Finnish shipowners SF Line (part of the Viking Line) sign a contract for the building of the world's largest car/passenger ferry with Wärtsilä. The order is believed to be worth £53.5 million. The 34,000 grt vessel will have accommodation for 2,500 passengers.

23 December
The Iraqi Navy reveals that they have sunk an Iranian salvage vessel while it had been attempting to save a vessel near Bandar Khomeini.

24 December
DFDS sells off the Nordana Line to Dannebrog Line for £2.4 million. This is just one more sale in the DFDS revival plan.

28 December
A Christmas cruise ends in protest when the Soviet cruise ship Mikhail Kalinin docks at Tilbury. Passengers claim the ship's crew were reluctant to let them go ashore, denied them use of the ship's phone system, and that the itinerary was not as advertised.

Problems and Progress in the Salvage Industry

by Nan de Halfweeg

Nan Halfweeg, Managing Director of Wijsmuller Salvage BV, is the author of this review. He has been with the Wijsmuller organisation some 26 years, and has been exclusively engaged in salvage work for the past 20 years. During this time he has been responsible for supervising many spectacular salvage operations, including, this year, the European Gateway *and* Ocean Ranger.

The effects of the continuing worldwide shipping recession, which shows no signs of abatement as these words are written, are many and varied. But, surely, nowhere is the effect more dramatically seen than in the salvage industry – the guardian of world merchant shipping.

Shipbuilding, fuel and crew costs have risen to such a level that it now costs around £1.5 million per annum to keep a large salvage tug on station; yet ship values are very low and getting lower, while salvage companies are faced with increasing problems over pollution and the ability to find ports or refuge for casualties. At the same time, as salvors repeatedly point out, awards are too little and too late.

Small wonder, then, that increasingly the major professional salvors are turning to other and more commercially viable work. But even here, in deepsea towage and anchor handling, there are problems, particularly in view of the downturn in the offshore drilling market, with newbuilding orders cancelled and existing units either idle or fighting for an ever-thinner slice of the cake.

The heavy-lift market, which some companies have embraced with great success, is also prone to over-tonnaging. Certainly the majority of heavy-lift transport operators are apprehensive about prospects, and some have described the immediate future as grim.

During the last six months of 1983, five new semi-submersible, heavy-lift carriers were added to the world fleet, while Japanese owners are also building some semi-submersible barges and the fleet has been further enlarged by conversions.

The Salvage Industry has gone through some profound changes in recent years: the available business has decreased, the shape of salvage tugs has changed, the OSV has taken much of the bread and butter work away from the purpose-built ocean salvage tugs, and all this in a time of recession in a trade which is already a hard, tough, and environmentally-ruthless task-master. To meet both new and old demands, the style of activity has had to change; semi-submersible heavy-lift ships, and compact anchor-handling tugs such as the *Typhoon* (shown) are now making their mark in a big way. (Cees van der Meulen)

The flexibility of the semi-submersible heavy-lift ship really made itself felt in 1983, both in the fields of transport and salvage. Ideal for the carriage of outsize and high unit-weight loads, the 'Super Servant' class have also blazed a new trail in the salvage of both *European Gateway* and the drilling-rig *Ocean Ranger*. (*Wijsmuller*)

In spite of the unfavourable market conditions, most operators have been able to keep their vessels reasonably employed, albeit at lower rates, but the newbuildings will obviously increase competition for the reduced cargo being offered.

However, as Paul de Vilder, managing director of Wijsmuller Nederland BV, points out, the superiority of self-propelled, heavy-lift vessels over towed barges and 'wet' tows has been proved during recent years. He believes that the market will pick up again as soon as economic conditions in the offshore and construction industries start to improve and transit times again become important. But he adds the warning that the total number of vessels available will be sufficient even in a more buoyant market, and further newbuildings

in the near future would certainly create a surplus which could affect rates for a long time to come.

Three of the five new vessels referred to were, in fact, the new-class *Mighty Servants* designed and operated by a Wijsmuller subsidiary (the other two were sister-ships to the *Divy Swan* and *Divy Tern*). The *Mighty Servant* vessels are among the most advanced of their kind in the world. Although they have been built to the same design as the highly successful *Super Servant* vessels, they are considerably bigger and incorporate a number of new features.

Wijsmuller blazed a trail in the heavy-lift market. Long renowed as a salvage and towage undertaking, Wijsmuller diversified and entered the transportation field in 1976 when it introduced two auxiliary-powered, semi-submersible barges of the *Ocean Servant* class – the first barges which could be submerged horizontally. In 1979 the company again introduced a new type, the *Super Servant* class. The concept was basically the same except that these vessels were completely self-propelled – something new in heavy-lift transportation.

Now, the combination of the three ultra-sophisticated *Mighty Servant* vessels and the three smaller *Super Servant* vessels means that Wijsmuller can claim to have the biggest and most flexible fleet of heavy-lift carriers to be found anywhere.

Like its competitors, Wijsmuller is finding the salvage market tough going. Although casualty statistics generally show a continuing trend of around one million tons gross being totally lost annually, which is of concern to the marine insurance business, the number of large, spectacular, high-cost casualties has declined quite dramatically over the past two to three years. This can be attributed to a number of factors, such as inert gas-freeing of tanks and so on, but undoubtedly a major contributory factor is the number of large ships, especially tankers, which are without employment; indeed, many are never expected to be reactivated. So the salvage industry loses out in this respect.

In addition, the shipping slump has thrown up a number of new problems and situations with which, legally, salvors are not equipped to deal. And overshadowing all else is the pollution nightmare.

When the Spanish supertanker *Castillo de Bellver* broke in two off South Africa in August, at an early

Mighty Servant 1, the first of three new semi-submersible, self-propelled, heavy-lift carriers to be completed in Japan for Wijsmuller. Picture shows the 23,800 dwt *Mighty Servant 1* in submerged condition during her pre-delivery trials. (*Wijsmuller*)

stage the accident threatened a crude oil disaster comparable to that caused by the *Amoco Cadiz*.

When Lloyd's Open Form was revised and brought into effect in May 1980 it included certain major changes, but the most important revision was the extension of the 'no cure – no pay' provision when salvors tackle a tanker laden or partly laden with oil cargo. Although this clause (known as the 'safety net') does not specifically mention the prevention of oil pollution, it was intended that this extension of the 'no cure – no pay' principle would encourage salvors to give prompt assistance to tanker casualties and thus minimise the potential dangers of pollution.

Although, generally, salvors welcomed what they saw as long-overdue changes to LOF, which is functioning quite well, some have since felt that perhaps there is room for another standard salvage contract to deal with cases where the potential salved fund is not sufficient. Also, there is no standard salvage contract for a case where a definite interest exists solely because of the pollution element.

On the other hand, salvors are acutely disappointed that governments have not yet taken one step to arrive at designated ports of refuge and cost-sharing agreements for them. All salvors are agreed that strategically located safe ports are essential for handling large-scale threats of pollution. Many well-publicised casualties over the past dozen years have demonstrated this need, for example, the *Amoco Cadiz, Andros Patria, Christos Bitas, Kurdistan, Montebello, Aquarius* and *Wafra*.

Governments or port authorities refusing entry to their ports does not solve the salvage problem. It not only delays the moment that pollution becomes real, but it also increases the risk of greater pollution by forcing the casualty to remain exposed to wave-bending forces and stresses caused by rolling and pitching.

In 1984 the International Maritime Organisation (IMO) is due to study the subject of 'whether the 1910 Salvage Convention should be revised or a separate convention should be prepared in order to cover those casualties which may cause a threat of pollution' according to what has been agreed between the IMO and the Committee Maritime Internationale (CMI), the latter charged with the job of exploring this question first.

The CMI has now completed a draft revision of the convention. The first thing in the draft that strikes one is that action to prevent pollution and other environmental damage has to be closely linked to salvage efforts. Consequently, there will be no action

One of the biggest jack-up drilling rigs in the world, the *Glomar Labrador I*, sits astride the semi-submersible, self-propelled, heavy-lift carrier *Mighty Servant 1* as she sets out from Dunkirk for Canada in October 1983. Delivered in August, this was the second transport performed by *Mighty Servant 1*. On her maiden voyage from Japan to Europe she transported another Global Marine Drilling Co rig, the *Glomar Adriatic IV*, from Singapore to Sicily. (*FotoFlite, Ashford*)

Few salvage contractors, if any, can afford to remain in business on the strength of salvage activities alone. This has forced the introduction of new types of salvage tugs, designed to operate in as many fields as possible while retaining an overall flexibility not required of any other ship type. This has caused the development of vessels such as the *Typhoon* and *Tempest,* which have high horsepower to size ratios and cutaway sterns to allow the handling of rig anchors. The latter play a major part in the activities of Wijsmuller's tugs nowadays. (*Bart Hofmeester*)

to prevent pollution in case salvage is not considered technically and/or economically feasible. Accordingly, there is no remuneration foreseen for these cases.

However, as Mr C P Srivastava, secretary-general of the IMO, pointed out in New York as far back as 1979: '. . . the prevention of marine pollution may often be of greater importance than the salvage of the ship itself . . .' So it seems that the IMO will not be satisfied with the CMI draft.

In the opinion of the salvage industry, the IMO must now accelerate the pace of the lawmaking process in order to be ahead of future maritime disasters.

Apart from the pollution problem, refusals by ports to admit casualties are causing severe problems for salvors in other ways. And these problems will multiply as long as the worldwide shipping slump persists. According to The Salvage Association, London, there have been cases of owners refusing to take redelivery of their vessels from salvors operating on LOF 80, and the salvor has had no option but to abandon the property at sea. This has emphasised, says the association, that owners must realise that Clause 2 of the contract requires the owner to co-operate fully with the salvor in respect of the salvage, including

obtaining entry to a place of safety to which the salved property can be taken, and, furthermore, promptly to accept delivery at such a place.

In disputes of this kind, the salvor finds himself in the classic situation of being caught in the middle – the reluctant owner not wishing to take responsibility for a casualty and the salvage company being unable to take the vessel to a safe haven. An example along these lines is described in latter pages of this Review.

The scenario, in its simplest form, is of a salvage tug appearing outside a port with an elderly ship in tow, frequently in a fire-damaged condition, which the salvor wishes to return to her owners. (In 1982 and 1983 there was a dramatic increase in engineroom and accommodation fires, and what is noticeable are the fires which are not confined to the area of origination, often leading to a vessel being declared a Constructive Total Loss by underwriters.) If the salvor tries to find a berth inside a port, the authorities expect the salvor to guarantee payment of port expenses for the time the ship is there. This could amount to several thousand dollars a day and would be especially prohibitive in the case of a larger vessel.

In any case, no harbourmaster wants to be left with yet another wreck on his hands, occupying commercial space and creating a hazard and nuisance to other port users.

This problem has prompted complaints from the International Salvage Union (ISU), while London maritime lawyers have urged salvors to exercise extreme caution when agreeing terms for taking in tow badly-damaged, low-value ships in case the owner refuses redelivery.

When the ISU held its annual meeting in London in October 1983, the 30-strong membership urged Lloyd's to amend the controversial LOF to reflect present-day conditions. The president, Mr Ron Scheffer, said: 'There is need to resolve ambiguities of wording which practical experience of the form has brought to light and also a need to ensure that the provisions of the agreement are appropriate to present-day circumstances.'

International agreement on a new salvage convention could take several years, and in the meantime the salvage industry wants Lloyd's to lead the way by reviewing the scope and wording of the form. One of the most effective actions, said the ISU president, would be to widen the 'safety net' to embrace noxious and hazardous cargoes.

But he added that salvors were facing problems which could not be resolved simply by formal wordings

of treaties and contracts. He followed the comments of The Salvage Association and lawyers by alerting members that salvages under LOF conditions were being jeopardised by the failure of some owners to fulfil contractual obligations and accept redelivery of their ships.

He said: 'Too frequently, serious difficulties are being experienced in obtaining security from ship and cargo and severe problems are being created by the indecisiveness and delays introduced by some governments when there is risk of environmental pollution.'

In the meantime, some legal opinion suggests that salvors could do something towards remedying the problem, which is a phenomenon of an extremely sick shipping market. Arbitrators could take a bolder line which would ensure that the present wording of LOF 80 is adequate to cope with this new situation.

Taking a technical overview of the salvage industry, every year there is usually at least one salvage operation that demonstrates the perseverance and ingenuity of the professional salvor, and 1983 was no exception.

It fell to Wijsmuller's salvage company to carry out, successfully, one of the most spectacular and widely-publicised ship rescues ever attempted. This was the uprighting of the capsized freight ferry *European*

One cause of a generally deflated market is the spread of the recession throughout almost all of the maritime trades. This view showing 'trots' of laid-up vessels in Greek waters, is but a small fraction of the total tonnage laid-up worldwide. (*Denzil Stuart Associates*)

If a salvor were to save a tanker worth, say £8 million, with a cargo of crude oil aboard worth, say £12 million, the total salved amount upon which the salvor's fractional percentage would be calculated would be about £20 million. In fact, however, the environmental clean-up could run to £500 million or more in an extreme case. If the salvage offered were on an 'open form' basis and the job looked doubtful from the salvor's point of view, a salvor could well find himself in a position whereby he just would not want to get involved. The only obvious way of overcoming this problem would be to *base* the salvage claim and award on the total value of *all* money saved by the prompt action of the salvor. (*Wijsmuller & Henk Honing*)

Gateway off Felixstowe, which was to prove a long and hazardous job.

The *European Gateway* was delivered into dry dock at Amsterdam on March 31. By early June, Wijsmuller was involved in yet another long and dangerous salvage, this time some 2,500 miles away in the inhospitable waters of the North Atlantic. This time the task was to raise the sunken and ill-fated drilling rig *Ocean Ranger*, which went down in a storm off Newfoundland in February 1982, and thereafter to tow the rig into deeper water and sink it.

But the *Ocean Ranger* was to claim yet more lives because, tragically, three men died during the salvage.

The *European Gateway* and *Ocean Ranger* operations were significant in that a semi-submersible heavy-lift carrier was used in both – the first time this type of vessel had been employed in a major salvage operation. *Super Servant 3* was the base and winching vessel for the *European Gateway* uprighting, while *Ocean Servant 2* was a key factor in the *Ocean Ranger* salvage.

The *Ocean Ranger* salvage involved a great deal of preparatory work underwater, and three divers, in two separate accidents, were killed while this was in progress. The operation continued, and the rig was eventually raised.

Death and injury in the salvage industry are nothing new – the risk is always there. When accidents like these do happen, however, they emphasise the dedication to duty which is the hallmark of the professional salvor.

The Salving of *European Gateway*

A photo feature by A J Ambrose

On Sunday evening 19 December 1982, while outward bound from Felixstowe, England for Zeebrugge, Belgium with a cargo of road vehicles and several accompanying lorry drivers, the 4263 grt roll-on roll-off ferry *European Gateway* was struck on her starboard side and severely holed below the waterline by the Sealink railway ferry *Speedlink Vanguard*. The collision took place in good visibility about two to three miles off the coast just outside Harwich Harbour. About a mile further out, the Captain of the Danish ro-ro *Dana Futura* watched his radar screen with horror as he saw the tracks of the opposing vessels merge. So started one of the most unusual stories of collision and subsequent salvage so far witnessed this decade.

On Christmas Eve 1982, against strong competition from other salvage companies, the contract for the salving of *European Gateway*, now lying on its side in about 20 feet of water, was awarded on Lloyd's Open Form to Wijsmuller Salvage of Ijmuiden, Holland.

Wijsmuller had handled many such salvage operations in their long established history, but this was an exception. *European Gateway* was lying on the hole which *Speedlink Vanguard* had made in her side, and was in a totally exposed position should a north-easterly gale develop. Thus, she would need to be brought upright first, then have her hole patched, and only then could she be fully pumped out. Provided, that is, that an easterly gale did not develop. It did, and the pictures tell the story.

European Gateway outbound from Felixstowe. Ten days after this photo was taken she was holed in the starboard side below the waterline by the ice-strengthened bulbous bow of **Speedlink Vanguard**. (*FotoFlite, Ashford*)

Six lives were lost as a result of the collision. That this figure was not considerably higher was directly attributable to the activities of the local Trinity House pilot launches, and the local lifeboats. (*A J Ambrose*)

◄

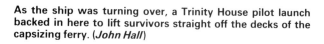

As the ship was turning over, a Trinity House pilot launch backed in here to lift survivors straight off the decks of the capsizing ferry. (*John Hall*)

Some of the trailers on the shelter-deck aft remained in position due to their securing chains which anchored them to the deck. (*John Hall*)

A selection of views of the capsized vessel. The hole is underneath. The bottom in that area is patchy consisting of either pebbles or mud. The effect of a mud bottom would have been to create suction on the hull of the capsized vessel making it harder to lift. The proximity to the coast and to the main channel can be seen: the IALA buoy just visible in some of these views shows the northern extremity of the deep-water channel. The officer in charge of *European Gateway* deliberately tried to steer out of the channel following the collision, in an attempt to run the ship aground on the soft-bottom to minimise damage and to prevent the ship from sinking.

Unfortunately however, the inrush of water into the engine room was substantial and this, coupled to a lack of watertight compartmentalisation (the fateful 'free surface effect' for which modern ro-ro vessels are notorious), caused the vessel to capsize on the gently sloping shelf. (*FotoFlite, Ashford and John Hall*)

◄
Having just completed their successful salvage of the jack-up drilling rig *Sagar Vikas* in Bombay on 21 December 1982, Wijsmuller's salvage teams were aboard an aircraft bound for Europe and the North Sea. Within 24 hours of the Lloyd's Open Form agreement on 24 December, salvage teams spent their Christmas organising and moving equipment into position in a race against the weather which takes no account for the niceties of the festive season. (*FotoFlite, Ashford*)

On 11 January 1983 the semi-submersible heavy-lift ship *Super Servant 3* arrived on the scene, and with the aid of a crane barge a series of eight winches were attached to *Super Servant*'s decks while anchors were put out from *European Gateway*'s keel. The intention was to winch *Gateway* upright using the hawsers under her keel as a fulcrum. (*FotoFlite, Ashford*)

By 30 January 1983, Wijsmuller's Managing Director and working salvage boss Nan Halfweeg, together with senior salvage captain Harry Hopman and his team of 50 salvagemen, were ready to start the pull. A set of 30-ton anchors had been positioned to seaward of *European Gateway* and affixed to her keel. *Super Servant 3* was anchored with another set of anchors laid to south-east. The winches and cantilever arms had all been fixed in position and connected with chains joined to the winches' cables. The vehicle deck had been plugged and pumping had started. All that was now needed was relatively calm weather.

Next morning, 31 January 1983 dawned fine. A reasonable weather forecast was received and the haul commenced. Tensions increased, both on the winches and the 60-plus members of the world's press present to watch the proceedings. By 11 am the ferry's list had decreased to about 60° with all looking fine. But, as the winching proceeded, the weather began to deteriorate, and a race between wind and winches developed. Within what seemed like minutes, a strong wind had appeared, whipping up 8-foot swells which were snatching *Super Servant 3* against both her own anchors and the winch cables. A larger swell suddenly hit *Super Servant 3* and the resulting movement caused a cantiliver chain to snap. The connecting winch shot overboard. The increased strain overheated another. The swell had by now started lifting *European Gateway* which had developed a perceptible sliding action along the bottom towards *Super Servant 3*. The attempt had to be stopped.

As the seas continued to rise, the dreaded north-easterlies appeared. Over the next weeks, the *European Gateway*'s exposed superstructure was battered by strong winds and waves, and all work had to stop. It was thus not until

The attachment points for the eight winch cables are affixed to *European Gateway*'s hull. Meanwhile, Wijsmuller's teams are plugging as many holes as possible on the ferry's vehicle deck so as to create some positive buoyancy to assist the winches in the lift. (*FotoFlite, Ashford*)

Saturday 26 February that the team were ready for a second attempt. To stop the sliding action, a pontoon was anchored to seaward with two heavy hawsers attached underneath *European Gateway*'s hull. Winching commenced again. This time, as the tension on the winches and anchors increased, *European Gateway* began to turn. (*FotoFlite, Ashford*)

By late afternoon, *European Gateway* was up. Now lying at an angle of only 14°, the damage wreaked on the superstructure by the onset of foul weather became obvious. Much of it had simply been wiped out. Added to this, the divers found that there were two holes in the starboard side: one about 5 × 15 metres, the other about 5 × 5 metres. A steel patch was fabricated in Felixstowe and positioned over the larger hole, while the smaller hole was left open and the compartment behind it was sealed. Conservation work on the ship's machinery, removal of debris, and mud, and pumping then began in earnest.

Soon, *European Gateway* was afloat again. *Super Servant 3* had sailed, bound for Venezuala, and the tug *Titan* was left to conclude matters. However, more problems were in store. The Harwich harbour authorities while content to allow *Speedlink Vanguard* to continue working, were not prepared to allow Wijsmuller to bring the floating *European Gateway* into the shelter of the harbour. To prevent this, they demanded Wijsmuller pay a $100 million indemnity along with equally massive harbour dues, while apparently forgetting that Wijsmuller had gone to great lengths to assure that no pollution would be caused by leakage from the *Gateway*'s fuel tanks. With such a sad show of mindless selfish insanity, Wijsmuller's tug *Titan*, which had assisted throughout, connected to the still listing *European Gateway*, and without further ado towed the vessel to Amsterdam.

Sadly, this was not the end of the story. Wijsmuller spent as much as £1 million on the salvage attempt on *European Gateway* which was insured for £13.6 million. Townsend Thoresen, the owners, did not want the ship back and the insurers decided to class the vessel as a constructive total loss. As a result, Wijsmuller made a massive loss on the venture, emphasising the point that salvage is a high risk business.

Passenger Shipping – 1983

1 – The Cruise Trade

by Russell Plummer

Russell Plummer is a professional writer covering several fields including both modern and historical short-sea passenger shipping. He is the author of Paddle Steamers in the 1970s, *editor of the specialist enthusiast's magazine* Paddle Wheels, *the compiler of the monthly* European Commentary *in the international enthusiast's magazine* Ships Monthly, *and still finds time to contribute regular articles and columns to journals such as the authoritative* Fairplay Shipping Weekly.

While the number of passenger ships running for British owners has paled almost to insignificance by historic standards, the names of Cunard Line and P&O have remained consistently in the public eye

although attention has too often been deflected from matters afloat by potential financial wheeling and dealing and, for Cunard at least, a whole series of controversies with political overtones in which even their patriotism was called into question.

Cunard's parent company, Trafalgar House, rocked the boat with a takeover bid for P&O that produced a series of furious exchanges before ardour was

P&O's *Canberra*, **totally refitted from stem to stern following her use as an assault ship during the Falklands conflict. She was fully booked for months thereafter, but has steadied down to her usual reasonably high load factor now.** (*P&O Cruises*)

Queen Elizabeth 2 has had a useful year but not without problems. In 1984 she boasts a new covered swimming pool and lido. (*FotoFlite, Ashford*)

dampened and the whole matter referred to the Monopolies and Mergers Commission. Despite their illustrious shipping antecedence, especially on the passenger side, both groups have diversified into other areas of commerce in recent times and from being wholly reliant on shipping for their profits a decade ago, this now represents less than half of P&O's assets.

Cunard put an end to speculation about possible new orders in 1983, when they strengthened their cruising fleet with the cash purchase, for a reported £46.5 million, of the Norwegian American Line vessels *Vistafjord* and *Sagafjord*, which are well established in the 'up-market' sector of cruising and came under Cunard control from October. The two ships, identified by Cunard as conforming with their traditional standards, are being retained on similar programmes, with *Vistafjord*'s time split between the Caribbean and Mediterranean/Scandinavia and *Sagafjord* continuing to run out of American ports, including the West Coast.

The two vessels are being re-registered in the Bahamas, a move that further angered British seafarers' unions, coming against a background of Cunard's continuing efforts for the flagging-out of the *Cunard Countess* and *Cunard Princess* in the United States.

Criticism of this policy was a major plank in P&O's takeover defence as all their seven cruise ships are British-registered and manned. The Trafalgar House bid values P&O's 60 ship fleet and energy and property interests at £290 million.

Unions in the shipbuilding and repair industry also reacted vociferously when Cunard first talked of ordering a replacement for Falklands casualty *Atlantic Conveyor* in the Far East and there was more flak from the same quarter when *Cunard Countess* was sent to Malta for a £2m refit at the end of her long stint in the South Atlantic. In fairness to Cunard it has to be pointed out that none of three British yards approached over the work on *Cunard Countess* would commit itself to the 40 days deadline with severe penalty clauses in the event of delay, and some executives expressed doubts whether the Maltese could do it either. Yet *Cunard Countess* left Valetta on schedule and resumed cruising out of Miami in July as planned.

Cunard had worries of a different kind when *Queen Elizabeth 2* suffered recurring mechanical troubles, including one embarassing weekend when the liner was a static tourist attraction anchored in Mounts Bay in SW England. Finally, transatlantic sailing and cruises had to be cancelled at the height of the season

Hapag-Lloyd Werft at Bremerhaven received the contract for the *QE 2*'s refit based on their experience with earlier passenger vessel conversions such as the *France/Norway* modernisation. (*Drawing: A J Ambrose*)

Scale: 1:1200

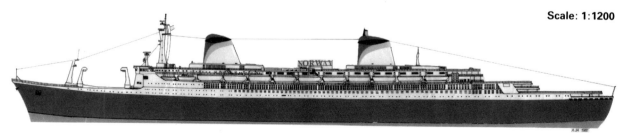

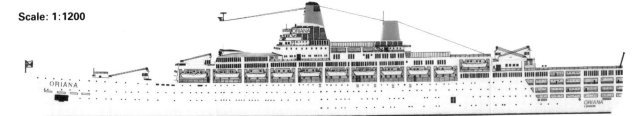

P&O's *Oriana*. (*Drawing: A J Ambrose*)

for the problems to be finally resolved at Southampton. The autumn brought another outcry when Cunard confirmed that *QE 2* was bound for Bremerhaven for extensive works including erection of an alloy Magradome over one of the two outdoor swimming pools and lido decks – although yet again the British yards had to admit their experience of such specialised work was minimal compared to that of the Hapag-Lloyd Werft who were responsible for the conversion of the former transatlantic liner *France* for cruising as the *Norway*.

Cunard's action with *QE 2* is no less logical than the decision to have Genoa-based *Vistafjord* refitted in Malta and *Sagafjord* docked in the United States, saving the considerable expense of bringing them all the way to British yards. During September Cunard did make a surprising entry into the sales market buying the 19-year-old passenger and car ferry *England* from DFDS and what's more, this veteran of countless North Sea crossings sailed for the Falklands with British crew and under a temporary British flag! Cunard secured the 19 month contract for conveyance of personnel and materials for the construction of the new Falklands Airport to the Islands from Cape Town at the eleventh hour after it seemed destined to go to Curnow Shipping, who also planned to use the *England*.

Cunard's purchase of the existing Norwegian vessels is rather against the cruising trend towards ships with substantially larger capacity. There has been a marginal increase in passenger cabins on *Vistafjord* and *Sagafjord* to boost profitability but carryings will remain well below the *circa* 1,500 berths of new constructions. Despite near saturation, particularly in cruising from the United States, massive building investment continues and after the debuts of significant newcomers such as *Song of America, Tropicale, Atlantic* and *Nieuw Amsterdam* even more ships are building and there have been further 'stretching' exercises to lift carryings on some of the first generation of modern cruise liners introduced with scope for between 600 and 700 passengers.

Among cruise ships currently taking shape is P&O's *Royal Princess* which, in many respects, will be a further development of the *Song of America*, delivered in November 1982 by Wärtsilä, Helsinki, and now on the seven day cruise circuit out of Miami. P&O still talk of a worldwide role for *Royal Princess* which is seem as an addition to the fleet rather than a replacement. Above all P&O look forward to having what promises to be an economical ship from the operating

point of view. Bunker costs of *Royal Princess* are estimated at 5 per cent of the total expenses against as much as 25 per cent for the flagship *Canberra*, one of a number of traditional passenger liners switched to cruising full time after advances in air travel rapidly destroyed their traditional routes.

Canberra's popularity, which soared in a return to cruising amid post-Falklands euphoria in the autumn of 1982, held firm last year with over 21,000 passengers carried in a 13 cruise summer programme from Britain. The rather smaller, higher quality *Sea Princess* has also established a foothold in Northern Europe after changing places and leaving the Australian market to the larger *Oriana*. But a casualty of the Falklands episode was the educational cruise series operated by

Oriana **now serves the Australian trade in the warm waters of the Far East. She is seen here in the unmistakable port of Sydney where she is now permanently based.** (*P&O Cruises*)

1982 saw several new completions in the cruise trade, among them being the Hapag-Lloyd flagship *Europa*. (*FotoFlite, Ashford*)

the popular *Uganda* which was used as a hospital ship during the confrontation with Argentina. *Uganda* went back to the advertised programme in September 1982 but the booking pattern had been interrupted and P&O cut their losses and chartered *Uganda* to the Ministry of Defence for a return to the South Atlantic in a supply role.

With her extensive dormitory accommodation the *Uganda* is proving ideal for moving troops of the Falklands garrison in and out of Port Stanley via Ascension. While cruising with school groups the vessel also carried a limited number of adult passengers in separate accommodation, and to cater for this continuing specialised demand P&O bought the Swan Hellenic operation which is best known for a long running series of lecturer accompanied cruises, mainly in the Mediterranean, and also a programme of Nile cruises in a similar format. The main Swan Hellenic Schedule has been in the hands of the chartered Epirotiki Line vessel *Orpheus* for the last decade and P&O saw no reason to make changes and retained the old-timer, originally the Irish Sea Ferry *Munster*.

The Falklands War and its aftermath continued to affect other companies, including St. Helena Shipping, the small but ambitious British West Country outfit that had been carving a useful line-voyage niche between Avonmouth and South Africa via St. Helena with the *St. Helena*, until the little passenger/cargo vessel was requisitioned in May 1982. *St. Helena* lingered in southern waters longer than most and did not return to the civilian route until last September, the larger Singapore-registered *Centaur*, on charter from Blue Star, holding the fort in the meantime but

proving too expensive to become a permanent fixture.

In November Curnow broke more fresh ground by joining forces with a South African travel agency to revive the UK–Cape Town liner service on a regular basis in the guise of Cape Albion Line with the 516-berth *World Renaissance* chartered from Epirotiki Line following a spell of Caribbean cruising in the colours of Costa Line. The launch of the service aroused considerable interest in Europe and South Africa and was seen as re-establishment of links severed when the historic Union-Castle/Safmarine service was terminated in 1977. Ironically, even before *World Renaissance* cast off on the first voyage competition was looming, Safmarine making moves to re-open a service to Europe with the West German passenger vessel *Astor*, reported purchased from Hadag by South African interests in October.

Although a modern unit, completed as recently as 1981, the *Astor* had been fighting a losing battle in the cruising market having fewer than 700 berths and this made the sale for a reported $50m less than surprising. Competition has certainly become keener among the cruise companies, and the need for greater flexibility in programme planning has been demonstrated by Norwegian Caribbean Lines who are bringing *Norway* to Europe for a 1984 series of North Cape cruises from Hamburg and Amsterdam. NCL still have a quartet of vessels running out of Miami which remains unquestionably the world's cruising capital with facilities to handle a dozen vessels simultaneously and a passenger turnover approaching two million in 1983.

While it might be expected that the influx of new tonnage would displace some of the older ex-passenger

Contrast in smaller cruise ships – Royal Cruise Line's purpose-built *Golden Odyssey* and the veteran Epirotiki Line motor ship *Orpheus* at Istanbul. Dating from 1948 and originally the British and Irish ferry *Munster*, the *Orpheus* has for the last decade covered the specialist cruise programme of Swan Hellenic that was taken over in 1983 by P&O. (*Russell Plummer*)

Continuing her regular cruise/line voyages between Europe and Canada is Polish Ocean Line's *Stefan Batory.* She has the possibly unique distinction that she almost always disembarks more people than she embarks, due to a prevalence for members of the crew to defect when the ship enters a Western sea-port. At one point a relief crew flown to Canada to take over the ship, following the former crew's mass disembarkation, also defected and yet another crew had to be flown out to bring the ship home. This aspect of operating a passenger ship was at its height in 1981–82 but has moderated somewhat this year. (*FotoFlite, Ashford*)

liners that have enjoyed a new lease of life in full-time cruising, this has not happened to any great extent and tonnage sold-off has simply been retained by new owners in similar services. Even rapidly expanding cruise giants Carnival Cruises with the impressive *Tropicale* already on stream, a sistership under construction in Denmark and a further pair of vessels on order from Sweden, still see a role for their trio of steam-powered ex-British vessels originally from such famous fleets as Canadian Pacific and Union-Castle. Another ex-liner from the same era, Greek Line's Clyde-built *Olympia* which had been laid-up at Piraeus since 1974, was rendered almost unrecognisable by a reconstruction in Hamburg which included replacement of steam turbine propulsion by Deutz diesels. Bought by a subsidiary of Finnish ferry specialists Rederi AB Sally, *Olympia* has started a Caribbean cruise circuit as *Caribe 1*, sailing out of Miami opposite *Boheme* and in Commodore Cruise Lines colours.

A strong Scandinavian influence remains in cruising and Oslo-based Royal Viking Line has now had all of its trio of vessels lengthened, the most recent insertion of a 28 metres mid-body section in *Royal Viking Sea* by A.G. Weser at Bremerhaven taking just 11 weeks. Royal Caribbean Line have sent vessels back to their builders Wärtsilä for a similar process, but small can also be beautiful in ship owners' eyes, with Sweden's Salen Group acquiring Lindblad Travel and continuing to operate the specialist cruise ships *Lindblad Explorer* and *Lindblad Polaris* to places off the beaten track all over the world. *Linblad Polaris*, sumptuously converted from a former Oresund ferry, takes just 76 passengers and there has to be a moral in that somewhere!

An elegant newcomer to cruising is Salen Lindblad's *Lindblad Polaris,* an almost yacht-like conversion from the one-time Swedish passenger ferry *Oresund.* Because of her small size *Lindblad Polaris* is able to penetrate inland waterways and visit locations well out of the reach of more conventional cruise vessels. (*Russell Plummer*)

Holland-America's *Nieuw Amsterdam* was the principal new entrant to the cruise market in 1983. She did not get off to a particularly good start however, as the builders Chantiers de l'Atlantique of France, did not have her ready in time for her maiden voyage. Nevertheless, when finally underway following her launch by HRH Princess Margriet of the Netherlands, she was well accepted by her US clientele, although continual construction faults have persisted to dog her progress.

She is of 33,930 tons, 214.65 × 27.2 × 7.4 m, has 11 decks, 21 lounges and bars, a 230-seat theatre, two 'outdoor' swimming pools, a whirlpool, gymnasium, massage rooms, saunas, 15 elevators, a passenger capacity of 1,354 (1,210 on cruising), and a crew of 559. All her 605 cabins have 'private facilities' (that's cruise market talk for toilet and shower/bath), radio, and colour television as standard fitments.

Power is provided by a pair of 7-cylinder Sulzer diesels, each developing 10,800 kW and driving 16 ft diameter 17-ton CP propellers. She has both bow and stern thrusters, a fuel oil capacity of 610,000 gallons and a service speed of 20 knots. She is registered in the Netherland-Antilles.

Nieuw Amsterdam on completion. (*Schart Fotografie*)　　　　Cut-away view of **Nieuw Amsterdam**. (*Holland America Line*)

At sea on trials in early 1983. (*Holland America Line*)

Named after the original Dutch colony on Manhattan Island, *Nieuw Amsterdam* enters New York at the end of her maiden voyage. (*Holland America Line*)

Interior views of *Nieuw Amsterdam.* (*Holland America Line*)

2 – The European Ferry Scene

by Russell Plummer

The near torrent of new ferry tonnage of recent years might have dried to a mere trickle, but that has not prevented new introductions from both the sales and charter markets in a 12 month period that has also been periodically dominated by the continuing trials of a single operator, DFDS! The Danish giant is now emerging with a considerably leaner look from a period of retrenchment and reorganisation following the lengthy spell of seemingly unchecked expansion.

It is now generally agreed that DFDS tried to go too far too quickly, as they gobbled up rivals on Danish domestic routes and the North Sea, at the same time as trying to establish their North American subsidiary Scandinavian World Cruises. Some drastic changes were necessary to pull the fat out of the fire and fairly severe axe wielding was applied to services out of Britain. Of the 11 passenger and vehicle carriers running from Harwich, Felixstowe and North Shields in the summer of 1982, just six vessels are in the schedules for summer 1984. Yet only two routes have gone by the board and while there are fewer sailings in

some directions, by better utilisation of larger ferries the loss of capacity is almost neglible.

In the space of little more than a year DFDS have been able to take out six ferries of 1960s vintage. *England* (1964) and *Winston Churchill* (1967) were retired from the North Sea services; the two Mediterranean routes were abandoned from October 1982 with *Dana Sirena* (1970) quickly sold for Red Sea use and *Dana Corona* (1969) chartered out for a 1983 summer stint for Viking Line consortium members S.F. Line between Kapellskar and Mariehamn; finally, the Copenhagen–Oslo run's sister units *Kong Olav V* and *Princesse Margrethe*, both dating from 1968, were replaced last October by *Dana Gloria* and *Dana Regina*, switched from the North Sea.

Apart from *England*, now in Cunard colours and enjoying a new lease of life running between Cape

---

Emblazoned with both Viking Line colours and DFDS funnel, *Dana Corona* is seen at Mariehamn in July 1982. (*K Brzoza*)

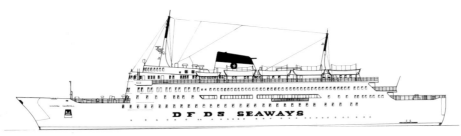

Scale: 1:1200

DFDS's **Winston Churchill** has now been retired from North Sea services. Built in 1967, she was, with her running mate **England,** an old favourite with passengers on both the southern (Harwich) and northern (North Shields) routes. (*Drawing: Michael J Ambrose/Jerzy Swiesnowski*)

Dana Regina has now been withdrawn from the Harwich–Esbjerg services in a reorganisation of Tor/DFDS/Prinz sailings from the port. (*A J Ambrose*)

Town and the Falklands on a 19 month contract conveying workers involved in the construction of the Island's new airport, the five remaining ships, all built at Genoa, have the limitation of originating in the days when multi-class accommodation had to be provided and in spite of improvements and alterations over the years, especially in the case of the ex-Mediterranean ships and those on the Oslo route, this legacy is very apparent internally.

Copenhagen–Oslo is potentially the most lucrative DFDS passenger route and it makes sense to bring in substantially larger and more modern vessels here, although there are many regular North Sea passengers who lamented the departure of the elegant *Dana Regina* after more than eight years and an estimated 1,250-plus Esbjerg–Harwich round trips. *Dana Regina* carried DFDS into the jumbo era ahead of the trend in uniformity of internal layout that so characterises the modern ferry, and combines high capacity with some of the styles and individuality of former ships through notable features such as the spiral staircase sweeping down from the Bellevue Lounge into the main restaurant.

The release of *Dana Regina* was effected by including the former Tor Line vessels *Tor Scandinavia* and *Tor Britannia* into the Esbjerg rosters opposite the DFDS flagship *Dana Anglia*, itself sold to Danish

banking and investment interests last year and then leased back. Additionally *Tor Scandinavia* and *Tor Britannia* provide three weekly round trips to Göteborg and since the beginning of May 1983 the Swedish sailings switched from Felixstowe to Harwich where a fourth ro-ro berth is now in the course of construction. DFDS claimed record carryings in the 1983 summer period and the Harwich–Hamburg service by the time-chartered *Prinz Hamlet* was especially busy and clearly gained traffic from the almost parallel Bremerhaven route withdrawn the previous winter.

The removal of *Dana Gloria* from a circuit providing North Shields with twice weekly summer connections with Göteborg and also a round trip to Denmark, fired speculation over the future of DFDS services from the Tyne and at one stage plans to scrap the Göteborg link, originally a DFDS-Tor Line joint venture, were announced. Eventually it emerged that new schedules were being worked out for North Shields to retain twice weekly sailings to Sweden, Norway and Denmark with the work shared by the chartered Fred Olsen-Bergen Line sisters *Jupiter* and *Venus*. However, as part of moves towards a corporate image, all North Sea routes are now marketed under the banner of DFDS Seaways with the use of the names of former operators Olsen-Bergen, Tor Line and Prins Ferries dropped.

Tor Scandinavia enters Harwich harbour following the withdrawal of Tor's services from their berth across the river at Felixstowe. (*A J Ambrose*)

Sold to a financial institution and leased back over a ten year period, was DFDS's 'flagship' and star of TV's 'Triangle' soap-opera *Dana Anglia,* which will continue to run on the Harwich–Esbjerg route. (*A J Ambrose*)

As far as British operators were concerned vehicle traffic did not reach anticipated levels in 1983, although on the shorter cross-Channel services passenger figures resumed their upward trend after a very lean period in the opening months of the year when even booming Dover suffered a loss of business that climbed at one stage above 7 per cent. Foot passengers and groups travelling by coach continued to be a growth area for all the companies at Dover and

Also 'DFDS' is the Harwich–Hamburg route operated by the chartered *Prinz Hamlet.* Her former running-mate *Prinz Oberon* which worked the Harwich–Bremerhaven route has now been withdrawn from service. (*A J Ambrose*)

Folkestone which helped off-set some decline in the demand for travel from the Continental side, especially France, where stringent new exchange controls and the decline in the value of the franc were a major deterrent.

Sealink and Townsend Thoresen continued their battle for Dover–Calais traffic and P&O happily sailed on with a three-ship shuttle between Dover and Boulogne after Sealink ended their own limited summer sailings on this route and decided to concentrate Boulogne operations on Folkestone. Sealink's Belgian partners RTM took further steps to upgrade their fleet and embarked on another long-term charter

The liner/ferry/cruise ship/cargo vessel *Black Watch* trades to the Atlantic islands in the summer and as the *Venus* in winter months on North Sea ferry sailings to Norway. (*Skyfotos*)

of Stena tonnage. *Stena Nautica,* introduced on a freight role in 1982 was renamed *Reine Astrid* and, despite speed limitations, put into the passenger service before the June arrival of the *Stena Nordica* (ex-*Stena Danica*) which immediately became the RTM's largest veesel.

The Stena ships now make two round trips from Ostend in each 24 hour cycle but *Renie Astrid,* fully repainted in the RTM livery, is allowed an additional 75 minutes for the crossing normally accomplished in around 3½ hours by other units. Back in the mid-1960s there were some who questioned the sanity of the then Townsend Brothers Ferries in attempting to establish a Belgian service from Dover. The independent company, now more widely known as Townsend Thoresen, started running to Zeebrugge and, 17 years on, celebrated the route's 100,000 sailing on 23 August when *Free Enterprise VIII,* one of three identical ships that are the mainstay of the service, made an afternoon crossing from Zeebrugge to Dover. Since then the nine-year-old *FE VIII* has been taken

Stena Nordica (ex-*Stena Danica*) is now RTM's largest vessel on the Ostend/Zeebrugge–Dover services. (*Stena Line*)

Townsend Thoresen Ferry's 'Viking' class *Viking Venturer* sails from Portsmouth in June 1983. Townsend Thoresen will be concentrating their western Channel assets on this port for the future. (*A J Ambrose*)

in hand for a major internal renovation to provide facilities on par with the more recently introduced trio of large ferries in use to Calais.

There has been increasing emphasis placed by the English Channel ferry companies on shipboard standards of service and passenger comforts and, indirectly, this is another concession to the increasing importance of the day trip trade. P&O instigated separate side boarding for foot passengers at Dover and Boulogne while Sealink sent *St. Anselm* and *St. Christopher* back to builders Harland and Wolff for extensions aft which incorporate duty-free supermarkets.

Sally-Viking, Ramsgate-based and highly ambitious off-shoot of Finland's Rederi AB Sally, have also set very high standards using a succession of former Scandinavian ferries on the Dunkirk service they took over in 1981. Now established as the route's year-round ship is *The Viking*, the former Danish Jydsk Faergefart

vessel *Kalle III* which had over £1 million spent on internal alterations including provision of an escalator to carry passengers from the car deck to public rooms. *The Viking* was re-registered under the Finnish flag in October 1983, the same month in which French operator Charles Schiaffino started a daily Ostend ro-ro freight service from Ramsgate.

At the end of September Sally had completed the first phase of a breakwater to protect the somewhat exposed Ramsgate berth, and by spring 1984 a second linkspan will be ready. Ultimately it is planned to reclaim 35 acres of land from the sea and to bring the total of berths to four with the necessary passenger terminals and wharfage facilities. Another centre of great development is Portsmouth Continental Ferry Port where a new berth for Brittany Ferries' St. Malo service will be followed by a fifth phase of expansion including a twin-level berth and substantial trailer parking areas for Townsend Thoresen, who will then concentrate all their passenger and freight sailings to Le Havre and Cherbourg on Portsmouth to the

Townsend Thoresen's *'Free Enterprise VI'* is similar to the later Free Enterprise class vessels and to the *Free Enterprise IV* and *Free Enterprise V*. Built in January 1972, and with slightly less gross tonnage than IV and V, she does nevertheless have increased power. Her passenger and car capacity remains the same at 1,200 passengers and 320 cars. (*Drawing: A J Ambrose*)

Scale: 1:1200

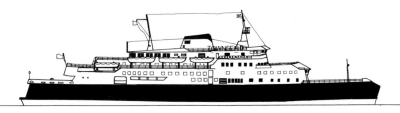

Sealink's latest and largest addition, the former *Prinsessan Birgitta,* chartered to Sealink (UK) Ltd and operating under the new name of *St Nicholas* on the Harwich–Hook of Holland route. (*A J Ambrose*)

exclusion of Southampton. Brittany was the first operator to put its faith into the establishment of Portsmouth as a major ferry port and Townsend Thoresen and Sealink, with a Channel Islands service, followed suit.

The route principally in the Sealink spotlight in a year when the first moves towards privatisation were awaited with some trepidation was Harwich to the Hook of Holland which had suffered the loss of much of its former prestige following the introduction of Olau Line's superb sisters *Olau Hollandia* and *Olau Britannia* between Sheerness and Vlissingen. Sealink's

plan to replace two smaller ships with a single chartered jumbo initially encountered considerable opposition at Harwich and at one stage Sealink even commenced talks with Dutch partners Zeeland Steamship Company on pulling out altogether. In the end logic prevailed and Stena Line's *Prinsessan Birgitta* was duly unveiled as *St Nicholas* in early June enabling *St. George* to go on the sales list and *St. Edmund,* absent for a year in the South Atlantic, to be sold to the Ministry of Defence and start a regular Ascension Island–Falklands supply run as *Keren* under Blue Star Line management. The onus is now on Zeeland to upgrade their contribution to the service, consisting of the five-year-old *Princes Beatrix* and the older *Koningin Juliana* which duplicates sailings as necessary. Two options are under consideration, one a plan to 'stretch' the *Princes Beatrix* by cutting the hull and inserting a new section amidships, and the alternative a charter of *Kronprinsessan Victoria,* the sister ship of *St. Nicholas,* and at present running Stena's Göteborg service. *Kronprinsessan Victoria* is due to be replaced by one of Stena's new ships building in Poland but delivery is likely to be delayed and Zeeland might have to wait!

Northern England's well-established Dutch and Belgian routes again had their share of problems despite finally getting *Norland* back after a lengthy stint in the South Atlantic, latterly running regularly between Ascension and Port Stanley. *Norland* resumed operations amid much ceremony at Hull and Europoort in mid-April but freight carryings on this service and the secondary route to Zeebrugge were affected by a long-running Hull docker's dispute that restricted loading of unaccompanied trailers on weekdays and made it impossible at weekends. Almost immediately normal working resumed in September after more

Harwich services made nearly all the news in ferry circles during the year. The *St George* was without help following the loss of *St Edmund* to the MoD. But the Dutch Zeeland Steamship Company maintained their *Koningen Juliana* and

the larger *Prinses Beatrix* in service on the route, and with the help of the *Prinz Oberon* chartered as a temporary replacement to the *St Edmund,* were able to handle all the traffic without too many hitches.

The impressive *Viking Saga*, which sails from Helsinki to Stockholm, and *Viking Sally*, which operates on Turku–Sweden sailings typify the move to larger tonnage on the Baltic routes. (*K Brzoza*)

Silja Line's *Fennia* put in an unusual appearance on the Irish Sea this year. (*K Brzoza*)

than eight months, Zeebrugge vessel *Norwave* was disabled by an engine room fire while outward bound and still in the Humber Estuary, and was off service for more than two months while repairs were made in Holland by Amsterdam Dry Dock Company.

Three notable Scandinavian ferries made first appearances in British waters during the summer months, two providing links with one of the more out of the way ro-ro destinations, Iceland. Two Icelandic companies joined forces to successfully launch Farskip with a weekly run from Reykjavik to Bremerhaven by the chartered polish ferry *Rogalin*, renamed *Edda*, which called in each direction at North Shields and generated encouraging business from Britain to both Iceland and Germany. An even larger newcomer was Smyril Line's *Norrona* bought by a newly founded company to take over the schedules linking the Faroe Islands with Scotland, Iceland, Norway and Denmark

previously covered by the Faroese Government Shipping Department's *Smyril* required in 1983 for inter-island services. *Norrona* was previously *Gustav Vasa* owned by Lion Ferry and used on the Malmö–Travemünde run of Saga Line (TT-Saga Line from 1980). This sale represented further dispersal of Lion Ferry interests, the Swedish concern also selling *Europafarjan III* from the Varberg–Grena service to Corsica Ferries before the route was acquired by Stena who brought in *Prinsessan Desiree*, now running as *Europafarjan*.

The other stranger was Baltic veteran *Fennia*, used by British and Irish who had to bow to Irish Government pressure and reinstate the Cork–Pembroke Dock service abandoned earlier in the year. A charter was necessary following B + I's sale of spare ship *Munster* to the Middle East and the 17-year-old *Fennia* coped admirably, having been displaced from the Silja Line schedules by a reduction in sailings between Stockholm and Turku via the Aland Islands. Silja, now a straight partnership between Sweden's Johnson Line and Finland Steamship Co (EFFOA), has ordered two new ships from Wärtsilä for the Turku service. These will be only marginally smaller than the giants on the Helsinki run, on which the introduction of a new Business Class reflects the way the overnight sailings are providing an attractive alternative to air travel between the two capitals. Conference packages are another increasingly vital ingredient for overnight ferry operators – including Olau Line on the North Sea – while even Stena on their three-hour Göteborg–Frederikshavn run make a big effort to get business afloat, and the impressive twins *Stena Jutlandica* and *Stena Danica* each have a flexible internal layout that can be changed to meet specific requirements from trip to trip.

Seen in her livery as a Jordanian passenger cargo ferry is the ex-British & Irish Steam Packet Co's *Munster,* now called *Farah.* Built in West Germany in 1968 the vessel now operates a regular service between Aqaba and Suez and isregistered in Panama. (*FotoFlite, Ashford*)

EFFOA's *Skandia* for service in this area as *Stena Baltica* but the biggest, and most surprising investment is Larvik Line's purchase of the previously unloved Gotlandsbolaget super ferry *Wasa Star* which has had a rather chequered career and was chartered to Vaasanlaivat immediately after completion but proved unsuitable for use in the Gulf of Bothnia and was laid-up until going to the Mediterranean last summer to figure in the Italy–Greece service of Karageorgis Lines. Fred Olsen Line added additional Norway–

Silja ferry *Skandia* at Turku, Finland, in the summer of 1983. (*K Brzoza*)

The newly completed *Stena Jutlandica,* sister to the 1982-built *Stena Dabica,* on trials in the English Channel following the handing over from her French builders earlier in the year. (*FotoFlite, Ashford*)

Stena are one of a number of operators putting new muscle into services between Denmark and Norway. Last summer they started a Frederikshavn–Moss overnight round trip in almost direct competition to Da-No Line's Frederikshavn–Frederikstad link and a decision to alter the name of *Prinsessan Christina*, the vessel concerned, to *Stena Nordica*, points to the success of the venture. Stena have also bought

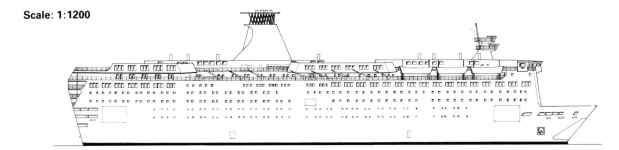

Scale: 1:1200

Profile of the new Stena ferries now building in Poland. Stena have had to wait so long for these ships that one despairs of ever seeing them at sea. At the last report, they were due in service during 1983, but do not appear to have yet materialised. (*Drawing: Michael J Ambrose*)

Silja's ferries are becoming larger again with the recent order for another two new ships from Wärtsilä. The likelihood of vessels such as *Silja Star* appearing in other waters in the future therefore increases. The Baltic ferries have shown a marked tendency to migrate south in recent years, and numerous examples can be seen trading in the North Sea and English Channel. (*K Brzoza*)

Paul Lindenau, normally engaged in the construction of medium-sized tonnage, has completed two new 'water buses' for trading on the Kiel Fjord. The 295 grt *Heikendorf* can carry 300 passengers. A 300 bhp engine allows her a speed of 12 knots. (*Gert Uwe Detlefsen*)

Denmark routes and have plans to revive a link with Britain in the summer of 1984 with *Bolera* due for a weekly Kristiansand–Harwich round trip.

Former European and Scandinavian ferries continue to find their way to the Mediterranean, and a significant purchase was Sally's *Viking 6* by the Cypriot Sol Lines for an Italy–Greece–Cyprus–Israel service as *Sol Olympia*. Sol are now in the market for a similar vessel to increase frequency on the route. One of the few new constructions to appear in the area during 1983, Turkish Maritime Lines' *Ankara* was advertised to go on the Izmir–Ancona service but was switched at the last minute to run between Istanbul and Izmir. Built at Szczecin in Poland and launched as *Masowia*, the ferry was offered to Turkey in repayment of Polish debts, and two sisters are to follow. Also in the Eastern Mediterranean as the Jordanian *Farah* is the former *Munster* and, in the opposite direction, part of the gap in services between Italy and Spain was filled by Miura Line with Gotland's chartered *Drotten* running between Genoa and Barcelona.

Fresh deliveries are few and far between. Sealink's pair of car ferries for the Isle of Wight run from Portsmouth were completed by the Sir Henry Robb Yard in Leith, and Caledonian-MacBrayne's new year-round Arran Ship is on schedule for a 1984 debut on the Ardrossan–Brodick service. Before the end of the year SNCF expect to boost capacity to Dover and Boulogne by commissioning *Champs Elysees*, sister ship to *Cote d'Azur*, but there is a noticeable lack of new orders apart from Silja and Danish State Railways decision to entrust the building of both replacement ferries for the Kalundborg–Aarhus passenger and vehicle route to the Nakskov yard. North Sea Ferries continue to ponder the question of a pair of ships for the Hull-Rotterdam route – although British yards have been asked for revised tenders – and Townsend Thoresen show no inclination to replace *European Gateway* either by new building or upgrading of one of three sister vessels to meet the specialised passenger/freight requirements of the Cairnryan–Larne route.

3 – The Maritime Highways of Washington State and British Columbia

by Graham Stallard and David Thorne

Thoroughly 'Canadianised' after 21 years in Canada, Graham Stallard is a City Planner by profession, with particular interests in the maritime highways and their operating vessels. An enthusiast/writer of long standing, he is presently working on a comprehensive shipping publication covering various aspects of the Northern American shipping scene, and is compiler of the Canadian section of Jane's World Shipbuilding.

The west coast of North America completely changes in character at the boundary between the continental USA and Canada. To the south, modest cliffs face the Pacific Ocean, wide sandy beaches are plentiful and harbours are scarce. North of the 49th Parallel the British Columbian and Alaskan coastline are deeply fiorded, island-studded, and sheltered waters abound. The most significant and extensive system of relatively sheltered water is virtually an inland sea. This is made up of Georgia Strait in the Canadian Province of British Columbia, Puget Sound in the US State of Washington, and Juan de Fuca Strait, shared by both.

Native peoples and the early colonial settlers were very much 'of the sea', and pioneer settlements were coastal or on the few navigable rivers. Transportation and settlement has, of course, spread into the interior in recent years, but development is very sparse by European standards.

The two dominant urban centres date from the late 19th Century and developed where trans-continental railways reached sheltered water by the Pacific Ocean. Seattle on Puget Sound has well in excess of 2 million people if the adjacent cities of Tacoma and Everett are included. Vancouver on Georgia Strait has over 1.2 million people, but other settlements are considerably smaller.

Because of the relatively sparse settlement pattern there are few 'trunk' ferry routes, but many minor services cross numerous straits, bays and rivers and provide links with small islands. When steamer services were the only form of transportation available, business was brisk and competition was intense. Increasing availability of private motor vehicles and the development of the highway system eroded much of the trade, and rising costs made most private enterprises marginal. The capital expenditures necessary to adapt to rapid increases in the demand for car ferry services in the 1950s and 1960s were not forthcoming from the 'private sector'. The transition to large-scale modern roll-on/roll-off motor vehicle ferries was left almost entirely to a small number of specially created public agencies. With one minor (and unconventional) exception, these were created out of economic and social necessity rather than political philosophy.

Washington State Ferries is a division of the State's Highways and Toll Bridge Authority and was created in 1951 after the financial collapse of the Puget Sound Navigation Company. It operates a network of services in the sheltered waters of Puget Sound. Two routes from Seattle are high-volume commuter trunk routes and the recreational service from Anacortes to the San Juan Islands has grown significantly in recent years. The fleet currently has 20 vessels, but two of these are elderly and may soon be retired.

The *Princess of Vancouver* was built in 1955 for the Canadian Pacific Railways route from Vancouver to Nanaimo. She is the last British-built ferry on the coast, and has recently been purchased by the B.C. government for the Highways Ministry's route from Comox to Powell River. Train carrying facilities have been removed and bow loading added. (*Drawing: D O Thorne*)

Scale: 1:1200

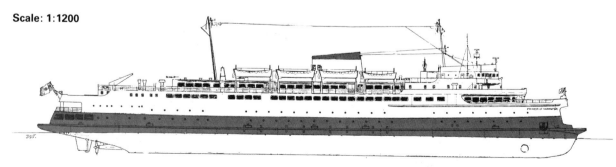

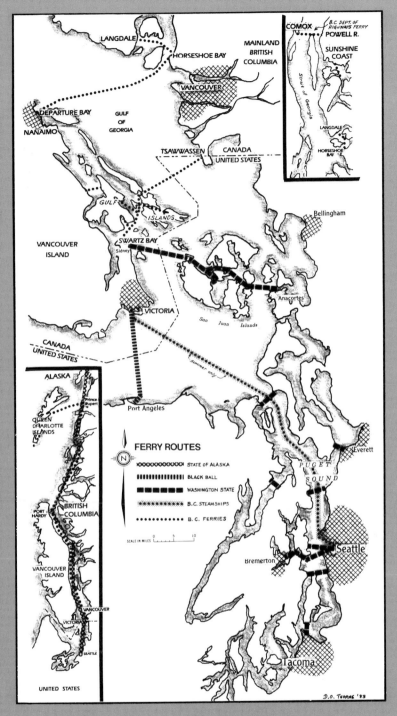

Inside the map:

LANGDALE

HORSESHOE BAY

MAINLAND
BRITISH
COLUMBIA

VANCOUVER

COMOX

B.C. DEPT. OF
HIGHWAYS FERRY
POWELL R.

SUNSHINE
COAST

Strait of Georgia

LANGDALE

HORSESHOE
BAY

DEPARTURE BAY

NANAIMO

GULF
OF
GEORGIA

TSAWWASSEN

CANADA
UNITED STATES

Bellingham

GULF
ISLANDS

VANCOUVER
ISLAND

SWARTZ BAY

Sidney

Anacortes

VICTORIA

San Juan Islands

CANADA
UNITED STATES

Summer only

ALASKA

Prince Rupert

QUEEN
CHARLOTTE
ISLANDS

Port Angeles

Port Hardy

BRITISH
COLUMBIA

VANCOUVER
ISLAND

VANCOUVER

VICTORIA

SEATTLE

UNITED STATES

FERRY ROUTES

N

xxxxxxxxxxxx STATE OF ALASKA

|||||||||||| BLACK BALL

▬▬▬▬▬ WASHINGTON STATE

xxxxxxxxxx B.C. STEAMSHIPS

•••••• B.C. FERRIES

SCALE IN MILES 0 5 10

Everett

PUGET
SOUND

Bremerton

Seattle

Tacoma

D.O. THORNE '83

A number of agencies operate ferries within British Columbia. The Ministry of Transportation and Highways (Highways for short) has developed a large number of river, lake and small island services. Its coastal operations tend to be relatively small and remote but it operates the last British-built major ferry on the coast – the *Princess of Vancouver* (built in 1955, 388 ft in length, 137 cars and 750 passengers) on a service at the northern end of Georgia Strait. Fifteen of Highway's fleet operate in coastal waters, but only three exceed 180 ft in length and a capacity of 30 cars.

British Columbia Ferries was established in 1959 to develop and expand the pioneering work of the Black Ball Company and to counter the steady decline of the Canadian Pacific Steamships services. This agency is now an independent Crown Corporation and operates large trunk routes on Georgia Strait, intermediate and small coastal and island services and since 1966 a long-distance coastal service. The corporation now has 25 vessels.

The only socialist government ever elected in this part of the world established a delightful anachronism.

The last passenger steamship on the coast is the *Princess Marguerite* operated by B.C. Steamship Corporation between Seattle and Victoria. She was built by Fairfields in 1948. (*Drawing: D O Thorne*)

B.C. Steamship Corporation operates the last operational passenger steamship – the *Princess Marguerite* on a 'summer only' tourist service from Seattle to Victoria.

When Alaska became the 49th State in 1959, the need for better communications with the continental USA was pressing. Alaska State Ferries was established and commenced operations in 1963. The trunk route operates along the so-called 'Alaska Panhandle' to Prince Rupert in British Columbia and was soon extended on a weekly basis to Seattle. Secondary services have been developed, and the fleet now numbers nine vessels.

The Alaska operation is described as the 'Marine Highway System' and this well describes the operating philosophy of all the major public ferry agencies. Yet ironically, while the ships are well adapted to the needs of the motor vehicle, much of the infra-structure has been inherited from an earlier era. For example, Washington State's biggest concentration of traffic focuses on a relatively small pier in the heart of Seattle. In fairness it should be noted that the Seattle to Bremerton trunk route has very heavy passenger traffic. Alaska State vessels often tie up alongside traditional wharves in smaller ports of call. B.C. Ferries purchased its Horseshoe Bay to Departure Bay route and terminals from Black Ball.

While the terminals on the latter route have been extensively rebuilt over the years, it has been the B.C. Ferries route, from Tsawwassen to Swartz Bay that is the most modern and innovative one. The traditional route from Vancouver to Victoria was from central locations in each city and took approximately five hours. The new route involved its own highway links and the shortest possible water crossing – 1½ hours. Terminals were also completely new and in the case of Tsawwassen it was located at the end of a 3 km causeway built across mud flats to reach deep water – a very efficient operation but involving a capital

investment in terminals, causeways and highways completely beyond the scope of private enterprise. All four of B.C. Ferries' trunk terminals have been rebuilt for two-level loading. While the terminals now resemble a Los Angeles freeway interchange, they do enable vessels carrying 400 cars to 'turn around' in about the same time as ferries with a third of this capacity a few years before.

A great variety of vessels have come and gone in these waters, ranging from stern-wheelers to Clyde-built short-seas passengers steamers. The forms have been familiar but the style has tended to be distinctive. Vessels typically have lived to a ripe old age and many have been modified out of all recognition. However, with the rationalisation of operators there has also

A recent photograph of B.C. Ferry Corporation's Tsawwassen Terminal, south of Vancouver, British Columbia. (*B.C. Ferries*)

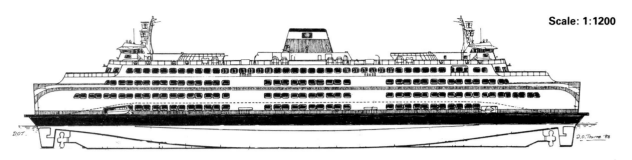

Scale: 1:1200

Profiles of B.C. Ferries' vessels *Queen of Coquitlam* and *Queen of Cowichan* are similar. (*Drawing: D O Thorne*)

Washington State 'Super' ferry *Kaleetan* tied up at the single link span wharf at Sidney, British Columbia. (*D O Thorne*)

Scale: 1:1200

been a concentration on two basic ship forms. Most of both types have been designed by two independent marine architects in Seattle, who have recently gone into partnership. Most modern ferries have been built locally, few have changed hands, and both basic ship types have been scaled up and/or drastically modified in recent years.

The doubled-ended ferry is familiar in rivers and harbours throughout the world. The local branch of this prolific family traces its ancestry to San Francisco Bay. In fact, many San Francisco Bay vessels migrated north, particularly in the late 1930s after the completion of the Golden Gate and Bay Bridges. The last of these vessels still serve in Washington, but in rapidly diminishing numbers.

Washington State's fleet is entirely composed of double-ended vessels reflecting the sheltered nature of its operations. Two-thirds of these ferries are less than

310 ft in length and of under 100 car capacity. The growth in demand in the 1960s led to the scaling up of this basic layout. Four so-called 'Super Ferries' were built in 1967 in San Diego, but to the design of Robert Nickum of Seattle. These vessels are 382 ft long, have a capacity of 160 cars and 2,500 passengers. This quartet was joined in 1972 by two 'Jumbo Ferries' of 440 ft length, 206 car capacity but with a reduced passenger capacity of 2,000. Due to the pecularities of design and tonnage calculations, gross tonnage figures have not been quoted as they can be quite misleading when compared to more conventional vessels.

The upward trend in scale of the double-enders has not been pursued in American waters. Washington State Ferries has recently concentrated on replacing

Profile of the Washington State 'Jumbo' ferry *Spokane*. (*D O Thorne*)

Scale: 1:1200

its elderly intermediate vessels. It was to be B.C. Ferries that went a step further when in 1976 they introduced a pair of double-enders based on the 'Jumbos', but still larger at 452 ft long with a 362 car capacity and licensed for 1,466 passengers. These Nickum-designed vessels were joined by a 'cut down' half-sister intended for commercial vehicles, and in 1981 by a pair of sister ships. The four car and passenger carrying sisters have enclosed ends and two-level loading. After initial operations on the southern trunk route, these vessels have been concentrated on the route between Horseshoe Bay and Departure Bay. The stated reason is to avoid the need to turn in the confined approaches to Horseshoe Bay, but it is rumoured that these huge double-enders are difficult to handle in Active Pass and on the exposed approach to the Tsawwassen terminal.

Mayne Queen **represents many small double-ended ferries in British Columbia and Washington. With her two sister ships she was stretched in 1980, and given 'Z Drive' propulsion similar to Sealink's new Isle of Wight ferries. (***Drawing: D O Thorne***)**

Queen of Cowichan **was completed in 1976, and is one of a class of four vessels that are the largest double-enders on this coast. (***D O Thorne***)**

Scale: 1:1200

B.C. Ferries and Highways both operate many small double-ended ferries on secondary routes. These are now quite modern and some are being stretched and updated. Page 111 of last years *Jane's Merchant Shipping Review* illustrated the *Quinsham* which is a 'British Columbia Ministry of Highways' vessel; not exactly a Canadian Government vessel as was stated.

A small number of B.C.'s secondary ferries, two-thirds of the B.C. trunk route vessels and all of Alaska State ferries have adopted the more sea-worthy and manoeuverable single-ended hull form. In these waters the single-ended car ferry traces its ancestry back to 1923 when Yarrows of Esquimault completed the *Motor Princess*, and 1927 when the former Great Lakes passenger steamer *Chipewa* was converted to a roll-on/roll-off car ferry. More conversions followed, most of which were quite utilitarian but there were exceptions. The *Kalakala* resembled an inverted aluminium bathtub with oversized port holes!

The first purpose-built car ferry was Black Ball's very advanced *Chinook* introduced in 1948. She was designed by Gibbs and Cox of New York and built in Seattle. It was to be a decade before she was joined by

a similar vessel, the *Coho*. This was to be the prototype of a series of ferries from the drawing board of Philip Spalding of Seattle. *Chinook* has recently retired, having spent two-thirds of her long life in B.C. service. *Coho* continues to operate the private

Chinook **was built in 1948 to a Gibbs and Cox design, and was the starting point of modern ferry design in these waters.**

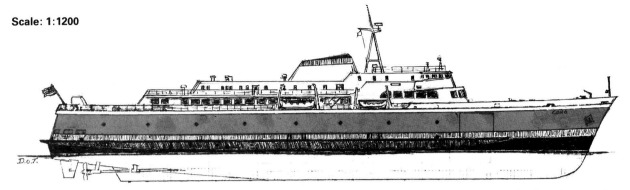

The _Coho_ of 1959 was the prototype of a large family of vessels that dominate the British Columbia and Alaska ferry fleets. (_Drawing: D O Thorne_)

enterprise service between Victoria and Port Angeles, little changed and still looking modern.

B.C. Ferries' first two vessels built to their own account were virtually indentical to _Coho_. The bows were blunt-nosed in contrast with the latter's conventional raked stem and flank doors. All three have similar stern doors. This pair was soon followed by an enlarged version that was to run to a series of seven vessels in the 1960s. While the original pair are little changed, the larger class have been radically rebuilt.

As designed, these vessels were 342 ft long and had a car capacity of 110. All have had a 'platform deck' added to increase car capacity to 132. Subsequently, or simultaneously, all seven vessels have been lengthened by 84 ft to 426 ft, and the car capacity raised to 192.

After the introduction of the huge double-enders, it was decided that there was a more cost-effective way of getting still more capacity. Four of the single-enders have undergone even more radical surgery. The superstructure has been raised and a new car deck inserted, doubling the car capacity to 400 vehicles. Sponsons have been added to counteract the considerable

increase in top weight. Interestingly, the marine architect for this latest conversion was K. E. Hansen of Copenhagen.

Alaska State Ferries' initial construction programme consisted of a trio of Spalding-designed vessels known collectively as the 'South Easters'. They were clearly based on _Coho_ with an additional deck for overnight accommodation. Two of these vessels have subsequently been lengthened from 352 ft to 408 ft, increasing the capacity from 105 to 120 and passenger capacity from 500 to 750.

In 1964 a smaller 'one-off' vessel was completed to serve the very exposed western coast of the State, including the Aleutian Islands. Since then a small number of short-distance vessels have been added to the fleet. These are much smaller than _Coho_ but clearly of the same family. All of Alaska State's secondary service vessels have been built in Wisconsin and Indiana while the trunk service vessels are Seattle-built.

The operation of foreign-built vessels is virtually prohibited by law for American companies, and it was therefore very unusual that Alaska State operated a second-hand European vessel for a short period. A

Three stages in the development of the B.C. Ferries' _Queen of Vancouver_. There were seven vessels built to the original configuration. All were subsequently lengthened. Recently four of this class have had an additional car deck inserted, doubling their capacity. (_Drawing: D O Thorne_)

CONVERTED 1981
(400 cars)

STRETCHED 1972
(192 cars)

ORIGINAL 1962
(150 cars)

David O. Thorne '81

Alaska State Ferries' vessel *Matanuska* approaching Prince Rupert, British Columbia. Prior to stretching the hull was virtually identical to *Coho*. (*D O Thorne*)

larger vessel was needed for the service to Seattle and the *Stena Britanica* (built in 1967) was purchased, renamed *Wickersham* and registered in Panama. This was approved on condition that an American-built replacement was ordered immediately. The latter emerged as *Columbia* in 1973, the ultimate version of the *Coho* family. She is 418 ft long and carries 180 cars and 1,000 passengers. Meanwhile, *Wickersham* has served as *Goelo*, *Viking 6* and continues her nomadic career under the Cypriot flag as *Sol Christina*.

B.C. Ferries initiated the long-distance service from Vancouver Island to Prince Rupert in 1966. Rather than emulate Alaska State Ferries, it was decided to adapt Hansen's design for Thoresen's earliest 'Vikings'. The *Queen of Prince Rupert* is very similar to Sealink's *Earl William*, but is slightly shorter and wider. European ferries are, of course, designed to accommodate European cars and this does not work out well for the larger American automobiles. The extra width built into the *Queen of Prince Rupert* enabled the car deck to be efficiently utilised. This

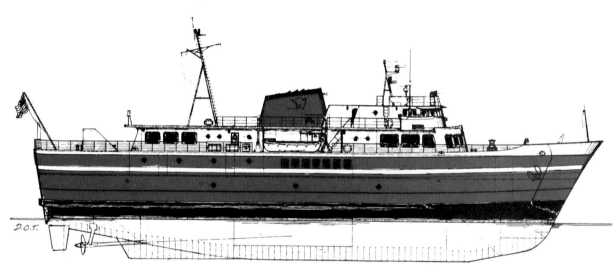

E.L. Bartlett is representative of Alaska's feeder ferries. She is much smaller than *Coho* but clearly is a Spalding design. (*Drawing: D O Thorne*)

Flagship of the Alaska State ferry fleet *Columbia* is the most recent and most elaborate member of the 'Coho' family. (*Drawing: D O Thorne*)

ferry was the last vessel built by Victoria Machinery Depot.

In 1974, B.C. Ferries bought the *Stena Danica* to provide extra capacity on the Georgia Strait services. This was a short-term measure and she was laid up with the introduction of the double-enders. In 1980 she was refitted, renamed *Queen of the North* and

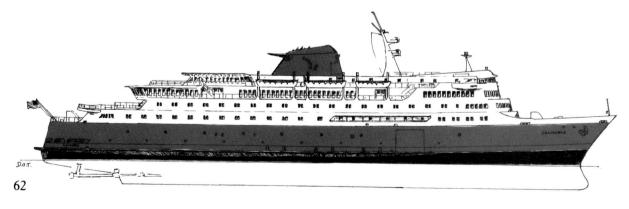

placed on the coastal run. At this time the service was extended from Prince Rupert to the Queen Charlotte Islands. The last private enterprise services had been withdrawn by then and one of the final non-government ships on the coast, *Northland Price*, has been in the news lately as the *St. Helena*.

An excellent excuse to investigate this fascinating coastline is attendance at 'The World Exposition on Transportation and Related Communications' – EXPO 86 for short. This will be held in Vancouver in the summer of 1986. Information can be obtained from:

EXPO 86,
P.O. Box 1986, Station A,
Vancouver, B.C.
V6C 2X5, CANADA.

B.C. Ferries two long distance ferries together off Northern Vancouver Island. *The Queen of Prince Rupert,* in the foreground, was locally built to a Danish design. *The Queen of the North* was originally the *Stena Danica. (B.C. Ferries)*

Sketch of the multi-level loading system used on both of the British Columbia Ferries' major route from metropolitan Vancouver to Vancouver Island.

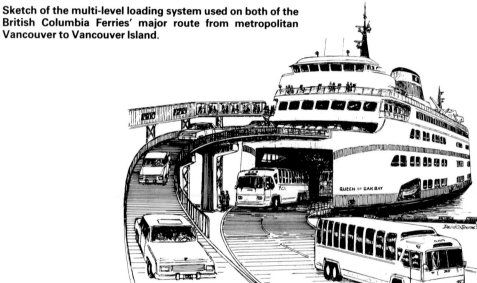

The last traditional cargo/passenger vessel on the coast of British Columbia was the *Northern Prince.* She was built in Vancouver in 1963 and was sold in 1977 and renamed *St Helena.*

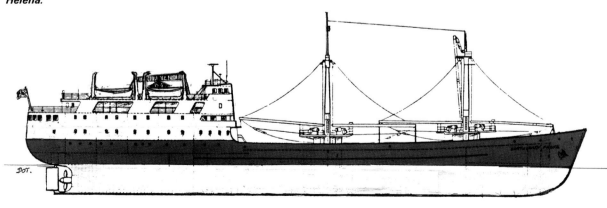

4 – The Decline of Steam

by Russell Plummer

The speed with which steam has been eclipsed as a prime mover for smaller passenger vessels and ferries has been dramatic to say the least. Although turbine-powered ships were being introduced well into the 1960s, in the whole of Europe and Scandinavia there was a solitary operator running steam car ferries in 1983 and it is necessary to look increasingly hard and sometimes far inland to find other traditional survivors.

A few ex-British units remain laid-up in the Eastern Mediterranean more in hope than anticipation of further work, and in 1984 enthusiasts will again look to the Isle of Man Steam Packet Company for opportunities to sail with style and no mean speed on the superbly turned-out *Ben-My-Chree* and *Manx Maid*.

A rare remaining example of the classic passenger steamer is seen at Tilbury when the Soviet flag *Baltika* makes seasonal appearances on the service from Leningrad but for other steamers the forlorn wait continues.

Libra Maritime's *Neptunia*, the former Irish Sea ferry *Duke of Argyll*, and Sol Lines' *Sol Express*, previously Sealink's English Channel ferry *Earl Siward*, are available for charter after remaining idle in 1983 and although in use, the role of the last steamer to run between Sweden and Finland, Jakob Line's *Borea*, is that of an unglamorous accommodation ship in Algeria. When in the Baltic the *Borea* just outlived Anedin Line's *Baltic Star* and the Viking Line vessel *Apollo III*, in competition on Stockholm's mini-cruise trade to Mariehamn, which each succumbed to diesel power in 1982.

Some paddle-driven veterans continue to prosper.

Manx Maid, seen arriving at Douglas in heavy weather, and sister vessel *Ben-my Chree* (1966), introduced drive-on car ferry services to the Liverpool–Isle of Man route but are side loaders with an internal spiral ramp aft which enables them to use existing quays at Douglas where there is a considerable tidal range. *Manx Maid,* introduced in 1962, and *Ben-my-Chree,* are powered by double reduction Pametrada geared turbines of 9,500 bhp. They exceeded 22 knots on trials and are still capable of over 20 knots in service. (*Richard Danielson*)

The Soviet passenger/cargo liner *Baltika* has been a regular summer visitor to Tilbury for a number of years on the Baltic Shipping Company's service from Leningrad and is now one of the last classic passenger steamers remaining in commission. Built in Holland and completed in 1940, *Baltika* was named *Vyacheslav Molotov* until 1957 and has turbo-electric propulsion with a pair of turbines driving generators connected to electric motors. There is accommodation for 437 passengers. (*Russell Plummer*)

The world's oldest side-wheeler, *Skibladner*, received a new boiler before commencing a 127th season on Norway's picturesque Lake Mjosa, and in Britain the

The Clyde-built *Waverley*, the last paddle steamer with seagoing capability, steamed just over 20,000 miles in a 1983 season lasting from late April through to the end of September. During this time the 693-ton vessel circum-navigated Britain and recorded 237,000 passenger journeys, a figure very close to record carryings in the previous year. Bought for just £1 from Caledonian-MacBrayne when retired from Clyde excursion duties, *Waverley* is operated on a non-profit making basis by Waverley Steam Navigation Company and 1984 will be the 10th anniversary of her return to service in enthusiast hands. (*Russell Plummer*)

much travelled *Waverley* will celebrate 10 years of operational preservation in 1984 having recorded over 230,000 passengers in each of the last two seasons while completely circumnavigating the mainland. *Waverley* has also been reboilered in recent times and internal accommodation is much improved from the almost spartan facilities offered in the first phase of her life as a Clyde ferry.

Steam still has one remarkable outpost at Instanbul, the city where East meets West and ferry connections

127 years young is the Norwegian paddler *Skibladner*, known locally as the 'White Swan of Mjosa' which was given a new boiler before commencing a short but intensive 1983 season of 120 mile daily round trips on the spectacularly beautiful Lake Mjosa, north of Oslo. Operated on a voluntary basis by enthusiasts, *Skibladner* has become a national institution and a special stamp was issued to mark the 125th anniversary in 1981. (*Russell Plummer*)

are provided between the shores of Asia and Europe by a fleet in which steam power predominates with even a few remaining examples of the coal burning two-deckers introduced before the First World War. Evening rush hour still presents an intriguing spectacle at Istanbul with ferries lining up three and four abreast and putting up clouds of smoke to all but obliterate the view of the mosques and minarets as they await the deluge of returning commuters.

The huge increase in building costs has tended to extend the lives of a number of old-timers on the lakes and rivers of Europe where operators have found it

Istanbul remains a steam lovers' paradise, and typical of the older two-deckers in the extensive fleet of the Turkish Maritime Bank (Denizcilik Bankasi) which run an intricate network of services across the Bosphorus is the *Kalender*, a twin-screw coal burner built and engined on the Tyne in 1911. Immediately behind is the funnel of one of a series of larger Dutch-built ferries now converted to burn oil. (*Russell Plummer*)

Inkilap is one of a series of nine handsome steamers added to the Istanbul fleet in 1961, all of them built on the Clyde at Govan by Fairfield. They are powered by a pair of interesting four-cylinder compound engines to a design of Christiansen and Meyer of Hamburg. Over 1,000 passengers are carried on the DB's principal ferry service to Haydarpasa and Kadikoy, plus longer runs across the Sea of Marmara. (*Russell Plummer*)

beneficial to keep steamers in service for high season back-up rather than opt for new construction. This applies particularly in Switzerland – where a strong preservation movement has emerged – and East Germany. The recession has hit hard in West Germany and Rhine operators Köln–Düsseldorfer Lines have been having a hard time to keep day excursion sailings viable over the stretch from Cologne to Mainz. A single paddle-steamer, the *Goethe* of 1913, was in use in the

last two summers while two similar vessels remained in lay-up.

Goethe celebrated 70 years of service in September 1983, and earlier in the summer similar anniversaries were marked on the Danube for the Austrian paddler *Schönbrunn* and in Switzerland for the flier of the Lake Lucerne fleet, the *Gallia*, a steamer still capable of over 31 km per hour. The Swiss have discovered that paddle steamers can be turned into tourist attractions in their own right. So too have the operators of the *Waverley* in Britain, pushing the same philosophy, although with more mixed results.

Paddle steamers have long been a familiar part of the Rhine scenery in Germany but now the 1913 vintage *Goethe* is the last of the Köln-Düsseldorfer Line's three serviceable side-wheelers to be in operation. Declining traffic in the midst of the European economic recession caused the KDR to lay-up first *Mainz* (1929) and then *Rudesheim* (1926) although both are capable of being brought back if traffic improves. *Rudesheim* was used in a static capacity as a restaurant in Cologne last summer. *Goethe,* seen heading upstream from Koblenz, ran over the whole Cologne–Mainz stretch on different services in 1983 and was also popular for river boat suffle evening sailings with live bands and dancing on the decks! (*Russell Plummer*)

The First Danube Steamship Company's *Schönbrunn* churns up the river at Spitz before being eased alongside the pontoon during a special 70th anniversary sailing in July last year. Built at Budapest and now the last paddle steamer in the Austrian DDSG fleet, *Schönbrunn* circulates on a three-day Vienna–Passau–Vienna roster with a pair of diesel/electric paddlers both now more than 40 years old. (*Russell Plummer*)

5 – Harwich – 100 Years On

by Russell Plummer

Few ferry ports have witnessed greater changes over the years than Harwich Parkeston Quay, although it has to be said that the greatest revolution has taken place in the last three decades with some of the world's largest passenger and car ferries now handled on a daily basis.

Apart from a gradual increase in the size of vessels, the pattern of passenger and cargo operations to the Continent hardly changed from the time Parkeston Quay was established by a Great Eastern Railway Company angered by the refusal of Harwich Council to allow expansion of existing facilities in the centre of the town.

The centenary of Parkeston Quay was celebrated in March 1983 with regular users already including the DFDS jumbo ferries *Dana Anglia* and *Dana Regina*. They were joined by *Tor Scandinavia* and *Tor Britannia* when the former Tor Line service to Sweden moved its UK terminal from Felixstowe and, in June, Sealink introduced their own imposing flagship *St. Nicholas*.

It is a far cry from the introduction of *England* and the start of drive-on car ferry serives in 1964. This vessel as a side-loader, but a pontoon berth for bow and stern loaders was commissioned in 1966 and two portal berths followed in 1967. Now construction of a fourth ro-ro berth is underway.

The DFDS passenger ferry *Kronprinsesse Ingrid* in 1963 in the area now occupied by the East Portal ro-ro berth. Astern, in what is now the container terminal are *Isle of Ely* and the train ferry *Essex Ferry*. (*Alfred Smith*)

Flushing day service departure in August 1964 with *Koningin Emma* underway and *Prinses Beatrix* loading – note car on quay waiting to be craned into the hold. (*Alfred Smith*)

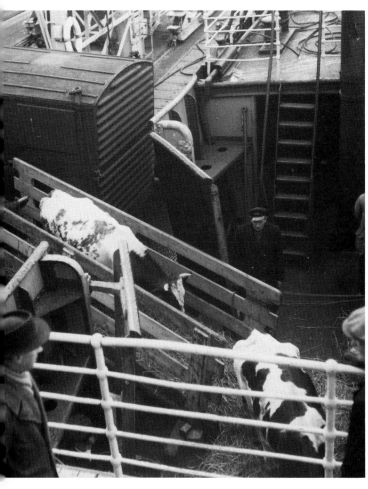

Prinz Hamlet prepares to depart for Hamburg from Parkeston Quay's original ro-ro berth in May 1983. (*Russell Plummer*)

Export cattle being loaded on the British Rail coal fired cargo steamer *Sherringham* in January 1957 — a year before her withdrawal. (*Alfred Smith*)

Zealand Steamship Company's *Prinses Beatrix* approaches the East Portal berth at Harwich in June 1983 after completing the day service from the Hook of Holland. (*Russell Plummer*)

Amsterdam, crack post-war steamer in the Harwich fleet, at Parkeston Quay in December 1959. She saw further service as a Mediterranean cruise ship in Chandris colours and remains laid-up and available for charter. (*Alfred Smith*)

Towering above Parkeston Quay, Sealink's *St Nicholas* loads via bow doors at Harwich while the stern extension to enable existing Hook of Holland facilities to be used can be clearly seen. Only the centre ramp is used, the two outer ramps are permanently closed. (*Russell Plummer*)

The Development of the Modern Salvage Vessel

by David Hancox

Based in Singapore, in charge of the operations of the premier Far Eastern salvage and towing comany, David Hancox has performed many complex salvage operations throughout the world and has a tendency to make the news in addition to writing about it (as is indeed true of several other writers in this edition). His individual exploits are too numerous to list here, as also are the 1983 activities of his company, Selco Salvage Ltd.

Generally speaking the maritime community associates the term 'salvage vessel' with large ocean-going tugs, and salvage operations concerning the rescue of disabled vessels at sea; yet this association describes neither the characteristics nor designed purpose of the 'salvage vessel' which has developed its own special features over the years. The salvage vessel's primary function is to provide a self-propelled working platform from which the various equipment to perform the following tasks can be easily deployed:

(a) Refloating of heavily stranded/damaged vessels;
(b) Raising of sunken or partly sunken vessels or wrecks;
(c) Recovery or removal of cargo from damaged ships;
(d) Location and recovery of aircraft/ordnance lost at sea;
(e) Accommodate and service large groups of divers and salvage crew.

To fulfil these roles adequately, the salvage vessel requires very different characteristics to those design

Dalhousie.

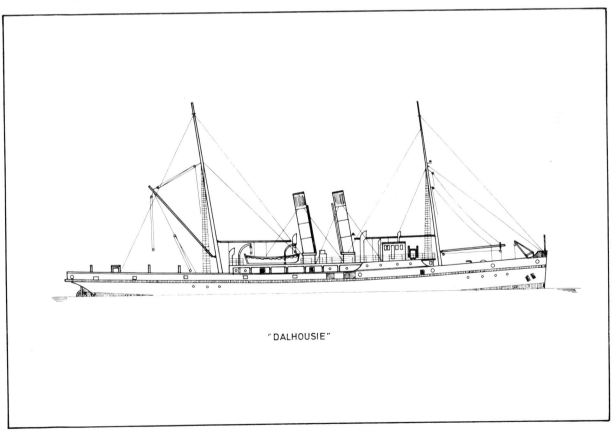

" DALHOUSIE "

features which allow the ocean-going tug to perform her assigned tasks. The ocean tug should have a relatively high and well flared bow design to allow the tug to proceed to sea in very bad weather; the tug must have deep draught aft to allow the propeller(s) adequate immersion to develop designed thrust; and the tug requires a large fuel capacity to enable her to remain at sea with the engines operating at full power for periods of between 50 and 60 days without refuelling. The modern ocean tug has very powerful engines, up to 20,000 bhp, to produce speeds of 18/19 knots with corresponding bollard pulls of 150 to 180 tons; the former necessary to have a minimum transit time to casualties requiring assistance, while the latter gives the tug the tractive power necessary to tow a damaged ULCC to a port of refuge. An old, but apt description of the design of such tugs reads '. . . an ocean-going tugboat is a tremendously over-powered machine filled to the brim with fuel'.★

The design features which give the ocean-going tug seakeeping ability, speed and towing power are not desirable in a salvage vessel which must work in shallow waters, be moored alongside wrecks, and handle a variety of anchors, chains and heavy moorings on a very restricted draught. Over the years the limitations of the ocean-going tug in an on-shore salvage role have become greater as ocean tugs have become larger and more powerful, and thus the salvage vessel has emerged as a separate and distinct type of vessel.

Probably the first purpose-designed salvage vessels were ships converted in the 1890s from old Royal Navy gun-vessels, the first being the Liverpool & Glasgow Salvage Association's ship *Ranger* which was built in 1880 and converted in 1892/93 for salvage purposes, serving in this role until 1954.

During the First World War, a number of old gunboats were converted into salvage vessels under

★ *A Sailor's Life* by Jan de Hartog (Hamish Hamilton Ltd, 1955).

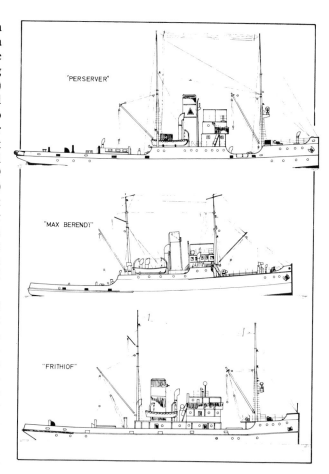

Salvage vessels *Preserver, Max Berendt* and *Frithiof*.

the direction of Captain (later Sir) Frederick Young. These conversions were performed quickly, using surplus or discarded material to produce operational vessels to commercial salvage requirements which have always tended towards expediency rather than technical and operational perfection.

Captain Damant, a senior Admiralty Salvage Officer, and later Director of the Rescue Tug Service (1939), commented on these conversions:

'The HMS *Racer* [an old gunboat] had been laid up for demolition until Sir Frederick Young, the bustling salvage chief exhumed half a dozen of her type, gutted them and installed engines from out of service [obsolete] destroyers. Damant was very wary about his choice of Young's salvage fleet because some of them had a pair of port engines out of twin-screw torpedo gunboats, and these propellers turned the wrong way'.★

However, notwithstanding Captain Damant's comments it should be realised that almost any small

★ Capt G C Damant in *Laurentic Gold* by James Dugan (p. 113), Cousteau's Underwater Treasurery – Hamish Hamilton Ltd, London.

Salvage vessel *Ranger* c. 1900.

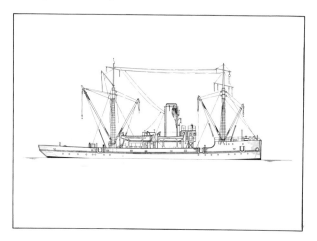

and robust self-propelled craft can be converted into a 'salvage vessel' if a salvage contractor so desires; the resulting conversion will be quite workable for a given geographical area, provided certain basic lifting gear and appliances are fitted to the vessel.

Between the end of the First World War and the beginning of the Second World War a number of interesting salvage vessels, the *Max Berendt*, the *Preserver*, the *Frithiof* and the *Salvage King* were built, all incorporating a considerable towing capability (lacking in earlier salvage vessels), in addition to diving facilities, a large workshop area and a good deadweight capacity for the carriage of salvage equipment and stores. The principal particulars of these vessels are shown in Table 1.

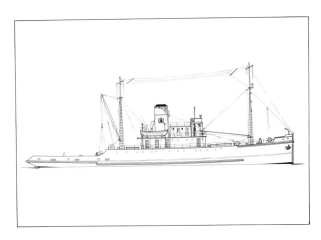

Salvage King.

TABLE 1

Vessels name	*Frithiof*	*Max Berendt*	*Salvage King*	*Preserver*
Gross tonnage	672	766	1,164	630
Nett tonnage	263	322	483	216
Length oa (m)	51.78	51.05	58.51	56.69
Length bp (m)	47.63	47.60	56.78	54.00
Breadth mld (m)	10.57	9.72	11.03	9.69
Depth mld (m)	4.81	4.96	4.93	4.93
Forecastle length (m)	7.31	30.7	42.66	10.36
Machinery	2 × diesels	1 × triple exp	1 × triple exp	1 × triple exp
Output (ihp)	1,220	875	2,500	1,500
Speed (knots)	14	13	15	14.5
Draught (m)	4.11	4.26	4.87	4.49
Year built	1921	1923	1925	1927

The Second World War created an urgent requirement for salvage vessels, and after pressing into service all available craft, and converting several vessels of opportunity, it was necessary for the British and American naval authorities to design and build new vessels especially for salvage services; each navy developed a distinct class of large and medium vessels. Although both the British and US large salvage vessels were developed from the *Salvage King* prototype (see above) each class of salvage vessel was totally different.

In the British 'King Salvor' class the towing capability of the prototype was sacrificed to produce a shallow draught, semi-lifting-craft design hull in which the salvage vessel clearly predominated, with

Built in North America in 1943 as the *Diver* this vessel has quite a history in salvage work. She is a twin-screw diesel-electric salvage vessel of 1,202 grt, and carries a good salvage suite in her 510 dwt. Now known as the *Rescue M* she has four main (oil) engines coupled to two electric propulsion motors driving a twin screw arrangement. (*C B Mulholland*)

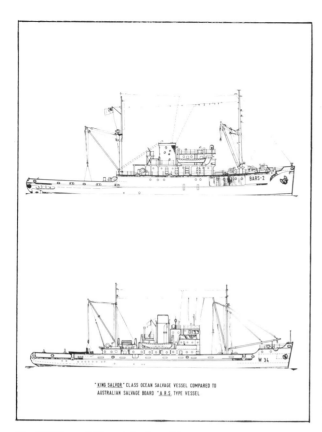

"KING SALVOR" CLASS OCEAN SALVAGE VESSEL COMPARED TO
AUSTRALIAN SALVAGE BOARD "A.R.S. TYPE VESSEL

The US Navy ARS and the Royal Navy 'King Salvor' class.

steam reciprocating machinery developing 1,500 ihp. The US salvage vessel was quite unlike the British ships, being a long forecastle design and propelled by diesel electric machinery of 3,000 shp which gave an exceptional towing capability to the vessels. The particulars of the two larger war-built salvage vessels are given in Table 2:

TABLE 2

Vessel's name	British 'King Salvor' type	US 'ARS' type
Gross tonnage	1,114	1,429
Net tonnage	370/380	720/740
Load displacement (tons)	1,680/1,700	1,970
Length oa (m)	65.83	64.91
Length bp (m)	60.95	63.09
Breadth mld (m)	11.30	11.91
Depth mld (m)	5.49	5.79
Draught (m)	4.14	4.64
Machinery	2 × triple exp SR; twin screws	4 × electric motors; twin screws
Output	1,500 ihp	3,000 shp
Speed (knots)	12/12.5	15
Range (n. miles)	4,500	9,400
Fitted with	1 × 20-ton 2 × 8-ton derricks; 1,000 tons per hour pump; two workshops; accommodation for 72 persons	1 × 20-ton 2 × 10-ton derricks; workshop; towing winch; accommodation for 90 persons

Vessels from both types were employed in commercial salvage work from the end of the Second World War until the middle 1970s by which time most had been disposed of. The US Navy retains a number of the ARS vessels in the fleet of tugs and salvage craft still operated by the Navy.

After the Second World War several vessels were converted for salvage duties, including a number of British LCT Mk VII (Landing Craft Tank), while the well-known US vessel *Salvage Chief* was converted from a standard LSI (Landing Craft Infantry) and fitted out with very heavy winching and ground tackle equipment for service on the West Coast of the United States. Of the few new buildings during this period, the Japanese *Hayashio Maru*, built in 1962, was another combined tug/salvage vessel, in which the salvage vessel predominated, while the Norwegian vessels *Salvator* and the (later) *Hercules* were more properly tugs, with some salvage capability incorporated in the design.

The development of the offshore supply vessel, commencing with the early Gulf of Mexico work boats, added a new and important dimension to the design of salvage vessels, with the recognition of the fact that clear, unencumbered deck areas were essential design elements in a successful salvage craft. Provision of adequate deck space had always been a problem in salvage vessels, largely because the accommodation areas had been situated amidships, with working areas on the towing deck and the forecastle deck. By compressing the accommodation into the forward part of the ship, as in a supply vessel, the effective deck area was doubled and a much more versatile craft could be designed to suit the requirements of salvage contractors. The sketches of the Nippon Salvage Company's vessels *Hayashio*, *Seiha* and *Koyo Maru* show that the split working area concept persisted up to the beginning of the 1970s in conventional salvage ship design where the towing function was considered very important.

At this point it is convenient to consider the phases

Converted boom defence vessels.

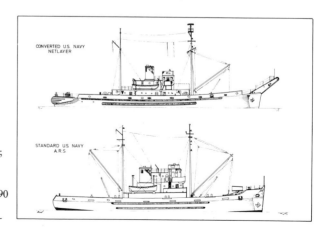

CONVERTED U.S. NAVY
NETLAYER

STANDARD U.S. NAVY
A.R.S.

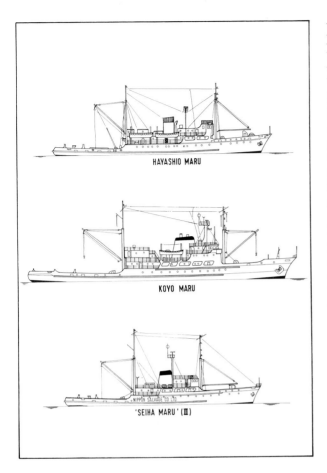

Japanese salvage vessels *Hayashio*, *Koyo* and *Seiha Maru*.

through which the US Navy's salvage vessel designs have progressed in the past 15 years before reverting to commercial salvage craft. The first major salvage vessels constructed for the US Navy since the Second World War were a class of three British-built ships known as the 'Edenton' or ATS (Auxiliary-Tug & Salvage) which came into service in the early 1970s. Apart from being extremely large, comparatively low-powered craft the 'ATS' were also extremely costly vessels to build and operate, even under military conditions. The wisdom of placing such a large capital investment in this size of vessel has always been questioned outside military salvage circles, and in 1974 Mr Salvadore J Guarino of Halter Marine Services Inc described a more cost-effective approach in his paper entitled *The Offshore Supply Vessel as a Naval Auxiliary*. This paper was presented to the Gulf Section of SNAME on 27 September 1974, and received much wider circulation when reprinted in the July 1975 edition of *Ship & Boat International*. Mr Guarino reviewed the development of the offshore supply/service vessel and proposed an 'All Oceans' class of tug/supply vessel known as the 'ATUS' (Auxiliary Tug, Utility Salvage) as a more cost-effective military tug-cum-salvage vessel. As such this project did not go ahead, but the US Navy subsequently ordered six vessels of the T-ATF (T-Auxiliary Fleet Tug) class from Marinette Marine Corporation, with the lead vessel *Narragansett* being delivered in 1979. (Particulars of this vessel are given in Table 3.)

The *Koyo Maru*. (*C B Mulholland*)

TABLE 3

US NAVY SALVAGE VESSEL DESIGNS SINCE 1945

	'ATS' Edenton	'A-TUS' Guarino proposal	'A-AFT-166' Narragansett	ARS Milwee proposal	ARS-50 type Peterson design
Length oa (m)	85.6	63.3	68.57	68.57	77.72
Breadth (m)	15.23	12.80	12.80	13.71	15.54
Depth (m)	7.31	6.09		6.70	7.31
Draught (m)	4.60	4.57 (5.18 max)	4.57	4.26	4.57
Load displacement (tons)	3,117	2,000 (2,546 max)	2,260	2,450	2,725 (proposed)
Machinery	4 × 1,700	2 × 3,000 twin screw	2 × 3,600 twin screw	2 × 2,000 twin screw	4 × 1,100
bhp	6,000	6,000	7,200	4,000	4,400
Max speed (knots)	16	15.5	15	15	13.6
Range (n. miles)	10,000	12,000	10,000		10,000
Bollard pull (tons)	70	80	53.6	60	64
Crew (normal)	93	18	20	48	87
Accommodation	102	12	20	24	99
Equipment	Towing winch; 1 × 20-ton cranes; 1 × 10-ton diving gear; salvage gear; ground tackle; bow lift ability 258 tons	Towing winch; workboat; crane	Towing winch; salvage gear; workboat; crane; traction winch	Towing winch; salvage gear; workboats; cranes	Towing winch; salvage gear; workboats; cranes; bow lift

Further US Navy thoughts on the design of salvage vessels were expressed by Commander W Milwee in a paper entitled *Considerations in the Naval Architecture of Salvage Vessels*, published in 1978 in the *Naval Engineer's Journal*, October edition. Cmdr Milwee, an experienced practical salvage person made the following observation, which is crucial in the design parameters of any successful salvage vessel:

'Of the principal dimensions, draught is the one most logically constrained. Shallow draught is necessary to permit the salvage ship to work without danger of becoming stranded. Deep propellor immersion to give greater efficiency when towing should not dictate increasing the draught. In the design of a salvage ship a maximum draught of 14 ft should be maintained.'

Various US Navy salvage vessels.

US Naval Ship *Narragansett*. (*C B Mulholland*)

The Milwee proposal is shown in Fig 7, and the outline dimensions tabulated with the STS, T-ATF and the new ARS-50 class vessels which are described in Table 3.

In 1981 the US Navy announced the award of a design and development contract to Peterson Builders Inc for the detail design and construction of the new ARS-50 rescue/salvage vessels, with an option for four additional vessels of the same class. The ARS-50 is a large vessel, with dimensions exceeding the vessel proposed by Milwee and certainly bigger than most commercial salvage vessels except the *Koyo Maru*, and the larger salvage craft owned by the People's Republic of China.

The commercial development of the salvage vessel from the larger anchor-handling tug/supply vessel is shown in Fig 8, depicting three conversions: the Smit 'Salvor' type, Risdon Beazley's *Seaford* and the Norsk Bjergnings 'Jason' class. Each of these vessels was extensively modified during conversion, which included fitting of additional winches, substantial cranes or derricks and fire fighting apparatus, in addition to diving apparatus and extra generating capacity.

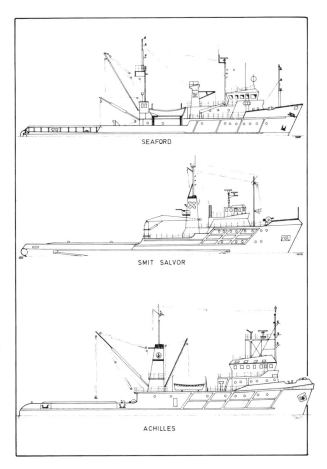

Conversions: *Smit Salvor, Seaford, Achilles.*

An example of a converted tug/supply vessel being used in the salvage role is apparent in Smit's *Smit Singapore*. Built in 1969 as the OSV *Smit-Lloyd 101,* she has a grt of 862 tons, a deadweight of 790 tonnes and is propelled by twin diesels driving two CP propellers. (*C B Mulholland*)

TABLE 4

COMMERCIAL SALVAGE VESSELS

	Smit 'Salvor' class	Beazlly's *Seaford*	Norsk Bjergnings 'Jason' class
Gross tonnage	856	791	933
Net tonnage	268	251	345
Length (m)	61.83	55.91	57.70
Breadth (m)	12.06	11.80	11.90
Depth (m)	5.35	5.20	5.50
Draught (m)	4.70	4.51	4.81
bhp	4,000	4,000	6,200
ihp	6,000	6,000	8,150
Speed (knots)	15	13.5	15.5
Bollard pull (tons)	60	55	72
Equipment	2 × 6-ton cranes; ground tackle	1 × 25-ton, 1 × 10-ton derricks; diving gear; sonar	1 × 20-ton, 1 × 10-ton derricks; diving gear;
Originally built	1970	1973	1973

The Smit vessels, *Smit Singapore* and *Smit Salvor*, were converted from large, rather uniquely designed tug/supply vessels in which the towing function had been predominant in the original design, consequently upon conversion very versatile vessels were produced. The *Seaford* (now *Smit Manila*), *Jason* (and sister vessel *Achilles*) were more of a supply vessel, with a towing capability, and the conversion of the *Seaford* was aimed at producing a more specialised deep sea cargo recovery vessel, with a salvage capability being developed as a result of the conversion. In the case of the two Norwegian vessels the conversion of two large North Sea type supply/anchor-handling tugs resulted in a salvage vessel with a good towing capacity, and some restrictions on the salvage role, due to a shortage

The salvage vessel *Salvista* is another conversion. She is seen here lightening a ship with the aid of a barge. In rapidly shelving and shallow waters such as these, the deep draught of a salvage tug is more of a liability than an asset. (*Selco Salvage Ltd*)

Converted trawler *Salviper*. (*Salco Salvage Ltd*)

of clear open working deck space. The *Achilles* and *Jason* are now owned by the Luzon Stevedoring Corporation of Manilla under the names *Regent* and *Royal*.

Three interesting and purpose-built salvage vessels were constructed during the 1970s; and two of these vessels were built prior to the conversions described above. The purpose-built salvage vessels are Smit's *Barracuda*, Sayremar's *Sayremar Dos* and Selco's *Salvenus*: the two first-mentioned being comparatively small vessels, and the latter being a large and relatively powerful ship for extended service, with a good towing capability and large cargo deadweight. The particulars of these vessels are given in Table 5.

TABLE 5

	Barracuda	Sayremar Dos	Salvenus
Gross tonnage	493	463	699
Net tonnage	151	240	228
Length oa (m)	45.00	39.65	54.00
Length bp (m)	39.20	34.85	48.00
Breadth (m)	11.50	13.00	11.00
Depth (m)	4.50	4.20	5.00
Draught (m)	3.50	3.00	4.56
Propulsion	Twin screw VPP	Twin screw VPP	Twin screw VPP
bhp	1,440	860	4,200
Speed (knots)	11	11	13
Crew	11	11	15
Extras (persons)	12	11	15

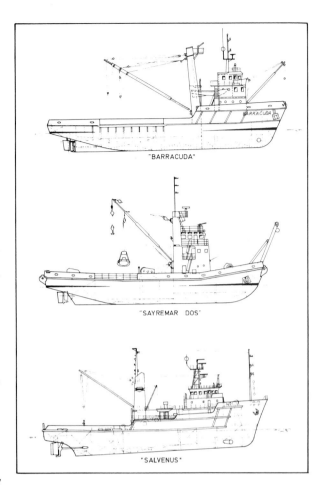

Purpose-built vessels, *Barracuda, Sayremar Dos, Salvenus*.

The salvage vessel *Regent* was also once an offshore supply vessel. Built in Holland in 1973 she is of 934 grt/1,351 dwt. (*C B Hulholland*)

Winches	Various forward and aft; towing winch	2 × 10-ton/ 2-drum; 2 × 10-ton/ 1-drum; derrick winches	4 × 5-ton/ 1-drum; 1 × 10-ton/ 2-drum; 1 × 20-ton/ 4-drum; derrick winches
Derricks	1 × 30-ton; 1 × 10-ton	1 × 25-ton	1 × 10-ton
'A' frame	Stern 1 × 100-ton; bow rollers/leads; stern roller	Bow 1 × 135-ton; 100-ton bow roller; 100-ton stern roller	Stern 1 × 80 ton; 50-ton stern roller
Equipment	Recompression chamber; fire fighting gear; ground tackle	Moon pool; recompression chamber; fire fighting gear; ground tackle	Recompression chamber; fire fighting gear; ground tackle
Built	1970	1976	1978

Salvage vessel *Salvenus*. (*Selco Salvage Ltd*)

Additionally these three vessels carry large quantities of diving equipment, workboats, rescue boats, anchors wires and buoys, pollution control equipment, and all can prepare and lay a 4-point or 6-point mooring system if required, without recourse to using their own bower anchors. Each vessel is a self-propelled work platform, with the prime function being to support underwater or surface salvage and/or diving activities on any conceivable salvage operation or wreck removal task.

The West Coast of the United States has produced two unique salvage craft, both being conversions from other vessels, and both designed to apply very high pulling forces on stranded vessels through an anchor system laid well offshore. Almost 30 years separates the conversion of the *Salvage Chief* and the *Arctic Salvor*, yet both vessels adopt a concept proven through many years of experience on the US and Canadian West Coast. Table 6 gives particulars of each craft, and the principal details of their operating systems, although space does not permit a more detailed

Proposed 8,400 bhp twin screw salvage vessel.

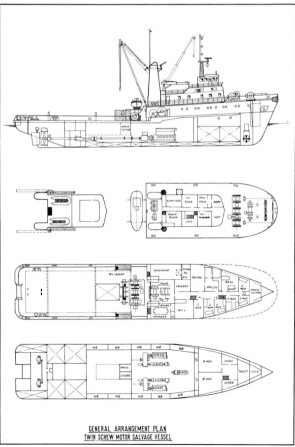

GENERAL ARRANGEMENT PLAN
TWIN SCREW MOTOR SALVAGE VESSEL

Smit-Tak's salvage vessel *Barracuda*. (*C B Mulholland*)

description of these most interesting vessels which are designed to work in the most hostile of all on-shore salvage environments – the surf zone! This writer has observed the *Salvage Chief* working in most adverse surf conditions on two occasions, and can only express great admiration for the way the vessel was handled, and the versatility and undoubted safety of the anchoring system used in the salvage operations.

TABLE 6

	Salvage Chief	Arctic Salvor
Built	1945	1970
Converted	(a) 1949	1980
	(b) 1982	
Gross tonnage	725	930
Net tonnage	275	632
Length oa (m)	61.56	64.91
Breadth (m)	10.43	16.15
Depth (m)	3.41	4.41
Draught (m)	2.89	3.65
Machinery	2 × 1,800 bhp	2 × 1,075 bhp
bhp	3,600	2,250
Winches	6 × Almon Johnston, each 90-ton pull	4 × Skagit DTW 150, each 156-L/ton pull
Anchors	6 × 6-ton	4 × 6-ton
Wires	2,800 ft per winch	3,950 ft per winch
Disposition	4 bow anchors	4 bow anchors
Cranes	2 × 25-ton;	1 × 40-ton
	1 × 20-ton derrick	
Crew	12	12
Accommodation	30	26
Helicopter	1	1

The drawing on facing page shows the general arrangement of a proposed modern salvage vessel, which would incorporate most of the operational requirements now demanded from such types, in a reasonably compact, and shallow-draught hull form. The principal particulars of the proposed vessel are:

Length oa	64.00 m (210 ft 0 in)
Length bp	57.90 m (190 ft 0 in)
Breadth mld	13.50 m (44 ft 0 in)
Depth mld	6.50 m (21 ft 0 in)
Load draught	5.00 m (16 ft 5 in)
Working draught	4.30 m (17 ft 1 in)
Load displacement	2,400 tons

The proposed machinery arrangement would comprise two 2,800 bhp diesel engines, and two 1,400 bhp engines; coupled on a 'father and son' arrangement to two variable pitch propellors. Propulsion power would thus be either 2 × 2,800 bhp or 2 × 4,200 bhp when all four engines were employed for propulsion purposes. Each 1,400 bhp engine would also be fitted to drive a fire fighting pump to 'Fi-Fi 1' standard, or an 800 kW salvage alternator, to allow large outboard power supplies to be provided. Either of the 1,400 bhp engine's salvage generators would provide power to drive an 800 hp bow thruster.

Deck machinery would be one 20-ton swinging derrick serving the after deck, and two 20-ton telescopic hydraulic cranes mounted port and starboard amidships to service both foreward and after working areas. Each crane would be fitted with attachments for a 3,500 litre/minute fire monitor to augment the vessels fire fighting capacity when fighting fires on VLCCs or ULCCs in ballast condition.

The winches would be one double drum (waterful type) towing winch with a 150-ton stall load brake system, and two treble-drum (in-line-barrel) working winches – one forward and one mounted on the break of the towing deck. Two wire storage reels would be provided for storage of ground tackle wires, spare anchor pennants and working wires. The centre drum on the three-drum winches would be specially strengthened for use as an anchor handling, working drum for recovery of anchors. Chain lockers to store ten shackles (270 m) of 3-in dia (76 mm) stud link chain cable [for use with the six 7,500 kg salvage anchors carried by the vessel] would be built into the hold space.

In addition to incorporating a landing area aft for a helicopter, and helicopter fuel storage tanks, the proposed design would have full decompression facilities for four divers and a complete outfit of surface supplied (air) equipment for four. If required, a 100-ton 'A' frame could be mounted either forward or aft, although it is envisaged that most work would be performed over the 7 ft (2.134 m) dia stern roller.

Each towing wire on the main winch would be 3,280 ft (1,000 m) of 7½ in dia wire, to suit the bollard pull of 75 tons developed by two 4-bladed controllable pitch propellers operating in fixed Kort nozzles. It would be unlikely that the vessel's fully laden service speed would exceed 14 knots, but this would be adequate for most salvage vessel situations. In any case the relatively shallow draughted, beamy design of the hull would preclude speeds of greater than 15 knots on the 8,400 bhp engine installation.

USS *Brunswick* (TS 3). (*C B Mulholland*)

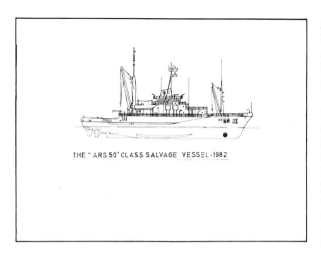

THE "ARS 50" CLASS SALVAGE VESSEL -1982

The new US Navy ARS 50.

Most normal cruising work would be undertaken using the two 2,800 bhp engines, although voyages at very economic fuel consumption could be made on the two 1,400 bhp engines.

The normal operating crew for the proposed vessel would be 14 men, which would include three seamen-divers and their tender-cum-boat driver. Accommodation for an additional 16 persons would be provided, with a lifesaving appliances certificate for a total of 36 persons. On present day building costs in the Far East a vessel of this general specification would cost between 8.5 and 9 million US dollars, which is somewhat less than the 50 million dollar-plus price being quoted for the US Navy's new ARS-50 type salvage and rescue vessels.

All salvage vessels are to some extent compromise units, being a balance between the hull available, the duties envisaged in the case of a conversion, and the finance available compared to the duties required of the vessel in the case of a new building. In describing the development of the salvage vessel over the last 80 years, the writer is aware that some significance or noteworthy 'salvage' craft have been omitted, and naturally it has not been possible to describe in great detail the equipment carried by salvage vessels in this brief historical review of this unique type. On a more personal note this writer has spent much of his sea service on salvage vessels of one shape or another, vessels either designed for or adopted to the purpose of salvage largely by the ingenuity and persistence of the salvage contractors and/or their crews concerned with the operation of the craft. In spite of the many cryptic and occasionally unprintable comments made about 'specialised salvage vessels' by their crews (and others) it has always been a most satisfying experience to arrive at a casualty after the large and rightly prestigious ocean rescue tugs have figuratively shaken their heads and given up, leaving the 'real' salvage work to the ubiquitous salvage vessel and her crew, who are frequently as unusual and independent-minded as their salvage vessel.

The Subsidy Syndrome
1 – A Future for Free Trade Shipping

by A J Ambrose

The editor is a former merchant seaman having served in a variety of small craft such as deep-sea trawlers, offshore supply vessels and tugs. Now a full-time journalist, he specialises in merchant shipping and defence subjects and has completed numerous articles in a variety of publications including Jane's Naval Review, Naval Forces, Jane's Defence Review, *and a number of other specialist journals. He is the Shipping correspondent to* NAVY international, *and editor of the new* Jane's World Shipbuilding *register and yearbook.*

With the present problems in the worlds of ship owning, operating and building being augmented by the emergence of both shipping companies and builders heavily supported by a generous donation of state funds, the future of the free-trade merchant fleets of the United Kingdom, Greece and the increasingly open market of the USA have been drawn into the limelight. Each of these nations has its own problems in differing areas, but the fundamental cause of these can all be traced to one specific source. That source is increased competition from subsidised national fleets both from

The Chinese *Guanghe* at Tilbury.
China has embarked on a massive fleet expansion programme recently, even though the recession has hit shipping hard. Massive subsidised fleets not working along normal commercial lines are putting many free-trade companies into the red. Will the free-trade operations survive? (*A J Ambrose*)

Nigerian National's *River Niger*. In addition to the 'dumped' tonnage appearing from Soviet quarters, several up-and-coming developing nations have been keen to establish their own national fleets. Of necessity heavily subsidised in their inception, these have contributed to the general over-capacity. (*A J Ambrose*)

the major fleets of socialist countries such as the USSR, but also from emerging Third World nations anxious to operate their own fleet and earn foreign currency. Even some of the major capitalist countries have contributed their own subsidies to the shipping world. Is there, therefore, a future for the non-subsidised operator, owner or builder?

Future options for non-subsidised fleets

As regards the amount of business available, the shipping situation generally is worse now than it was last year. However, with the widespread tightening of belts that has been prevalent over recent recession-troubled times, those companies that are still in business, and their employees who still have jobs, can face the future with at least a guarded level of optimism.

The shipping industries today are substantially trimmed down from their halcyon positions of just a decade ago. An improved situation has definitely emerged in 1983, but inherent problems brought into perspective by the recession have forced many companies into liquidation, others to apply for greater levels of state subsidy and, at the very least, have forced trimmed-down operations, lay-offs of workers/crews, and in most cases reduced or non-existent levels of profitability.

There are few fleets of few nations emerging from the recession unscathed. While some Arabian fleets have managed to continue their expansion within the realms of their bank balances, others, particularly in the Third World, have continued to build up their national fleets with no considerations apparently being given to the commercial viability of their expansion plans. Even the large Sanko orders in Japan appear to suffer from a nebulous approach to this latter factor. These activities simply enhance the big problem of the

world's shipping and shipbuilding industries today. The problem is of course, overcapacity. And this applies both to the shipping and shipbuilding trades alike.

To summarise the worldwide situation in very simple terms, the world's fleets expanded by nearly 4 million gross tons in 1982 alone, while the world demand for shipping generally has decreased by about double that figure over the past two to three years. Thus, on 1 January 1983 we had about 12 million tons capacity too much. This rather large problem manifests itself most in the large tanker trades and latterly in the bulk carrier trades too, but all areas felt the capacity glut to some degree or other.

As such, charter rates on the open market dropped drastically, and orders for new constructions became fewer. Many vessels were put into lay-up, as their operating overheads exceeded their working income. State-subsidised vessels dumped themselves on a poor market, and the problems grew worse and worse. In an effort to reduce the contraction pains, some nations adopted widespread protectionism, and reserved their own trades exclusively for their own national vessels. This latter factor was to squeeze the free-trade and cross-trading nations substantially, as the vessels of

BP's *British Tamar* in for refit at Falmouth. If private buyers are not found for Britain's ship repair yards they will be closed, according to new BS chairman Graham Day. British Shipbuilders can not afford to continue to subsidise them. Actually however, although apparently due for the chop, the Falmouth ship-repair yard runs at a profit. (*A J Ambrose*)

protectionist countries were still free to dump themselves in the more 'open' markets too. All told, an investor in the shipping sphere during the early 1980s had to be either one of two things, and sometimes a little of both: brilliant, or insane. And to paraphrase the old saying, 'the dividing line is thin'.

The problems of overcapacity are quite simple to identify, but the answers, unfortunately, are not so easy to evolve. The UNCTAD 40:40:20 liner code which took effect in October 1983 was destined to alleviate some of the present problems, particularly in the area of protectionism. In the tanker market, a policy of scrap and rebuild on a 2 out – 1 in ratio was advocated. Both of these policies will no doubt help, if that is, owners and operators will be bound by them. Other developments are also needed though, if stability is to be returned to the building and operating spheres of the shipping industries.

One problem that will not just go away is the state-subsidised versus free-trade operator/builder conflagration, which is enhanced in effect by aspects of protectionism. In the operating sphere, the only answer put forward to date which seems to have a ring of workability about it, is to ban vessels of protectionist subsidised fleets from operating into the ports of the free-trade countries. Unless of course, bilateral agreements exist between these nations. However, even this proposal is fraught with problems of its own. To use some examples of how this policy would work, or not work as the case may be, one could find an obvious case in the British cruise market.

British cruise companies are unable to offer cruise business from the Soviet Union's ports as this is protected for Soviet ships (assuming that is, that Soviet people could afford to cruise anyway). However, the USSR still operates an intensive cruise programme out of the Port of London area from Tilbury Landing Stage in the River Thames, and from several other UK ports over the course of the year. Under the tit-for-tat protection scheme proposed, all these Soviet cruise ship sailings would be banned – unless of course, P&O or Cunard or whomever, were allowed to operate cruises out of the Soviet Union. In itself, this example appears quite simple to put into effect, but in practice there are many problems.

If the USSR were to open its door to UK cruise companies, there would be nothing to stop the USSR from operating competitive cruises, heavily state-subsidised which, due to their cost differentials, would remove almost all the Soviet-generated trade from any UK vessels. As such, the Soviet cruise ships would still be free to trade from the UK, but no British cruise company could afford to subsidise the USSR-generated trade and there would therefore still be no UK vessels operating from the Soviet ports!

A simpler answer (in appearance only) is for free-trade states to ban *subsidised* vessels from competing in their home markets. The problem here is identifying what constitutes a subsidised vessel however. In the above-mentioned case for example, the USSR does not admit that its Tilbury operations are subsidised.

Probably the only workable answer is for both the above aspects to be taken into account, and for the adoption of a port-state-control licensing system that would view each application with a flexible policy related to what mutually advantageous operating rights and facilities were *available*. Nevertheless, with each application being studied on its own merits, numerous complications would undoubtedly ensue.

As regards our example, the present British government's apparent view of this situation is quite straightforward and laughably simple: if the USSR wishes to subsidise British passengers and cargoes, let them carry on. In the final analysis, it is the passenger/shipper who benefits and not the ship operator, in this case the USSR. The latter simply keeps losing money at no cost to the UK. This is, after all, the true capitalists position: if one cannot make a profit from operating ships, then get out of the shipping trades and let somebody else lose the money.

In fact, this appears to be an active policy of both the United Kingdom, which operates no protectionism whatsoever, and the USA which operates a protected coastal fleet, and what must rank as one of the most complicated Anti-trust shipping laws that exists, but which, under the present Administration, is having its sharp teeth drawn.

In short, these governments do not care if the USSR subsidises their cargoes, they actively encourage it. In the long run, it theoretically leaves the UK and the USA better off. Why should they care if the Soviet Union and other protectionist countries want to carry their cargoes at a loss? The UK and USA can therefore invest their money in other, more profitable international trading activities.

If an example of this policy were necessary, one

Formerly the British flag *Manchester Concorde,* this 12,040 grt container ship has now been sold to Panama and renamed *Char Lian.* In 1980/81 Manchester Liners operated a large fleet of container ships; now they have none. (*Drawing: Michael J Ambrose*)

Scale: 1:1200

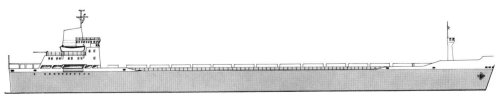

Mentor, Methane Progress and *Princess,* and numerous other vessels laid up. All these ships are at just one location,

King Harry Ferry in Cornwall, and some of these will never work again. The basis of a reserve fleet? (*A J Ambrose*)

---

need look no further than the British merchant fleet. In the last few years, this fleet has declined to almost half its former self, and there is no immediate prospect of this decline halting. There has certainly been no governmental action to halt it. Instead of wasting money trying to retain the former fleet in bad market conditions they have simply let it wither away, retaining only those units that can operate profitably. If the present glut of overcapacity should fall bringing better prospects to the market, then British investors will again start to acquire new hulls and the fleet will expand. If not, investment hasn't been wasted. This is, after all, good business.

Unfortunately however, this fleet trimming is not good news for the British seaman who loses his job. Furthermore, it lowers the level of strategic sealift assets available, as is detailed in the final chapter of this Review. Also, if a sudden market upturn takes place, Britain will not have a fleet able to make the most of the improved situation, and will not have the trained crews ready to man these ships which do not exist.

Once again, there appears to be a commonsense answer, but as put forward in an earlier article, 'governments only apply commonsense once all other options have been exhausted'. What seems to be the obvious answer is the establishment of a reserve merchant fleet of laid-up ships, consisting of the most economic older vessels which are likely to be in short supply – either militarily or commercially – when

needed. Likewise, a pool of trained reserve merchant seamen would be created to man these laid-up vessels if the need arose. Such a fleet already exists in the USA, where a two million deadweight tonne-plus reserve fleet can be called into service in a matter of days. Although this US fleet exists for strategic military contingencies, there seem to be no obvious reasons why such a policy could not be extended to cover commercial exigencies too.

While such policies could perhaps aid ailing merchant fleets, they would not alone provide any support for the equally ailing shipbuilding industries. Once again, the problem is painfully simple: there are too many shipbuilders competing for too few orders. And again, the dreaded protectionism subsidies are all too commonplace.

There can be few shipbuilding industires worldwide which do not receive some form of subsidy from their respective governments. Even in the USA and United Kingdom where one would expect these practices to be minimal, millions of dollars and pounds find their way from the public purse into the pockets of the shipbuilders. There is hardly a deep-sea ship built in the USA which is not subsidised, and in the UK there are several 'intervention fund' payouts each year, the most well known of these for 1983 being the subsidy for the Cunard G3 class Con-ro building at Swan Hunter. Nevertheless, British subsidies are small compared to those of some other countries.

2 – US Shipbuilding

by A J Ambrose

In the merchant ship building sphere, it is the United States of America which, compared to its former prowess in this field, has fared worse than any other of the world's shipbuilding nations. Only three significant true merchant ship orders were placed with US shipyards in 1982, and it must have been with some trepidation that domestic builders watched United States Lines place their massive order for twelve 4,000 + TEU container ships with Daewoo in Korea!

Big changes have taken place under the Reagan Administration which circumvent the former merchant shipping acts to a great degree. These laws required that US flag vessels be built in US yards in order to qualify for certain subsidies and operating rights. Now however, US Lines can buy abroad at prices as low as a third of the cost of a US-built vessel. Naturally, this does not exactly excite the traditional US merchant ship yards, but as the US government had been footing as much as 50 per cent of the bill for each new ship built, it was quite clear that the old practice could not continue.

Meanwhile, the US merchant fleet had been in a permanent process of decline. It is about ten million grt smaller today than it was 25 years ago. It had progressively decreased in size every year since the close of the Second World War, and the Reagan government was determined to halt this process. They did. But unfortunately, not through the efforts of US shipbuilders.

In 1981, temporary authority was granted for ten US flag operators to build 36 new ships outside of the USA. In addition, some of the legislative handicaps of owning US ships were removed, and with these factors combined, were destined to herald the start of a new period of prosperity for the US Merchant Marine. This newly adapted legislation (known as the Senate Shipping Act of 1983) has certainly improved the lot of a US ship operator by allowing him once again to enter into healthy competitive activity in foreign trade, although the Jones' (protectionism) Act which reserves all coastal and inland traffic for US ships, still applies in full. Nevertheless, while much new life has been breathed into the merchant fleet, the new legislation has effectively 'winded' the nations merchant shipbuilding industry.

Whether or not the merchant ship construction yards will ever be revived again however, is a question to which no clear answer has yet emerged.

Although the oft quoted recession is almost always blamed for the present problems, the disease lies elsewhere. For far too long now, the US politicians and industry chiefs have sat on their haunches in a position of world prominence, from which they have gazed at the world shipping and related industries, smug in the knowledge that their petro-chemical expertise, high technology, and prominence in the offshore trades would bring them full order books for the future. Then came the oil crisis. Suddenly, from the booming offshore growth of the 1960s and early 1970s, a period of stagnation had set in. New and sophisticated drilling rigs and exploration equipment orders simply ceased to materialise. There was an industry, and then there wasn't! Yards fell silent, employees were laid off, and many belts were tightened. It was trauma in all directions. Having relied on subsidies or petro-chem and high technology shipping markets, US builders were then in a sorry position – up the creek without a paddle, so to speak.

Now, the US shipbuilding industry must consider the future: do they sit there and wait for the tide to turn in their chosen specialisation? Or do they build a new paddle, and use their skills in other areas?

Firstly, an upswing in the offshore industries must inevitably take place. Timing is the important factor here, and although this cannot be controlled, the tide will nevertheless flood again as the ocean exploration

President Lincoln and her two sisters, *President Washington* and *President Monroe,* are the first US-built container ships for 30 years to be powered by US-built low-speed diesels. (*Drawing: Michael J Ambrose*)

Scale: 1:1200

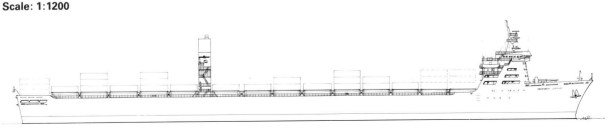

programme moves into deeper waters, with the prerequisite need for US high technology exploration and production equipment. Secondly however, and perhaps more importantly, another string is needed to the US shipbuilders' bow, not only to give work for the present, but to secure the industry's future existance.

To list definitively, the reasons for the present shape, scope and problems of the US shipbuilding industry would be a complex task. However, a straightforward summary can be adequately expressed in two words: labour costs.

As the USA is an environmentally and socio-economically rich nation, internal labour costs are high – far higher than those faced by Far Eastern industries. Naturally, this factor increases substantially the cost of having a ship built in the US, and therefore favours the industries of the less developed countries such as Korea and Taiwan, Brazil, Spain and so on. Thus, ship for ship, US prices are uncompetitive. Nevertheless, this does not mean that the US shipbuilders cannot compete anywhere in the building spectrum. In fact, the economic and technological stature of the US can almost monopolise certain spheres of the shipbuilding industry without really trying! But these areas are limited at present.

Spheres of high potential for US builders centre

The 1983-built *Falcon Leader* is theoretically a merchant ship. At present she is another vessel for Military Sealift Command charter. (*FotoFlite, Ashford*)

mainly on vessels which other nations simply cannot build, ie the ultra-sophisticated oilfield units, in which marketplace the less developed countries cannot compete due to lack of the required skills.

The aforementioned points are of course generalisations; less sophisticated ships are built in the US, and high technology vessels are built elsewhere. But as a general overview, recent years have borne testament to the former pattern.

Unfortunately, as a result of this tendency US

The new Sulzer RTA engine has made an early breakthrough into an unlikely market. All five of the 30,000 dwt 'T5' class tankers building at American Shipbuilding's Tampa yards will be fitted with a RTA76 low-speed diesel of 16,450 bhp and 95 rpm. (*Sulzer*)

The 1983-built *Point Liberty*. It is only in the field of supply boat construction that the US really uses the production techniques for which they were once famous. (*Halter Marine*)

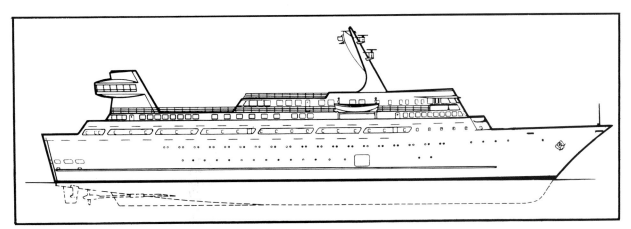

Tenders were invited in late 1983 for the construction, in US yards, of two small cruise ships for US owners. Known as the Contessa project, they are surrounded in secrecy. It appears however, that even these vessels are not totally commercial-based, as a recent application was made for Federal Maritime Aministration subsidy for two vessels to be on optional call-up access to Military Sealift Command for hospital ship duties.

builders have swung into the technology market more and more, while the conventional low technology shipbuilding fields have been largely ignored and have taken on the guise of the poor forgotten relative.

Now however, with high interest rates, the slump in the oil markets and the consistent poor trading results of the oil companies, capital is not being re-invested on the same scale and thus US builders have no orders. Added to which is the obvious tendency now appearing of the less developed nations encroaching on this domain promoting their own high technology constructions. Thus, even if a massive upturn in growth took place now, the US industry would be unlikely to achieve its near total domination of this field again. And as such, it needs to think very carefully about its conventional shipbuilding capacity in the retrospective light of the last few years activities (or lack of them).

Short of reducing shipyard workers' wages, or following the retrograde 'subsidised syndrome', just how can the US regain their competitiveness in the conventional shipbuilding scene? The answer, or at least one option, is to alter the direction of shipyard technology towards the old Henry Ford and Liberty ship styles of 'production line' building of standard designs. In which context it is perhaps both relative and interesting to note that of the large numbers of standard design 'Liberty Ship Replacement' concepts, such as the best-selling 'SD14 type' and 'Freedom' ships which have emerged, not one has been from a US builder! Thus the production line ship is a concept the USA has given the world, and to date, has thrown away itself.

Perhaps, therefore, US shipbuilders should be looking again at that area of the industry, and using their technology and design skills to produce better, more capable, safer, fuel-efficient and futuristic

vessels, using completely modernised and efficient production-line building techniques which are less labour intensive. Only then will they be able to negate some of the high initial-cost disadvantages with which US merchant ship constructions are presently troubled. In the final analysis, if US design skills can make these production line ships cheaper to operate, then a slightly higher initial capital cost may prove to be quite acceptable to a prospective purchaser. Failing that, one does not see much future for an industry which must charge a customer three times the going rate of the Far East, and is no longer automatically supported by its own merchant marine. At present, US shipbuilders still exist, but almost exclusively on the strength of the naval and naval auxiliary building programme, which cannot last for ever.

The *President Monroe*, last of a series of three 'C9' class ships completed by Avondale. These were the largest container ships built in the US to date. Will they also be the last? (*Avondale Shipyards*)

More than 400 tons of steel formed into dozens of rooms is lifted carefully over the *Estelle Maersk* by four cranes at Bethlehem Steel Corporation's Sparrows Point yard. The new deckhouse was lifted in early October from a pre-outfitting area on the ground to its permanent location just forward of the ship's existing superstructure. *Estelle Maersk,* the first ship completed in the US Navy's Maritime Prepositioning Ship Program, is scheduled for delivery on 31 August 1984. Owned by a consortium of banks, the ship will be operated by affiliates of Maersk Line Ltd of New York City and chartered to the Navy's Military Sealift Command. In addition to the construction of the deckhouse shown above, a major portion of the work has involved the construction of a 48 m (157-foot) long mid-body section, which lengthens the ship to 230 m (755 feet). Such work forms a major part of US shipyard activity at present. (*Bethlehem Steel*)

Non-naval completions in 1983 have included the third American President Line 'C9' class 40,000 grt container ship *President Monroe* from Avondale Shipyards who also completed a 42,000 dwt tanker *Exxon Charleston* for Exxon. Bath Iron Works completed a 33,869 dwt tanker, the *Falcon Leader*, for Falcon Sea Transport, and the *Essayons*, a 6,000 dwt dredger. Bethlehem Steel have been building a series of tug/barge combination vessels in conjunction with the famous small-vessel builder Halter Marine. Halter have been responsible for the tug sections, while the 47,600 dwt barge sections *Groton, New York* and *Baltimore* were completed by Bethlehem's Sparrows Point yard in mid-1983, with two others approaching completion for late '83/early '84.

Launched on 1 March 1983 for New England Power/ Keystone Shipping was the *Energy Independence*, an appropriately named coal carrier designed to supply New England Power's generating stations direct from the Norfolk coal fields while operating on its intrinsic cargo, ie coal. This 36,000 dwt coal-fired turbine steamer is the fifth to emerge in the last 24 months. The other four are Australian.

As previously stated, Halter Marine have completed the pusher tugs for the Bethlehem barge-vessels, and have also completed a good number of their staple diet of OSVs, including their largest yet, the diesel-electric *Kodiak I.* Other sisters are to follow, and several other US yards are able to keep active constructing various examples of offshore supply and support vessels. Strangely, the technology-intensive diving and oilfield support vessels one might have expected to emerge from US yards are, in fact, all built elsewhere.

Levingston have completed one 36,000 dwt the *Spirit of Texas* bulker. Mangone of Houston have completed the *Northern Sun*, a 2,600 dwt coastal tanker for Sun Transport. NASSCO have delivered *Hunter Armistead*, a 37,500 dwt tanker, and *Delaware Trader* and *Potomac Trader*, two 44,000 dwt tankers for American Trading Inc. Newport News have completed a 35,000 dwt chemical tanker for Union Carbide, while a similar sistership has been delivered by fellow East Coast yard Seatrain Shipbuilding, also for Union Carbide. Tacoma Boatbuilding have finished two incinerator vessels for Appollo Marine, and with one 4,000-ton train ferry under construction at Upper Peninsular Shipbuilders and with a number of other small MFVs and OSVs, this effectively completes the list of US merchant ship construction for 1983.

In itself, the above list is small enough. But when one looks at the list of new orders, the pessimistic atmosphere comes over a lot stronger. Avondale have two 42,000 dwt tankers for completion in 1984; Bath Iron Works have one 36,000 dwt tanker due off the slips in 1984, and that is it!

Possible future contracts are also thin on the ground. There are tender applications out for two small cruise ships and a few smaller vessels of below 4,000 tons, but little in the way of larger merchant ships. US major Lykes Lines, now back in Lykes family ownership after a spell as an LTV corporation subsidiary, is planning a major fleet renewal programme, but as with the United States Lines and Delta Steamships orders, most of these vessels are likely to be built abroad.

However, a better picture is apparent if one includes the auxiliary naval vessels being constructed for the US Central Command (formerly the Rapid Deployment Joint Task Force): Waterman Steamships have two 23,500 dwt Conros now fitting out at Sun Shipbuilders, General Dynamics are building five TAKX ro-ro vessels and the third Waterman 23,500 dwt Conro at Quincy; Avondale have three auxiliary tankers building, and the American Shipbuilding Company of Tampa have five 30,000 dwt products tankers under construction for Ocean Carriers Inc for long-term charter to the US Navy. Even with these vessels, however, there is precious little room for optimism about the survival of the US merchant ship building industry.

In South African Waters

by David Hughes

Author of the book In South African Waters *(from which the title of this article was taken), David Hughes is the representative and motivating force of the Southern African region of the* World Ship Society. *Based in Durban, he is well known for his articles on shipping activities in this significant area of the world's oceans, and is editor of the local nautical newsletter* Bluff Signal.

The most widely publicised event in South African waters in 1983 must without doubt be the tragic loss of the VLCC *Castillo de Bellver* in early August. Following a fire caused by an explosion, the vessel split in two about 30 miles off the South African coast in the Atlantic north-west of the Cape in about 1,000 ft of water. All but three of the crew were saved. En-route from the Arabian Gulf to Spain with a cargo of some 250,000 tons of crude oil, the five-year old ship became perhaps the most unlikely loss so far recorded for these massive vessels, as not only was she fairly new and equipped with all the latest safety aids including Inert Gas Systems (IGS), but she was also, as previously stated, full loaded! Under these circumstances there was no obvious reason for her loss as she was in the safest condition in which a VLCC can be found. It was only in later days that a possible explanation for the accident materialised. This was, it is believed, that she had a leak from one of her cargo tanks into one of her non-IGS protected ballast tanks wherein the original explosion took place, soon spreading its force upwards into the main oil-laden heart of the ship.

After the ship had broken in two, the stern section sank, leaving in its wake about 40,000 tons of crude oil which formed slicks that spread for miles but luckily did not close the coast. The bow section which remained afloat was subsequently towed out to sea and sunk by Safmarine's *John Ross* approximately 200 miles further west of the coast. Thankfully, the pollution from the 271,540 dwt vessel was not too serious, as most of the oil sank with the separate sections of the ship. However, while perhaps the most newsworthy happening in 1983, it was not the only significant development in this sphere of shipping influence during the year.

With its open economy, South Africa's shipping markets are inextricably tied to worldwide trends, and the current international recession has therefore left its particularly unwelcome stamp on the region's exports and imports alike. Furthermore, an over-tonnaged world fleet is exacerbating the local problems by depositing surplus capacity from other areas into the South African market, thus destabilising those areas where the recession was formerly least felt.

Taking the above factors into consideration, it is therefore evident that South Africa's own merchant shipping is experiencing an extremely difficult phase. The two most important shipping companies operating from South Africa are South African Marine Corporation Limited (Safmarine) and Unicorn Shipping Lines. These two companies are studied in some depth in the pages that follow. Apart from these two 'giants' in South African shipping there is little else to report on. The financial position and power which these two

Safmarine's *SA Alphen*. (*David Hughes*)

companies hold virtually make any operations by so-called 'one-man operators' impossible. There have been several attempts in the one-man operator field since the post-war era, but all have folded after short operating periods.

Within the general South African shipping circles competition is presently fierce. Shipping lines, ship-owners, ships' agents, freight forwarders, ship-builders, ship-repair yards and stevedores are all battling for their very survival. Furthermore, rates are being drastically cut as all these undertakings struggle to retain their portion of a rapidly diminishing market.

Safmarine, South Africa's most important shipping line, appears to have emerged successfully in 1983 despite current trade problems. At present the company is committed to the building of three new bulk carriers. They will be 35,000 dwt each. Added to this there are two new reefer vessels of 12,000 dwt. The last new vessel to enter service was the container vessel *SA Vaal*, in June 1982. She was slotted into the Far East trade on the Conference Shipping Lines 'SAFARI' trade. In 1983 she is a successful partner on this run.

The most successful route of the company in 1983 has been the European service, viz the container run between Durban and Southampton. Improved labour and port conditions at Southampton, for instance, have considerably helped this trade in 1983. Support for the southbound service, both cellular and ro-ro, has also maintained a high level of success. Examples of the ships on this run are the *SA Sederberg*, *SA Waterberg* and *SA Helderberg*.

They are 55,000 gross tons each, and replacement or withdrawal of other certain Conference Shipping Line vessels on the European trade have indicated that South Africa's contribution, by Safmarine, is fully

One of Safmarine's multi-purpose freighters, *SA Van der Stel*, seen entering Durban harbour. (*David Hughes*)

permanent. A recent proof of this fact was OCL's *Table Bay*, which was withdrawn and transferred to that company's Pacific service, having been renamed in the process.

Refrigerated cargo in the European cellular service also continued with improvements in 1983, underlining the importance of the container as a major mode of transport for perishable products.

Safmarine's United States trade has also performed well of late, with weekly southbound sailings and a fortnightly sailing from South Africa. Cargo flow, however, is now at lower levels.

One of Safmarine's latest moves has been the acquisition of the Hadag cruise liner *Astor*. She was purchased for R60 million and will serve on a new passenger service between Durban, Port Elizabeth, Cape Town, and North European ports. The full route still has to be established at time of writing, as the service is due to commence in April 1984. It originally appeared that the liner would not call at any British ports but with the decision by Curnow to withdraw from this line, an additional call at Southampton is envisaged.

Safmarine have not involved themselves in any form of passenger liner trade since the Union-Castle Line shared mailship run between the years 1966 and 1967. The ships then operated were the *SA Oranje* (formerly *Pretoria Castle*), and *SA Vaal* (formerly *Transvaal Castle*). *Astor* still has to be renamed but will operate a 'mailship type service' along with a second passenger ship, which will be built for presumed delivery at a later stage, eg 1985. The company has therefore, in 1983, endeavoured to enter a new area of passenger ship operations most courageously when most other world shipping lines have long since discontinued passenger ship operations.

SA Waterberg, one of Safmarine's container ships on the Durban–Southampton service. (*David Hughes*)

Sugar carriers form an important role in the Safmarine fleet, and above the *SA Sukumbi* is seen in Durban. (*Safmarine, Cape Town*)

The Bulk Carrier division of the company has expanded its worldwide activities of late. This has subsequently resulted in the carriage of increasing volumes of raw materials to the Far East, Europe and the USA. Examples of such bulk carriers are the *Victory*, *Venture*, *Sukumba* and *Skukuza*. The last two named are sugar carriers, which forms an important portion of the bulk carrier trade. Other certain bulk carriers are 'contracted out' from time to time. Examples of these are the *Sishen* which carries iron ore from Saldanha Bay to overseas destinations, and the *Vanguard* which had been chartered to outside interests.

The large Safmarine fleet consists of a diversity of vessels. There are also the reefer vessels, although the traditional reefer fleet has been reduced in 1983. More chartered tonnage has been employed on reefer schedules, one move which is obviously geared towards a greater involvement of trade between South Africa and countries of a more 'delicate' political nature.

The South African Perishable Products Export Control Board has continued strong support for the company's reefer trade.

Tugs and anti-pollution vessels also form a strong part of the fleet. There are two salvage tugs, the *John Ross* and the *Wolraad Woltemade*. These tugs are based in South Africa, although they can be drawn upon, from time to time, for necessary world-wide service. They were among the world's most powerful salvage tugs in 1983.

Safmarine has a standard contract with the South African Department of Transport for the patrolled safety of South Africa's coastline, which underlines the company's excellent reputation for their continued involvement in international towing and rescue operations. Recent incidents involving large fully laden tankers off the South African coast underline the necessity for such arrangements.

The above operation is furthermore backed up by the fleet of six 'Kuswag' class anti-pollution vessels. One of these ships is based in each South African port, in order to keep a close check on harbour and off-port limit areas where pollution is concerned. Should any major (or minor) shipping disaster occur in South

The Safmarine salvage tug *John Ross*, which in 1983 is still one of the world's most powerful tugs. (*Safmarine, Cape Town*)

Shown above is *Berg,* one of Unicorn Lines fully cellular container ships. (*David Hughes*)

African waters, the whole fleet is called up to undertake the necessary clearing duties. The anti-pollution fleet along with the two salvage tugs are therefore fully manned and operated by Safmarine on a strict 24 hour basis from South African ports.

To conclude, Safmarine has since its inception into world shipping in June 1946, managed to weather the storm of shipping recessions and world trade problems. The fleet is a strong one, with no signs of reduction at the present stage. However some pruning of older multi-purpose vessels such as the *SA Alphen* or the *SA Van der Stel* will eventually become a necessity within the next three/four years. Only one vessel, the *SA Huguenot,* of 18 years vintage, was disposed of in 1982. Therefore we see ahead the continued growth of an already powerful shipping company which presently comprises 40 per cent of operating liner trades from South Africa to overseas destinations.

Having stressed the trade routes served and operated by Safmarine, we are now going to look at Unicorn Shipping Lines. There are some interesting comparisons to be made between the two operating divisions of these two companies. They do not compete on any same trade route, and yet there is no strict written agreement that they should not. Apart from the SA coastal route, with a few exceptions, Unicorn lines trades primarily to Third World countries, whereas Safmarine trades on older, traditionally developed routes. This point is of major importance when comparing services operated by South Africa's merchant marine.

In 1983 Unicorn Lines celebrated the 50th anniversary of the registration in Durban of its one-ship parent line, African Coasters. The actual company Unicorn Lines was formed in 1966, from the amalgamation of three former coastal shipping companies, viz African Coasters, Smiths Coasters and Thesens Steamship Co.

Before looking at various trade routes served by this company, mention should be made that in September 1983 Unicorn Lines took over control of Cape Natal Line, a minor coastal shipping company. The latter had been badly hit by the recession, and as a result Unicorn Lines once more have full control as operators on the coastal container/break bulk cargo trade. Cape

Unicorn Lines *Umfolozi,* which operates on the Zimcorn service. (*David Hughes*)

Natal Line had lasted for little more than three years.

Relevance should therefore be placed on the importance of the coastal service operated by Unicorn Lines, as this is clearly their largest trading area. All ports are served in the Durban and Walvis Bay range, by a number of highly versatile vessels. First there are the fully cellular container ships *Berg* and *Breede*. They currently serve all ports between Durban and Walvis Bay. Then secondly, a main Durban to Cape Town service which during 1983 was being maintained by the *Kowie* and the *Nahoon*.

Further to this, a back-up service between Natal and Cape ports exists, currently being operated by the *Ridge*. All of these vessels named so far were built during recent years by Durban shipyards.

Other ships on the coastal run include the *Buffalo*, a tanker serving various ports, and the *Mkuze*, which is a car-carrier.

Unicorn Lines ships are in the main named after South African rivers, whilst Safmarine vessels have various name sources, although the large container ships of Safmarine are named after South African mountains.

On the coastal run, however, Unicorn Lines have dispensed with the traditional type of coaster, and in recent years all surplus or unwanted tonnage (some ships being rather elderly) were all disposed of.

Therefore, in 1983 Unicorn Lines operated a successful coastal service which is certainly vital in terms of South Africa's coastal trade and as a back-up for foreign trade.

Besides the coastal service, there are a number of other routes worth discussing which Unicorn Lines serve. They include the Indian Ocean Islands service, the Zimcorn service to Israel, the service to the West and East coasts of South America. Unicorn also act as agents for a service to West Africa. All of these services were in 1983 operated by a sufficient number of highly versatile container/break bulk multi-purpose vessels. Certain vessels are also occasionally chartered by the company for some of these services.

In more detail, we shall look at two of these trade routes. The Zimcorn service to Israel operates under a joint agreement with the Israeli national carrier, Zim Lines. A monthly container service between Durban and Eilat is backed up by vessels suitable for the carriage of large tonnages of bulk commodities to Eilat and Israel's Mediterranean ports.

Unicorn Lines *Buffalo*, a tanker serving the Southern coastline. (*David Hughes*)

Unicorn Lines *Ridge,* one of a number of the company's multi-purpose back-up ships. (*David Hughes*)

The second is the company's Indian Ocean Islands service. This covers the islands of Mauritius, Reunion, and Malagasy. Unicorn and the Mauritian shipping company Societe Mauricienne de Navigation have jointly developed a container service to Mauritius and Reunion, backed up by a conventional service for break bulk cargoes. In 1983 Unicorn Lines multi-purpose vessel *Tugela* was the partner on this run.

Durban's Maudon Whalf harbour area is the nerve centre for Unicorn Lines and rightly so, as it was from here in days gone by that the operations of the various coastal shipping companies were undertaken. The company's Marine Division is therefore a large one, and in workshops in Durban (also Cape Town) carry out all types of repair and maintenance work. The company also has, in recent years, taken a big role in the training of South African seamen. This point had more importance than ever in 1983, when an increasing number of black youths are being trained to be future Deck Officers and Engineers. The company started its role in this area in 1973 with its initial training programme.

Therefore in 1984 Unicorn Lines can also look ahead to the future with a great deal of confidence, as it has already contributed greatly to the building up of the

Durban's day cruiser *Royal Zulu.* (*David Hughes*)

Pakard Shipping's *Judith II*, which caught fire off the Comores Islands. (*Pernell Mizen, London*)

Republic's sturdy maritime trade. Indeed its history is largely a chronicle of Southern Africa's coastal shipping developments.

To conclude a brief look now at other South African shipping concerns. As already discussed, the Cape Natal Line, which at one stage looked a ready contender for competition on the coastal trade, no longer exists.

Pakard Shipping is a small South African shipping concern on the Indian Ocean Islands run. In 1983 at time of writing they were awaiting delivery during the month of October for a new ship the *Anna* which will re-open their service to the islands. Their previous ship, *Judith II*, became a total loss when she caught fire recently off the island of Comores.

Another company which is without an operating ship at present is Zambezi Africa Lines. The current recession badly hit their only service, from South African ports to Mocambique and East Africa. As a result, their chartered tonnage promptly ceased. Time will tell if this company will survive to operate another year.

Also in the news as a newcomer in 1983 was Durban's passenger ship line, Royal Cruise Lines. Previously known as Lloyd Cruise Lines, (which ran into financial embarassment in 1982) the company operates a day cruiser from Durban along the Natal coastline. The vessel is called the *Royal Zulu*, and was originally built in 1964 as a Spanish inter-island (Balearic) ferry called the *Santa Maria de la Nieves*. At present no immediate expansion is envisaged for Royal Cruise Lines, as their one-ship operation will hopefully manage to keep its head 'above water'. The ship is capable of carrying 250 one-class (deck) passengers.

No other formal South African shipping companies exist. There are a number of agencies operating chartered tonnage, for independent 'non-conference' shipping lines, but none of these ships or companies may be termed members of the South African merchant marine.

Therefore the post-war rise of South African shipping operations has been meteoric, and it has been remarkable that in 1983, despite the recession, trade facilities were still widely operative by most concerns to various parts of the world. Economic or political trends shall no doubt outline future expansion, and perhaps in 1984 there may hopefully be an eventual upswing towards increased foreign trade once more. It is vital and imperative that South Africa's trade links through its merchant marine are kept alive for the benefit of world-wide trade.

Chips on Ships

by A J Ambrose

Modern micro-electronic technology has provided the shipping industry with many cost-effective labour saving devices, gadgets, and ship operating enhancements. The fields of communication, navigation, shipping intelligence, ship management, design, engineering and operations are all now well served by one micro-electronic package or another.

A measure of the advance of electronics and modern technology is well evident in the advertisement of one leading equipment supplier which closes by proclaiming 'Call Earth Satellite Station 10 for further details'. A

Seeing where one is going is becoming an old-fashioned idea nowadays. Modern technological advances in the electronics fields are causing more reliance to be placed on sophisticated radars. The container ship *Dart Europe* enters the Harwich estuary, passing over the spot where the *European Gateway/Speedlink Vanguard* collision took place in December of last year.

sign of the times!

Nevertheless, although modern technology has provided us with some mind-boggling multi-million megabyte computers, it has not yet achieved the manufacture of any computer that can match either the memory storage and speed of operation or flexibility of the human brain. And even were such a machine to exist, it would be physically far larger than the human equivalent.

There is as yet no radar that is as discerning as the human eye. There is no robot as inherently flexible, dexterous and capable as the human body. Yet still there is talk of reducing crew levels further and further towards the 'ultimate' unmanned and fully automated merchant ship. That most dangerous of vessels comes ever closer.

To adopt a naive and head-in-the-sand stance to the appearance of technology could however be just as dangerous for a ship operator and his crews. It could

heads by substantial margins and allows profitable operations to be a realistic target, even in recession troubled times.

Automation aboard ship today, while not yet able to replace man aboard ship entirely, can nonetheless be a competent assistant and an extremely useful ally. Provided of course, that the 'chips' assets and liabilities are fully appreciated in the first instance.

Altogether too much reliance is still placed on the 'chip', reliance on radar in particular being a contributory cause to many accidents. The *European Gateway* sinking by Sealink's *Speedlink Vanguard* was a prime example of how two ships with sophisticated ARPA radars managed to collide in good visibility. It must be remembered that radar is an *aid*, *not* a replacement for the human eye or lookout.

spell the end of his operation if he is unable to compete on the same levels of cost-effectiveness as those who have adapted to the electro-economic revolution.

Nowadays, electronic loadmasters, engine monitors, navigational equipment and information/communications systems can provide a captain/engineer/operator with precise details on the best course to steer, engine speed, cargo loading and voyage timing, to produce the most cost-effective and economic exploitation of the ship's capabilities. This reduces operating over-

Computerisation both suffers and scores from its inherent flexibility: on the one hand, a machine which performs the same function time and time again with no deviation is a useful tool to possess. On the other, if something out of the ordinary takes place and things go wrong (and the internationally applicable 'Sods Law of the Maritime Environment' will always assure that it does), then this inflexibility becomes a disadvantage as the machine is unable to compensate for the altered working environment. And man is

Literally packed with electronics, Western Geophysical's *Western Ocean* searches for possible 'oil-containing sub-strata' in the English Channel. (*SkyFotos*).

Part of a recent advertisement. A sign of the times?

needed to put matters straight. Only then, when the liabilities are fully appreciated, can the immense assets of the 'chip' really prove their true worth.

SATNAV

The first of the wondrous spin-offs from the original military satellite system was, as far as merchant shipping is concerned, the SATNAV or satellite navigation receiver. A full shipboard installation nowadays can, typically, consist of a small receiver not much larger than a portable radio set, an antenna, a bit of cable and a few interfaces, and can cost as little as £1,500 complete.

SATNAV is basically a deep sea system. It is not particularly useful for coastal navigation, as due to the movement of the satellite in its orbit a position 'fix' cannot be obtained at all times.

The satellites serving these navigation systems travel continuously in a series of fixed orbits around the earth, and a ship can only obtain a 'fix' during a 'pass' of the satellite. Depending on the ship's location, these 'passes' can be as infrequent as every five hours or as often as one pass per hour. During the satellite's pass,

The component parts of Demek's satellite navigation system. The sets are so compact that they can even be fitted in a small yacht, as indeed they are in hundreds of examples. (*Delta Marine*)

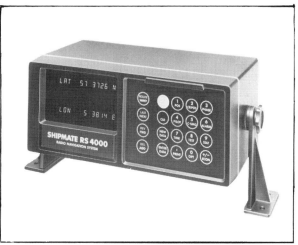

Another small system used extensively in ships and yachts as small as 20 ft in length, is Demek's RS4000 navigator which uses the Decca Navigator chain of Radio Direction Finder transmissions to provide an extremely accurate 'fix'. (*Delta Marine*)

a position fix is obtained, and this fix will typically be to within 0.05 nautical mile. While this is extremely accurate at the time of the 'fix' the ship would, nevertheless, have to wait until the next pass of the satellite before another accurate fix is possible. Thus, it can be seen that for a ship navigating in close confines to the coast there are other systems which would be more useful, such as radar, Decca Navigator, etc.

However, once out of sight of land SATNAV really comes into its own. In open seas, radar becomes useless as a position-fixing device, and while the excellent standard of Decca Navigator is fine in a Decca-covered area, these areas constitute only a small proportion of the world's seas and oceans.

In order to improve the capabilities of the SATNAV between satellite passes however, most SATNAV sets now possess a range of interface abilities to provide the navigating officer with a constant update of the ship's position. These interfaces allow the SATNAV set to draw information from a number of other primary sensors such as the ship's compass/gyro compass and ship's log (ie the ship's speedometer), and drift indicator.

These additional information inputs allow the SATNAV's internal computer to calculate by DR (dead-reckoning) a running update of the ship's position between satellite passes, which is typically accurate to within about a mile or so.

The next satellite pass then updates and corrects the DR information in a 'position-jump', and so the process continues automatically, displaying an LED or LCD readout of the ship's latitude and longitude at all times. Also displayed is the 'time to next pass' of the satellite, the course for the ship to steer to correct for drift, etc., and depending upon the sophistication of

the set various other navigational information too.

Most SATNAV sets can now also 'talk' to the ship's Autopilot, and in so doing effectively navigate and control the ship automatically with no apparent need for a 'human' operative. However, these items are not flawless, and while many ships nowadays do sail about with no one at the helm there is nonetheless an important requirement that an officer or seaman is on the bridge at all times to monitor the system for failure and to keep a lookout for other ships and uncharted obstacles.

The silicon chip has also made its mark in training ships' officers. This illustration is entirely computer generated on the University of Wales' CASSIM training simulator, which can simulate almost any conditions found at sea, virtually at the push of a button, by use of a new Computer Generated Imagery (CGI) called Tepigen. (*Marconi*)

Racal-Decca's new ARPA radar bridge-mounted display unit is no larger than most conventional radar's yet its capabilities are enormous.

Radar inputs

Yet another enhancement on the total-automation front is for the ship's radar to be linked up direct to the SATNAV and autopilot. In so doing, the radar can identify most other ships and obstructions, and feed this information in electronic form to the autopilot which can then program a series of collision avoidance movements which the ship will follow automatically each time the radar establishes a contact on a converging or close vector course. Likewise, by use of other programs and interface units, 'traditional' navigation devices such as the Decca Navigator can also be linked to logic sensing devices which in turn are linked to the ship's main navigation computer. In this manner, all of the logic circuitry devices and many of the analogue devices can be linked together to provide a totally computer-controlled navigation system.

As yet however such automated set-ups are not in commercial use aboard merchant ships, and present trends do not really indicate that they ever will be; at least, not in the forseeable future, as aside from the practical difficulties of the radar's inability to ascertain some subjects, there is also the international legal requirement that a permanent watch be maintained with human eyes. This latter factor assures that an owner/operator who has to pay a crews' wages anyway, is not also going to shell out for an expensive set of automated navigational equipment that he/she does not need. Nevertheless, the technology exists and it is therefore likely that at some stage in the future we may see some more pronounced steps in that direction.

As for the discernible effects of today's technology in use on merchant ships, it is really the ARPA or 'Automatic Radar Plotting Aid' that has recently risen to prominence, even though its prominence is occasioned more by the new IMO legislation on the prevention of collisions rather than any particular cost-effectiveness or popularity with owners.

These new regulations, which have not yet been universally adopted, call for all ships in excess of 40,000 grt to be fitted with an operational ARPA set, while certain ship types such as LNG and LPG tankers must be fitted if they are greater than 10,000 grt. Some nations have taken the IMO resultion even further, and are requiring that *all* ships in excess of 10,000 grt have an ARPA set fitted.

Automatic Radar Plotting Aids

The ARPA is actually a sophisticated radar with a computer attached which assesses all the data input derived from its primary source (ie the radar scanner, etc.).

With the normal radar, the transmitted signal is reflected off the contact (ie another ship or the coastline, buoy, etc.), and the time taken for the RF signal to be broadcast, reflected back, and received back at the scanner is measured to provide a fairly precise 'distance off' of the subject contact. This is achieved because the frequency of the radar pulse and its speed of travel are known factors. In fact it is quite possible to hear radar transmissions on a domestic radio on various frequencies, and particularly in the short wave bands where one can often hear Soviet, US and British 'over the horizon radars', most usually when one doesn't want to. They are distinguished by a 'woodpecker' sound, usually with a pulse rate of

The ARPA's display unit. Surprisingly, the controls are not that difficult to master although they seem so at first sight. The 'joy-stick' on the bottom left hand corner of the display can be used to paint pictures on the CRT, such as guard zones, digital mapping, and acquisition of contacts which the operator considers especially significant.

precisely which direction the contact is as well. On the normal radar, this information is then displayed on a CRT or Cathode Ray Tube. With the ARPA however, other things take place first.

By measuring two or more separate returns from the scanner, the ARPA's computer can establish the direction in which the contact is travelling. It stores this information in memory updating it with every transmission. From the host-ship's autopilot or gyro-compass, the ARPA ascertains what direction it is travelling in itself, too. By comparing the projected tracks of the opposing contacts and its own track, it can then deduce whether these tracks will cross at all. If they do when projected forward in what is termed a 'vector', then the computer will ask its own autopilot for the ship's speed (this having been entered by the ship's log), and will project the host-ship's tracks forward on the screen, telling the operator where his ship will be if he maintains his present course and direction at timed points along the projected track. By establishing the same information about the other contacts, by measurement of the distance they have travelled between the radar's reception of their reflected signals, the computer can then put this on the screen too, and in so doing can calculate precisely what the closest point of approach (CPA) will be in regard to any of the contacts it sees.

This is exactly what the ARPA then does. If it decides that any of the contacts look to be approaching in a dangerous manner it sounds an alarm so that the

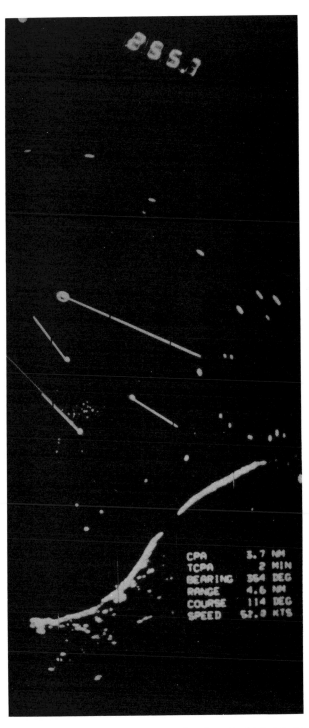

A section of the ARPA's screen, showing the 'data block' which contains details of, the CPA, time to CPA, bearing of the contact, its range, course, and speed. By use of the joystick to 'acquire' a contact, the operator can request a display of this information for any ship within a theoretical range of about 90 miles.

around 10 to 16 per second. However, we digress.

As radar transmissions travel in a more or less straight line, the radar set can also establish in

Additional devices that can be obtained to plug in to your Racal-Decca ARPA set. The cost of a typical ARPA is around £40,000 ($60,000), and you can upgrade this to a full naval specification for as little as £70,000.

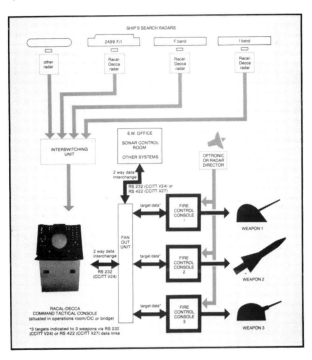

The modern ship's bridge has little in common with the wet and windy bridge of the past. The Swedish *Thebeland*'s bridge/wheelhouse is packed with electronics. Note the ship's wheel, which is duplicated. The forward helmsmans position can just be discerned. (*Brostrums AB*)

lookout (assuming he exists and is not 'below' having a mug of tea or the like – the cause of more than one collision on record) can then alter course accordingly. Displayed on the CRT at that time will be a precise CPA figure along with the time to elapse before the two ships reach that point. For example, the following information may be given as a data block on the radar's CRT or on a separate VDU panel built into the set:

CPA   8 nm.

Time
to
CPA   16 min.

In addition to these features, the ARPA set has numerous other attractions too. These include the ability to superimpose navigational charts over the CRT. These charts could take the form of a stretch of coastline, a deep water channel, a navigational mark, a minefield, a wreck's position, etc. Should the ship then approach these marks, as with the collision warning, an alarm will be sounded to make the lookout aware of the dangers.

These data-maps can either be committed to the radar's memory, or established and entered in by the operator as he likes during the course of the journey. If they are entered in memory, when the radar reaches the point in the journey where the data-map is to be displayed it will identify its reference landmarks and automatically display the map. If there are no landmarks for the radar to use as its 'switch-on' co-ordinates, it may instead obtain its position fix from other navigational devices which can interface together, such as a SATNAV, for example.

There are many other features and facilities on the ARPA set too numerous to detail thoroughly in the space available here. Furthermore, some manufacturers are offering additional plug-in facilities too. One manufacturer at least offers such additional features as plug-in circuit boards and the like, which can expand your conventional merchant ship ARPA set into a complete naval 'Command Tactical Console', able to offer surveillance facilities which interface directly with tracking/guidance and fire-control systems for Seawolf anti-missile missiles and other similar weapons systems. And while there may not be a stupendous demand for these latter devices among the somewhat staid world of the Baltic Exchange, there may be at least a tongue-in-cheek interest for such a device among any shipping company making regular pickups at Kharg Island for example! A ULCC with its own self-defence missile system would surely qualify for reduced insurance rates for *that* journey at least!!!

Satellite communications

While missile-armed ULCCs may sound ridiculous today, not so many years ago it would have seemed just as ridiculous to suggest that in 1983, from a ship at sea, we could telephone our family from the other side of the Earth using the medium of a satellite spinning round in space! Yet, on 1 February 1983, The International Maritime Satellite Organisation (INMARSAT) were able to announce that in the past 12 month period they had recorded a growth rate of a staggering 60 per cent!

From its first commercial beginnings in 1976, when three maritime communcations satellites were launched from the United States, maritime satellite communications have expanded daily. For commercial purposes (other naval-orientated SATCOMS exists), all maritime SATCOM facilities are under the control of the one body, INMARSAT. This organisation trades as a profit-making international company in its own right. The 'shareholders' consist of 38 member

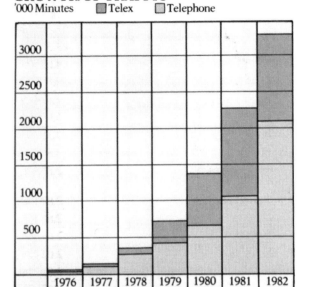

GROWTH OF TERMINALS

Number

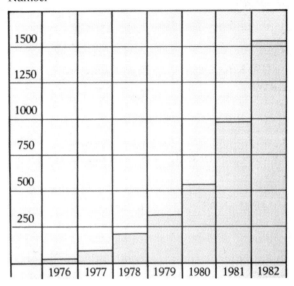

The growth of satellite communications traffic and the corresponding growth in the number of ship earth stations is evident from the above graphs. (*INMARSAT*)

Distribution of INMARSAT's ship earth stations, February 1983. (*INMARSAT*)

Distribution of ship earth stations, February 1983

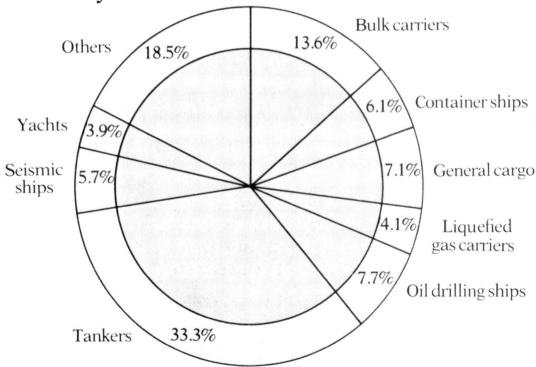

countries of a strange mix, the principal members being the USA, USSR, UK, Norway and Japan, in that order.

There are three principal components to the INMARSAT system, these being the satellites, the coast-earth stations and the ship-earth stations.

The basic fundamentals of the system are quite simple: the ship transmits its signal to the satellite,

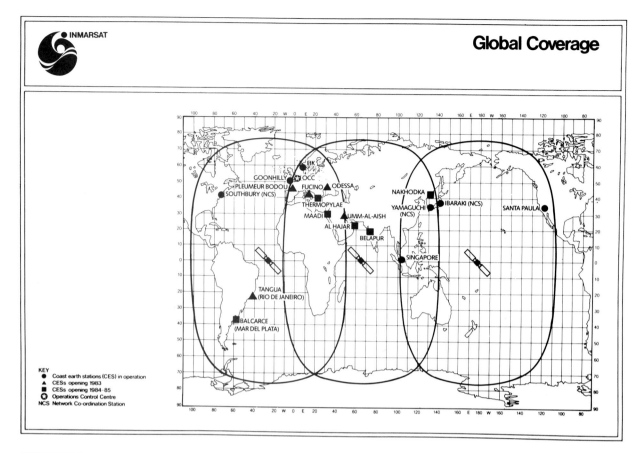

KEY
● Coast earth stations (CES) in operation
▲ CESs opening 1983
■ CESs opening 1984-85
✪ Operations Control Centre
NCS Network Co-ordination Station

INMARSAT's geographical coverage and locations of earth stations. (*INMARSAT*)

A schematic illustration of the INMARSAT system showing the ultra ultra-high transmission frequencies used. (*INMARSAT*)

---

and the satellite relays this to the coast-earth station from whence it is connected into the national telecommunication system for onward transmission. There are presently six satellites serving the major oceans of the world, and there are now few, if any, places that are outside the transmission and reception zones of the satellites which are located in orbit 36,000 km above the Equator, over the Atlantic, Pacific and Indian oceans. The satellites are termed 'geostationary' which in simple terms means that they do not move far in relationship to the Earth's surface.

The coast stations each maintain an antenna which is permanently pointed at the satellite. At time of writing there are seven coast stations, but others are

---

A recent development in satellite communications was the establishment of an emergency distress system based on the use of the satellite to ensure rapid contact between the vessel in distress and the coast rescue co-ordination centre. Known as the EPIRB, this network will allow far quicker response times than are presently possible. In the salvage industry for example, the time saved by the EPIRB system could well enable a salvor to rescue a ship which might otherwise be lost. (*INMARSAT*)

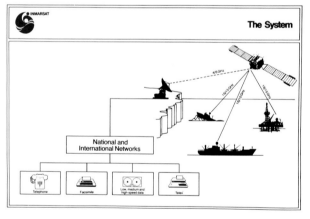

● INMARSAT

The System

National and International Networks

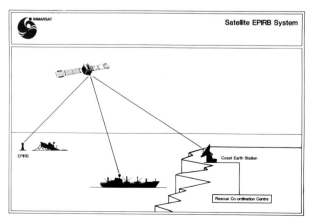

● INMARSAT

Satellite EPIRB System

being added and it is expected that there will be at least 14 in operation by the end of 1984.

The ship station consists of an antenna which is kept pointed at the satellite at all times by a clever stabilising system mounted inside a 1 m diameter dome, which also contains the ship's parabolic antenna. The ship stations prevalent at present are all of one type which give the ship one telex channel and one plain language telephone channel, although other ship stations are now coming on the market which allow the user a complete set of telex and telephone lines. Basically, this is in answer to the demands imposed by cruise ships for example, where one telephone line is obviously insufficient.

At present, INMARSAT's customers range from tankers (the largest sector of their market) through drilling rigs, container ships and tugs, to private

The ship installation consists of a single antenna mounted externally and the internal telex and processing equipment. Until very recently, there was only one type of ship installation available, which offered only one voice and one telex line. Known as the 'Standard A' installation, the antenna is easily identified, being mounted just to port of the sea search radar in this view of the Liberian *Ambia Fair*. (*SkyFotos*)

yachts, with over 1,600 ship stations now in operation.

And finally, the bottom line: a typical ship-installation will cost from around $50,000 (£34,000). But with the present trends of having to wait hours, and sometimes days, to get a radio telephone call through to a ship, coupled to the increased interference from a quantitative rather than qualitive expansion in radio traffic, to a ship that is costly to operate that £50,000 could be money well spent.

The German Coaster Fleet – From Sailing Barges to Con-Ro Types

by Gert Uwe Detlefsen

Motor vessel *Sigrid Wehr* was the second coastal ro-lo vessel built in Germany. Three yards co-operated to build the ship, but not spontaneously. The hull was constructed at Howaldtswerke-Deutsche Werft, Kiel, at their steel construction department. The fitting out was started with the Kremar Yard at Glückstadt, but after their bankruptcy Rickmers Werft at Bremerhaven completed the 999 grt/2,600 dwt vessel. By special means the vessel is able to trade without hatch covers, as seen here when she was carrying a tower for an oil drilling platform from the UK to France. (*Oskar Wehr KG, Hamburg*)

Well-known shipping commentator, journalist, and maritime photographer based near Hamburg in the Federal Republic of Germany, Gert Uwe Detlefsen is the author of many first-rate shipping publications including Flensburger Fordeschiffe, Einladung: Monographien zur Schiffahrtsgeschichte, *and his latest technical handbook* Vom Ewer zum Containerschiff *which was published in 1983.*

No other coaster fleet has experienced such radical changes in tonnage as the German Fleet has in the last 50 years. Right into the middle of the 1920s it was still possible to see a large number of German sailing vessels

◄ Very popular with German owners are the 'Rhine-Sea-Traders' built by various yards for many owners. The *Aladin* was completed in 1982 by Hugo Peters at Wewelsfleth. This 499 grt/1,768 dwt vessel with the usual flat superstructure is owned by Matthiesen Shiffahrt of Hamburg. (*Gert Uwe Detlefsen*)

of all types and sizes owned and used in the North and Baltic Seas. They were mainly employed in the local distribution trade, known in Germany as 'farmer's shipping'. However, a few of them were occasionally employed far from home: the Haren/Ems-owned 'Pünte' *Helena* of 220 dwt sailed twice to Brazil in 1892 and Blankenese-owned 'fruit-yachts' sailed regularly to the Mediterranean. In 1900 the German fleet of sailing vessels consisted of 2,288 vessels, 2,000 of them being coastal craft. It was only after the First World War that many of them were equipped with auxiliary motors.

The development of the German coaster fleet nearly stagnated between 1910 and 1926. The majority of the small yards along the coasts failed to make the change-over from timber construction to iron and steel. On the one hand they did not have enough of their own capital to invest in new machinery, and on the other they could not find suitably qualified men in the small ports. Also the owners themselves did not have faith in the new material, since their expertise over the centuries had been in wooden-built sailing ships.

The situation changed radically however after the First World War, when a rail network was built connecting nearly all places of importance. This made the armada of small craft of 50 tons and under too expensive to operate in competition with the state railways.

The Dutch neighbours were quicker to react to the changing situation as they expected that only modernised coasting vessels would have a future. They had already built sailing-coasters with motors called 'motorsegler' (motorsailers), and when their own needs

Not a coaster any more, but a good example of many similar ships ordered by coastal owners is the *Oriolus*, named in Latin after a bird, completed in 1982 by J. J. Sietas. The 3,980 grt/7,785 dwt vessel is specially designed for the container trade and is fitted with two 36-ton cranes. Her owner, J H Breuer, is the present chairman of the German Coastal owners organisation. (*J J Sietas*)

were satisfied the Dutch yards looked around for other markets. They found them in Germany, where there was little competition, and they were able to deliver a large number of modern sailing coasters with motors between the wars. Sails became relegated to a secondary position, assisting with the stability and giving a little extra speed under the right conditions.

It was not until the late 1920s that German yards started to make modern coasting vessels with both sails and engines. Surprisingly enough, they were mainly built by yards which had not been engaged in constructing coastal ships before. In 1926 one of them, the Nobiskrug yard, delivered the first two pure German motor coasters of 170 dwt each, the *Elisabeth-Auguste* and *Marie Mathilde*, although they were not ordered by a traditional coastal shipper but by the Belt-Reederei.

The Nobiskrug yard experienced a great success with their old-fashioned looking, but modern conceived 3-mast-schooner fitted with motors of the 'I earn' type.

Until the Second World War a larger number of newbuildings entered the trade, gradually beginning to look more like the coasters of today. At the same time, older and smaller vessels were motorised and in

Views of the *Condock III,* a multipurpose vessel which can carry all the wide range of bulk and general cargoes with additional abilities for the transport of roll on/roll off cargoes, containers and heavy lift objects. However, the special feature of the vessel is the capability to load floating units semi-submersible, by means of floodable tanks. The 1,599/4,600 dwt-vessel was completed in summer 1983 by Husumer Schiffswerft for Condock-Reederei Wolfgang Bauer. (*Gert Uwe Detlefsen*)

order to pay for the engine, lengthened, occasionally more than once. The rigging was simultaneously cut back and the vessels lost their old-fashioned look.

During the Second World War, the German coaster fleet lost a large number of ships of all types and sizes, and when the building of replacement tonnage started in 1949, only the most modern motor coasters were constructed.

In the 1930s, the average size of the German coaster was about 200 grt and about 300 dwt. By the 1950s, they averaged 299 grt and about 400/450 dwt. Only a few vessels with less than 299 grt have been built since that time, and then mainly for special trades supplying, for example, the Frisian Islands.

There were of course a lot of changes after the last war. Only a comparatively short stretch of the Baltic coast remained with West Germany, and trade altered accordingly. The armada of small tramp steamers of between 200 and 1,000 dwt had been decimated by the war, and what was left only found employment in the years of the shortage of tonnage in the early 1950s. Later it proved to be uneconomical to run these ships. The tramp steamer trade was taken over by the coasters, and this new generation of post-war vessels were now also engaged in the timber trade from Scandinavia, once a domain of the smaller steamers, and in the coal trade from the UK to the Continent and Scandinavia. The deadweight rose and soon the step to the next 'paragraph-section' had been taken and a series of 499 grt-vessels had been built. The deadweight ranged from 700 up to 1,000 dwt and in the last 15 years rose further to 1,500 dwt and in a few cases even to 1,900 dwt. The majority of modern German coasters are constructed as free- or shelterdeckers with a 'tweendeck. They are measured only up to the 'tweendeck, all space between 'tween- and maindeck is 'not registered' which means the coasters have a high cubic volume, which is required in the timber, coal and general cargo trade, cargoes of a greater value than the bulk cargoes. Different rules ie in the Netherlands, where the length of a ship is the important factor, lead to different types of ships, the UK and Dutch owners still having a preference for singledeck tonnage.

Many yards were founded or became engaged in the construction of coasters and larger ships after the war, some only existing a few years. However, they managed to complete a large number of new vessels during this period. At that time the European coaster fleet was not overtonnaged, so modern and economical vessels proved highly profitable. Once half of a newbuilding price had been earned, an owner sold his ship to another and then moved up into a higher class of vessels, and ordered himself more modern newbuilding, a couple of hundred tons larger. Since 1950 the majority of German coasters have been engaged in the cross trades and developed increasing trade between foreign ports.

The remaining small coasters, many of them still with sails, had established themselves in their last domain, distributing goods to the Frisian Islands and along the German coast. The coastal trade was then lost to road-haulage and when ro-ro ferries started to connect the Frisian Islands with the mainland at the beginning of 1960, they lost this trade also and there was no other alternative than to scrap the ships or lay them up. The money obtained for the scrap was seldom enough to finance a larger and more profitable ship.

In 1951 the German coaster fleet consisted of 478 motor-sailing ships, of which 336 units were over 30 years old, and 542 motor coasters, about the half of which were less than 20 years of age.

In 1960 the German coastal owners organisation counted 1,041 units. Of these, 562 vessels were between 200 and 500 grt, forming 76 per cent of the total fleet. 500 units were older than 30 years, but they accounted for only 26 per cent of the total tonnage.

The picture changed considerably in following years up to 1983. Today's fleet of the German Coastal Owners Organisation contains only 604 units but with a greater tonnage of 493,640 grt and 1,095,243 dwt (1960: 253,832 dwt/378,820 dwt; 98 units have a deadweight of less than 500 dwt, and only 48 vessels had been built before 1950. The majority are less than 15 years old.

There were, of course, many reasons which led to this fantastic development. One is the enormous increase in building costs. In 1955 a 1,000 dwt coaster cost about £190–200,000; to build a 1,100 dwt vessel today would coat about £1–1.4 million. It is no longer economical to build coasters of less than 1,100 dwt, as they can no longer operate profitably. The modern class of 499 grt is manned with the same size of crew as older 499 grt vessels. However, the modern example can carry 1,500 tons of cargo while the same vessel of 20 years ago carried only about 800 tons.

Hove is one of the many German container- timber carriers. The large and wide hatch allows rational transportation of many cargoes. The 999 grt/2,560 dwt vessel was completed in 1976 by J. J. Sietas and is owned by Arnold Fischer. (*Gert Uwe Detlefsen*)

Two German coasters, 'out of fashion' but still successfully trading, in the Kiel Canal. The 499 grt/1,200 dwt *Hermes* dating from 1966 is overtaking the 1961-built *Annelies* of 297 grt/444 dwt. (*Gert Uwe Detlefsen*)

Despite that, there is still a demand for small units of 300/600 tons as there are still many shallow-water ports where the larger vessels cannot call. Furthermore many shippers and receivers prefer smaller units because they can then minimise storage expenses, as the turnround of smaller cargoes is of course quicker than that of larger ones. The price of older vessels remained good because the costs for newbuildings were rising rapidly, and even after 10 to 15 years of trading the vessel brought more in sale than it had cost as a newbuilding. So all owners who invested money in newbuildings between 1950/60 earned quite a considerable amount when selling their ships later, and could therefore order much larger replacement vessels.

In the 1960s the German coaster fleet took over the leading role in Europe. German owners were flexible and reliable and yet remained extremely competitive with foreign coaster fleets. In countries such as Sweden where the development of coastal shipping was retrogressive, the Charterers took German ships because it was cheaper. The main reason for this was the Swedish scale of wages which were higher than in Germany.

When container and ro-ro shipping started to take over in the general cargo and coastal trades, German owners were among the first to follow the signs of the times and immediately ordered container ships designed specially for the coastal trades.

In 1966, the *Bell Vanguard* came into service exemplifying the trend towards semi-containerships. After that date, nearly all of the larger coasters incorporated large hatches, allowing to accommodate either general cargoes or containers.

With the influence of containers the timber trade

The 1981-built *Roma* was completed by Werftunion at their Emden works. She has one hold and, as shown, can carry containers on top of her hatch covers. The *Roma* typifies much of modern German tonnage. (*FotoFlite, Ashford*)

from Scandinavia changed completely. The timber was no longer shipped in single deals, boards and battens, this proving to be too expensive in man-power, but now in unitised packets. Both container and timber parcels required a new type of ship, a vessel with open hatches and no understow. Cranes were used to lift cargo, and man-power could be reduced to a minimum in order to balance the rapid increase in wages of employees afloat and ashore. This new generation of open-hatch coasters was suitable for all kinds of cargoes, for containers, timber, general cargo and also bulk cargoes, because for all commodities open hatches were an advantage.

Since the first years of building up a new coaster

The *Detlef Schmidt* seems a fairly large vessel at first sight, yet she is only 499 grt. Nevertheless, she has a 1,610 deadweight. She was built by Werft Nobiskrug in 1978.(*A J Ambrose*)

The advantages of vessels such as *Castor* are their large open holds which can accommodate conventional cargoes or 20/40-ft containers. *Castor* was built by Martin Jansen in 1969 and has a 1,408 dwt capacity in a gross of only 484 tons. (*A J Ambrose*)

Two generations of coaster at Teignmouth in southern England. *Union Mars* has a collapsible mast to facilitate her transit up rivers/canals where low bridges are a problem to the conventional coaster. They are known under the peculiar title of 'low air-draught' vessels. (*A J Ambrose*)

The 1962-built *Plancius* contrasts starkly to the deadweight capacities of the modern German coaster such as the *Roma*. *Plancius* (formerly the *Noval*) is of 399 grt with a deadweight of 560 tonnes. (*A J Ambrose*)

fleet the majority of ships were not individual constructions but more or less standardised. All yards engaged in the construction of coasters had a few types of ships which were built for various owners, with only minor equipment alterations. As such, building costs could be kept to a minimum, an attraction for many ship owners.

In 1978 another type of coastal vessel began to emerge, the ro-ro type. The main characteristic, the large open hold and hatch was combined with a stern ramp in order to take on rolling equipment as well.

The owners of these vessels had not only the smaller ro-ro trade routes in mind, but also the Scandinavian timber-products trade where the shippers could cut costs by loading by both ro-ro and conventionally. Scandinavia is one of the new 'home trades' of the German owners. Also in general trade on nearly all routes it is an advantage today to have ro-ro facilities. If there is no rolling cargo to load at some of the ports one can utilise the ramp at least for the speeding up of loading and discharging operations.

More than two thirds of today's newbuildings for German owners are in the 999 grt and 1,599 grt brackets. This size is still regarded as a coaster, the manning and safety regulations for coasters still apply and this offers considerable advantages in the short and medium range trades. The vessels are permitted to sail with a fairly small crew and in respect of pilots, port-dues, etc they are cheaper than ships with larger tonnage, taking their large deadweight into consideration.

The German coaster ship yards, of which there are now very few left, and the German 'coaster factory' J. J. Sietas are well known, at least all over Europe, and have an unique ability to utilise the last inch of space to construct a large deadweight but a small gross-tonnage measurement.

With the flexibility and the reliability the German ship owners have built up, they maintain a high reputation with international charterers so that they nearly always find employment for their ships, even if it is not always as satisfactory and as profitable as one would wish.

Many owners who earned good profits in the better days of shipping started early to build ships in classes which no longer can be considered to be true coasters. It is obviously more economical for them to operate two 7,000 tonners than seven 2,000 tonners or 14 vessels of 1,000 dwt. The majority of German coastal owners, even if they have no more coasters, are operating their fleets as 'armchair owners' from their own homes, with only the family as staff. They normally do their chartering via their 'house-brokers', although this can be understood to mean different things to different people!

If a German owner is offered a two-year time charter, he will build exactly the ship required since the first two years are always the hardest to finance. That is possibly one of the secrets of the (more or less) successful German coaster fleet.

The Changing Face of Offshore Vessel Types

by A J Ambrose

The offshore supply vessel and its running mates are now fast becoming the most numerous types of craft to be seen. Their proliferation effectively began about 20 years ago, when the necessary technology to allow the search for oil and gas to proceed further offshore into deeper and deeper water became reality rather than fantasy. The growth rate in the search for fossil fuels was in those days quite dramatic, and as the drilling rigs and production platforms moved further and further from the shore, the demand for specialist vessels to support these rigs increased proportionately.

With the passage of time, greater sub-sea resources were discovered in more locations than had previously been considered possible. With these discoveries, new problems in the exploitation of these resources demanded increased technological resourcefulness to combat the harsh natural environmental conditions. Technology advanced, the search spread, and hitherto unheard of areas of the seas and oceans began sprouting rigs and platforms in steadily increasing numbers. The demand for supply boats and specialist support vessels increased to new heights almost on a daily basis. Demand was strong, although supply was initially weak. Those were halcyon days for the operators of supply vessels, but they were not to last.

As offshore prospecting increased, supply caught up with demand, and by the start of the oil price-led recession in the late 1970s, some areas of the supply boat market were facing overcapacity. Nevertheless, a skilful operator could still ensure work for his craft if he was prepared to move them from one area to another.

A typical example of the regional ups and downs of this relatively new industry were clearly apparent

The extremely capable multi-purpose OSV *Maersk Runner* is just one example of a proliferating type. Note the characteristic rounded under stern (sometimes refered to as a stern-roller) which aids in anchor handling duties, and the added enchantment of four fire monitors fitted above the bridge. (*FotoFlite, Ashford*)

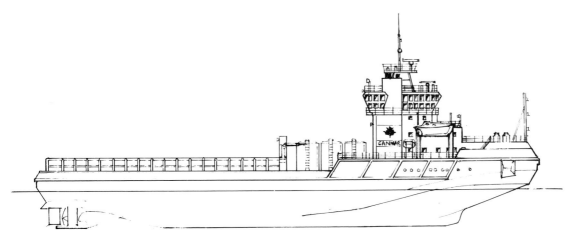

Cunard's offshore supply subsidiary was building a series of tug/supply vessels of the 'Shore' class in the late 1960s and early 1970s. *Canmar Supplier VII* (ex-*Polar Shore*), built in 1971, is an example of this type. Today however, these vessels do not compare favourably with the more modern MP designs and can be chartered at rates of little over US $1,500 (£1,000) per day. (*Drawing: A J Ambrose*)

One of the more unusual types of OSV to emerge in late 1982/early 1983 were the Canadian icebreaking supply vessels *Robert Le Meur* and sister.

The exploitation of large new oil fields inside the Arctic circle is likely to bring a large number of these vessels into service over the next decade, serving in both the Arctic and the Antarctic. (*Drawing: Michael J Ambrose*)

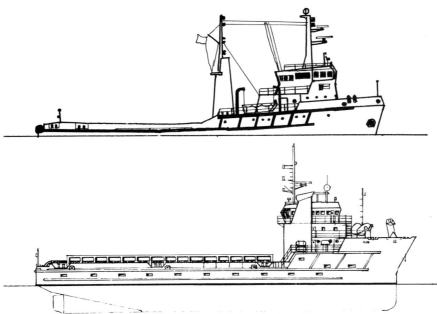

Seaforth Emperor and sisters were completed in 1982 and fitted with massive forward anchors to enhance their anchor-handling role. These anchors give the OSVs greater tugging abilities when starting to lift the 100-ton plus anchors fitted to many rigs. (*Drawing: Michael J Ambrose*)

during 1982. In the US Gulf, 1982 saw a deflated market. New supply vessels were still emerging from the builders' yards in vast numbers. Thus, considerable overcapacity was visible in the US market, and a number of American vessels were forced into lay-up. However, across the Atlantic in the North Sea rates were still high, and a typical supply vessel could still earn as much as $7,000 per day.

But as 1982 drew to a close, a dramatic decline in the charter rates had established itself, and by August

1983 the same supply vessel could expect to earn less than half its 1982 rate in European waters. By September, North Sea supply vessels had been fixed on charter rates as low as $1,350 (£900) per day! Others went into lay-up. Such are the ups and downs of investing in supply boats.

In a measure to alleviate some of these 'helter-skelter' aspects of the market, de-specialisation of supply boats grew in fashion. Supply vessels became tugs, anchor handlers, firefighters, anti-pollution vessels, safety attendance standby vessels and, to quote an extreme, some even became naval patrol boats! This was not a new event for 1982 however, as this development had taken place over a period of several years. By 1983 though, this trend had established itself as a major pattern in new supply boat

Two of the largest and most powerful OSVs in the world are the 1982-built *Wimpey Seahorse* and *King Supplier*. Both have true multi-role capabilities which are demonstrated on the frontispiece to this edition where they are shown towing the rig *Chris Chenery* in the English Channel earlier this year. (*FotoFlite, Ashford*)

construction, and the building of multi-purpose supply vessels had become the norm rather than the exception.

By 1982, Wimpey Marine of the United Kingdom had completed two of the most powerful multi-purpose supply vessels ever built in the shape of their *Wimpey Seahorse* and *Wimpey Seahunter*. These were to be followed in late 1982 and 1983 by a number of these powerful jack-of-all-trade OSVs from a variety of yards. As 1983 progressed, more and more of these vessels entered service and began encroaching to a greater degree on a wider variety of potential markets.

The concept behind the appearance of these multi-role types was quite clear. While they were more expensive in their initial cost, modern technological developments were such that operating overheads could be reduced to a certain degree, thus making the large new MPV only marginally more expensive to operate than a conventional supply boat. As such (and

taking into consideration their greater attractiveness to potential charterers) their multi-role abilities could allow them to command higher earnings, as in addition to moving cargoes between shore-bases and rigs, on arrival they could act as safety-attendance vessels, be available for firefighting duties if necessary, re-position rig anchors, and even move the whole rig if required.

This factor was not their only advantageous point however. If the market was depressed, it would be the multi-purpose vessel that would likely win any spot-charters (albeit at reduced rate) in preference to a one-duty vessel. Furthermore, if supply runs were not available, rather than go into lay-up the MPV could look for work in other areas, such as conventional towage, rig-moves, even marine salvage if the opportunity presented itself. As a last resort, the flexibility of the MPV is such that rather than suffer the depreciation expenses of lay-up she could accept a role as a safety attendance standby vessel which, although not allowing her to make a profit, could nevertheless help her owners to stay ahead of some of her capital and operating costs. As option, it is marginally better than the no-income depression of owning laid-up tonnage.

The very flexibility of this new breed of supply vessels did not go unnoticed however, in the ranks of the specialist craft operators of the towage, salvage, and safety attendance industries. A profound change was therefore apparent in the new designs of former ocean towage and salvage tugs as was detailed in Capt Hancox's article in the last edition of this review. In Britain, United Towing's *Salvageman*, in Holland Wijsmuller's *Tempest* and *Typhoon*, and latterly even Smit's massive new salvage vessel, were constructed with stern-gate rollers rather than with conventional sterns, to allow them to handle the large rig anchors so they too could now enter the domain of the anchor-handling supply vessel and, as it were, fight back

Wimpey Seahorse and sister *Wimpey Seahunter* were earning rates of around US $ 4,500 per day in 1983, compared to more than US $7,500 per day during the 1982 season. (*Drawing: Michael J Ambrose*)

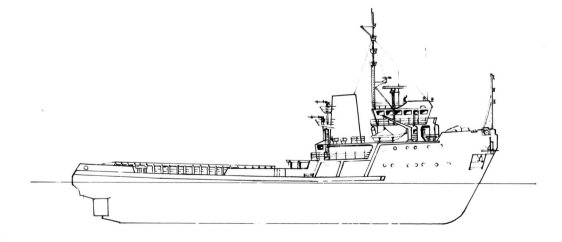

Exemplifying the movement of the OSV into the conventional towing market is this view which shows the multi-purpose fire-fighting, anchor-handling tug, supply vessel *Maersk Runner* towing a semi-submersible drilling rig without the assistance of any other vessel. (*FotoFlite, Ashford*)

Most of the safety attendance vessels in use today are converted trawlers such as Claridge's *Mustique*. While the poop deck contains a clear area which can accept helicopter winch-transfers they are hardly ideal vessels for the job. Many of these are fairly old, the trawler types having changed more to the stern-trawler variant in the last decade. (*FotoFlite, Ashford*)

against the massive influx of supply vessels into the tug's traditional trades.

Although even the largest of present MPV supply vessels can not handle all the tasks of the specialist ocean towage and salvage tug, there is nevertheless much credence to the view that the MPV supply vessel and the ocean salvage tug are following close and increasingly parallel paths of development. It is possible that future progress in design could well bring these two different types of vessel together as the *multi-purpose salvage, towage and supply tug*. Indeed, that day draws closer.

Even the safety attendance vessel is not sacrosanct from the OSV's inroads. While it has been put forward that the low cost of the safety ship makes the duty unattractive to the OSV operator, increasing insurance premiums, environmental and government pressures have occasioned the need for more sophisticated and capable safety ships. If cost-effective operation can be provided, safety vessels equipped with some measure of fire-fighting and oil-pollution control apparatus such as towed oil-booms, suction tanks, etc could become commonplace.

Already, new purpose-built safety vessels are entering the market, such as the Sentinel-designed *Sentinel Maria* class. Taking over the duties of former converted trawlers, these are sophisticated and capable little ships and, as the life-span of many of the present trawler-safety vessels removes them from service, numerous examples of these specialist units can be expected to materialise.

As the cost of these new vessels could increase with their improved capabilities, the price differential

First of two 'Sea Titan' class anchor-handling tug supply boats to emerge from the US yards of Halter Marine in 1983 was the 12,280 bhp diesel-electric *Kodiak 1*. She is the largest and most powerful OSV built in US yards to date. (*Drawing: Michael J Ambrose*)

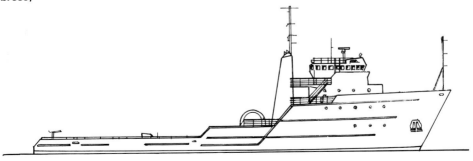

Converted trawlers are now engaged in a variety of other offshore activities including research work. In this view, the former trawler *Northern Horizon* is seen firing her array of compressed air guns which are trailed from beams just visible on her stern-quarters. These air guns fire a series of blasts into the sea bed, the shock waves of which are measured to gauge whether the sub-sea area could contain oil or gas reserves. *Northern Horizon* is shown here working off Eastbourne, England. (*FotoFlite, Ashford*)

Operating in similar vein to the *Northern Horizon* is the 685 grt *Western Atlantic,* a purpose-built seismographic survey vessel completed in 1980. Her seismic streamers can be clearly seen in this view which catches them precisely as they are detonated. (*FotoFlite, Ashford*)

between the supply vessel and the safety vessel is bound to lessen as the earlier supply boats pay-off their annual depreciation figures. Thus, unemployed supply boats could make a larger mark in the safety vessels market if additional inducements are not provided by the latter's operators.

Some of these inducements are clearly apparent in

the new Sentinel vessels, and progressive development could well improve their capabilities further. Future development of the safety vessel is likely to incorporate greater attention to helicopter compatability as the helicopter annually proves itself as by far the best initial rescue facility. The helicopter is finite in its capacity however, and so a larger survivor reception facility is needed close by. The specialist attendance vessel answers this need.

Other enhancements that could materialise are some form of connection between the rescue vessel and the

Yet another unusual offshore vessel type is the 1974-built 929 grt research vessel *Oil Hunter.* She is another example of a converted stern-trawler. In 1983 she has been operating in conjunction with the seismographic research vessel *Northern Horizon.* (*FotoFlite, Ashford*)

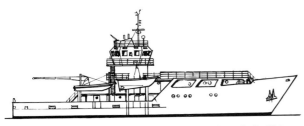

Sentinel Maria. First of a completely new breed of offshore safety attendance vessels which are destined to become quite numerous in future years. (*Drawing: Michael J Ambrose*)

rig. The only obvious form for this facility is evacuation chutes of a similar nature to those now carried by many merchant ships for discharging passengers and crew into liferafts. There are practicality problems to this course of action however.

Firefighting, anti-pollution and pollution control are other areas where the specialist safety vessel must now concentrate. Progress here could lower insurance rates which must otherwise rise if the incidence of blow-outs and the like continue or even possibly rise. The lowered insurance rates would therefore meet to some extent the increased cost of the new breed of 'safety vessel' thus assuring its continued attractions to the oil companies, and by extension, the profits of the safety vessel operators.

Additional impetus in favour of the specialist safety vessel equipped with pollution control equipment is also on the cards following West German demands for tougher penalties for those responsible for oil spillage. The West German government, backed by several others, was given EEC support for a high-level conference on this subject in 1983, and with the MARPOL agreement also taking effect in October 1983, these two developments have developed a significantly increased demand in this field of operations. It can, therefore, safely be assumed that all of the new 'Sentinel' vessels entering service and under construction during 1983 will find no shortage of work. However, original plans for these new vessels anticipated only *Sentinel Maria* and *Sentinel Cathinka* actually entering this mode of operation in the first instance, the remaining three of these vessels finding work in the diving field.

Sentinel Maria, the first of the new type, entered service in late 1982 working the Norwegian fields, while *Sentinel Cathinka* entered service in April 1983 in the UK market. Three more vessels of the class

Making her debut at the oil port of Aberdeen, Scotland, is the British-registered Norwegian safety ship *Sentinel Cathinka*. Completed in April 1983, she visited Aberdeen in May prior to taking up duties in the UK sector of the North Sea. (*Jim Prentice*)

The more modern stern-trawler types such as the ex-Grimsby trawler *Boston Lincoln* are even less suitable as safety attendance ships than are the older side-trawler variants. Removal of the after mast/gantry and replacement with a helicopter deck however, would make these far more useful in the offshore trades. (*FotoFlite, Ashford*)

were completed in 1983, and further vessels to an improved design will enter service in 1984.

Packed into their 499 grt are a wealth of features including capacity for up to 310 survivors, a 16-bed sick-bay and a three-bed intensive care unit. Two 'man overboard' (MOB) rescue craft are carried, and the flat deck forward of the bridge is built to accept helicopter transfer of survivors winched down to the ship, in stretchers if necessary. This deck is served by a lift of sufficient size to accommodate the stretchers. The forward deck could also accept small helicopters landing-on in an emergency, but winch operations have to suffice for the larger units such as Sea Kings and similar.

The propulsion machinery consists of two 1,125 bhp Caterpillar diesels each serving a rotatable ducted propeller mounted forward of midships. This arrangement allows greater manoeuvrability and furthermore, means that survivors can be picked out of the water at any point aft of the bridge utilising the various boarding nets and ladders carried aboard.

In addition, fire-fighting equipment is carried, and two spray booms are fitted to allow the vessel to combat oil-pollution. A hydraulic derrick, fitted aft of the bridge, is used to handle the primary MOB resuce boat, and with minor conversion the design allows a quick transfer of duties enabling the vessel to act as a mother ship for a remote-operated diving vehicle (ROV) used for pipeline inspection and ROV/survey work.

In conclusion, it is clear that fundamental changes are taking place in the various offshore vessel types expected to be operational in the second half of the 1980s. The transition from supply boat to multi-purpose offshore service tugs is taking place already and is likely to reinforce itself with the manifestation of larger anchor-handling salvage tugs and more powerful supply-vessel tugs. By the mid-1990s these types could all be one and the same form of ship, each capable of handling the duties of supply, anchor-handling, firefighting, ocean towage and possibly even salvage. The increased capital and operating costs of this sophisticated new type is likely however to limit or curtail entirely their use as safety attendance vessels.

The increasing ages of the present fleet of trawlers engaged in rig safety attendance, and their lack of compatability with helicopters, coupled to increased demands for better safety conditions and more effort in the control of pollution, will see a decline in the numbers of converted trawlers working the safety ship markets. In their place will come new breeds of purpose-built safety attendance vessels, better equipped and more capable than their predecessors.

Hopefully, these two new types will aid in more cost-effective exploitation of sub-sea resources and, perhaps even more important, will improve the safety conditions pertaining around the numerous rigs and production platforms which, as deeper waters are prospected, will also likely change their forms.

From a Soviet Seaman's Eye

by Captain Vladil Lysenko

Captain Lysenko has had many years sea-going experience on a variety of ship types as a former trawler and cargo vessel captain in the Soviet Merchant Marine. After leaving the Soviet Union, he joined the Swedish Merchant Marine where he continued his sea-going career. He is the author of the non-fiction work A Crime Against The World *(Gollancz). The following article 'From a Soviet Seaman's eye' is taken from a series of papers formerly published as* The Challenge of Soviet Shipping' *by Aims of Industry and the National Strategy Information Centre.*

The Soviet merchant fleet has expanded enormously since the close of the Second World War, and even amid a worldwide shipping contraction it continues to grow at a tremendous pace. The *Bratsk* is one of the many new vessels completed for the USSR in 1983. She is one of a class of 20,000 dwt ro-ro general cargo vessels with significant ice-breaking facilities. (*FotoFlite, Ashford*)

According to the 1980 edition of *Narodnoye Khozyaistvo* (The National Economy), the Soviet Union's annual statistical handbook, the average monthly wage paid to a worker in the field of maritime and internal-waterway transport in 1978 was 227.5 rubles (roughly $340 or 1,400 Swedish crowns). In

ХУДОЖНИК ПАХОМОВ
ЛЕНИНГРАД

Soviet merchant tonnage has had a dramatic effect on many of the liner routes, forcing Western companies to pull out of the formerly lucrative trades. That they can achieve this is due to the extremely low cargo tariff they adopt when competing against Western shipping companies. These low rates are achieved by low overheads and a large measure of subsidy. (*A J Ambrose*)

1979 it was 228.9 rubles, and in 1980 232 rubles indicating an increase of somewhat less than 1 per cent in the first case, and slightly more than 1 per cent in the second case.

Taken at its face value – that is, disregarding camouflaged inflation and the gap between official State and black-market prices, which are basic realities in the USSR – this monthly wage would seem a lot. The Soviet seaman earns 65.5 rubles (40 per cent) more than the same statistical handbook tells us, is the monthly salary of the average wage-earner or *homo sovieticus*. The contrast with the 'cultural worker', who earns only 104.7 rubles a month, is even more striking: the average Soviet seaman earns more than twice as much!

We know next to nothing about the methods of calculation used in the compilation of such statistics: whether, for example, they take into account payments for food on board, wage increases for service in polar regions, and bonuses paid out in foreign currencies.

For seaman's wages in the USSR vary greatly from one maritime enterprise to the next. Seamen working for Black Sea companies, for example, are not entitled to the 'polar' bonuses paid to seamen employed in northern companies. Even in the Black Sea the wage paid to a seaman employed, let us say, on the Zhdanov–Poti line will differ from that paid to a seaman on the Zhdanov–Naples route. The difference is due to the foreign-exchange bonuses which are paid only to seamen in ships touching at foreign ports.

Such being the case, I am going to try to show – not on the basis of unverifiable statistics, but of my own experience of conditions in the Soviet and Swedish merchant marines – how Soviet seamen really live.

Up until 1975 the monthly wage earned by a Soviet merchant-marine captain varied between 195 and 250 rubles a month (or from 1,170 to 1,500 Swedish crowns). The salary earned at that time by a Swedish sea captain was roughly 11,000 crowns, or 1,833 rubles at the official rate of exchange. Depending on his status, a Soviet seaman at that time earned between 78 and 88 rubles a month (468 to 528 Swedish crowns),

The *Boris Zhemchuzhin* (5,627 grt) handling cargo at Gravesend on the south bank of London's River Thames in August 1983. Soviet ships can almost always be seen at this berth. (*A J Ambrose*)

whereas a Swedish seaman's monthly wage was around 3,700 crowns (or 616 rubles).

In 1975 wages to sea-faring officers and sailors were increased – the average for a captain rising to 250 rubles, and for a merchant seaman to about 110 rubles. These wage scales still prevail today. In Sweden seaman's wages are subject to an automatic annual rise based on the level of inflation and retail price increases, but nothing comparable exists in the Soviet economy, and consequently in the Soviet merchant marine.

To have a precise idea of what Soviet seamen actually earn, one must add all sorts of bonuses paid out to them for their success in 'realising' or 'exceeding' the assigned quotas of the Plan, for the transport of dangerous goods, for repair jobs undertaken at sea, etc. These bonuses take the form of percentage increases calculated on and added to the basic salary or wage. In this way a captain, for example, can earn up to 350 rubles, while a seaman can hope to earn 130

The *Mikhail Lermontov,* a Soviet cruise ship which is one of many trading in the West European cruise market. She is seen here berthing at Tilbury Landing Stage in summer 1983. There are more Soviet cruise ship departures from the UK than there are British or any other nationality's. (*A J Ambrose*)

rubles a month. The potential increase for a captain is thus 100 rubles, compared to a maximum of 42 rubles for the most hard-working of seamen. (Unlike the percentage bonuses, taxes vary little and usually amount to between 10 per cent and 13 per cent).

Now let us see what 130 rubles actually represent for the Soviet seaman in terms of what he can buy on the home market. In the USSR official State and unofficial (black-market) prices differ widely for two important reasons: the chronic shortage of foodstuffs for the Soviet seaman in terms of what he can buy on the home market. In the USSR official State and unofficial (black-market) prices differ widely for two important reasons: the chronic shortage of foodstuffs and the poor quality of consumer goods manufactured at home. A Soviet-made suit may cost 130 rubles in a State store, but a pair of American blue jeans will cost 250 rubles on the black-market 'bazaar'. Soviet-made shoes cost between 25 and 40 rubles a pair, but Swedish-made shoes are hawked at prices ranging from 60 to 200 rubles. Meat, when available in a State store, costs from 2.5 to 3.5 rubles per kilogram, but on the black market it costs from 5 to 10 rubles. And so on.

At the official exchange rate prevailing in 1981, the

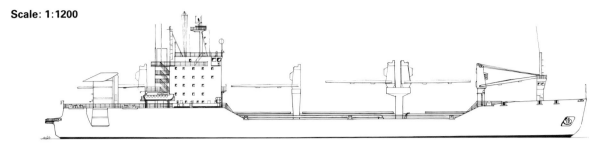

The Soviet SA-15 class ro-ro icebreakers of the 'Norilsk' class are building in large numbers at Finnish yards. They have a number of military utilities in addition to their mercantile facilities. (*Drawing: Michael J Ambrose*)

State-fixed prices in the USSR were approximately equivalent to those for similar goods in Sweden. But the wages earned by a Swedish seaman in 1981 – 5,141 crowns, or 856 rubles – were still, even at the official exchange rate, six times higher than the comparative earnings of a Soviet seaman.

There has never been a shortage of applications for employment on Soviet merchant marine vessels touching at foreign ports. The main reason for this is the tiny bonus paid in foreign currencies to seamen on such ships, which amounts to roughly one dollar for each day at sea. These small sums are enough to buy foreign products that are unobtainable in the USSR and which can be profitably sold at the end of each voyage in Soviet ports or cities. Soviet seamen call these dealings '*bizness*' (derived from the English word, business).

To no Western seaman would it occur to operate *bizness* in baby milk-bottle nipples. But Soviet seamen buy them in Sweden for half a crown (8 kopeks) apiece and sell them for 5 rubles each after their return to the USSR. A neat profit of 6,250 per cent!

Here is another example. A Soviet methane gas tanker was laid up for a long time in a Japanese port to undergo essential repairs. For a price of $60 (54 rubles at the official exchange rate) crew members bought portable sewing machines which were later resold in the Soviet Union for 25,000 rubles each. A *bizness* profit of 46,296 per cent!

I myself used to buy synthetic boots in Göteborg at a cost of 18–20 Swedish crowns a pair – roughly equivalent to three days' worth of my foreign currency bonus. In the Soviet Union I was offered from 150 to 160 rubles for those same boots. There is a thriving *bizness* for Soviet seamen in cheap synthetic products of all kinds: umbrellas, synthetic (mohair) wool, chewing gum, shirts, women's lingerie, pornographic magazines, lipstick, records, guitar-, violin-, or doublebass strings, and so on. All this, of course, involves the payment of bribes to harbour and customs officials, police inspectors, and even to KGB officers.

Particularly profitable, though dangerous, is the *bizness* done in literary works that are forbidden in the USSR. A small book by Solzhenitsyn, for example, can fetch up to 250 rubles (or five years of imprisonment for 'idealogical deviation'). In this way, by exploiting the very weakness of the Soviet economic system, its closed, secretive character, its rampant corruption and its idealogical absurdities, Soviet seamen manage to assure themselves and their families a relatively tolerable existance. But I must repeat the *caveat*: this is true only of seamen working on vessels involved in international trade and receiving foreign-currency bonuses. Those who are unable to visit foreign ports and who cannot indulge in any form of *bizness* live, on the contrary, in conditions of dire poverty.

Let us now have a a look at the vital problem of food allocations at sea. In the mid-1970s the sum allocated to each merchant seaman to cover food costs was 1.4 rubles a day. In 1981, as a result of repeated seamen's complaints and an investigation by a specialised medical committee, these starvation level allocations were raised to 1.8 rubles a day. It is highly doubtful if this improvement did much to increase the number of calories absorbed each day by a working seaman in the 1980s. For in the interim the prices of essential foodstuffs had risen substantially.

I am not referring here to officially announced price rises, but rather to those of a camouflaged variety. For example, the so-called 'Leningrad sausage' (15 cm long and 1.5 cm thick) which used to be sold for 1.90 rubles a kilogram in State stores suddenly disappeared. In its place appeared a new 'Neva' sausage, of no better and often poorer quality. These new sausages, 10 cm long and 2 cm thick, were put on sale for 2.20 rubles. (Let no one insinuate that this is a form of inflation! A new product has simply been put on sale.)

To cite another example: a fish called merluza used to be sold for 40 kopeks a kilogram. One day it disappeared, and in its place there appeared a 'silver hake' (lovely name isn't it?), which was put on sale at 70 kopeks a kilogram. In reality, it was the same fish. I myself fished it, and on my trawler we had to change the labels on the crates containing it.

In the Soviet Union ships are supplied with foodstuffs from the warehouses and depots of an organisation called *Torgmortrans*. The prices charged are the same as those practised in State stores, but the quality is much inferior, particularly for vegetables. Forced to obtain their food supplies from this *Torgmortrans* system, seamen have no choice as regards either quality or price, and have to accept whatever is in stock.

Both the liner and break/bulk tramp trades are areas of considerable Soviet involvement. The 1983-built *Pyer Puyad* is an example of a growing Soviet interest in container ships. It is noteworthy that they do not include the larger vessels in their register such as are the converse fashion in the West. (*FotoFlite, Ashford*)

To make matters worse, each Soviet seaman is assigned a prefixed ration of so many grams of flour or starch items, meat or fish products. Regardless of what may or may not be desired, one is obliged to load on board the exactly stipulated quantities of those various products. We who were employed on a fish-processing trawler-factory ship had to buy canned and other fish products from the depot before we put to sea. It is also pertinent to note that while we paid a wharf price of little more than 1 kopek (for a crew of 96) for each kilogram of sea perch we fished, we were obliged to buy the same perch at the depot at a price of 2.10 rubles a kilogram.

In accordance with a directive (No 193) issued by the Soviet Finance Ministry in cooperation with the Ministry of the Merchant Marine and that of Fisheries, one was allowed to buy perishable foodstuffs in foreign ports after a period of 20 days at sea. The sums allocated for this purpose amounted to 45 kopeks per crew member – this sum being included within the 1.80 rubles assigned to each seaman per day. This directive remained unchanged for years, unaffected by the increase in the cost of foodstuffs abroad, so that we saw the purchasing power of our 45 kopeks a day steadily dwindle. Nor were we allowed any leeway if, for example, we were not able to put into a foreign port until we had been 30 days at sea. The ten days elapsed beyond the original 20 were not counted, and all we had the right to buy were perishable foodstuffs for the number of days it was reckoned it would take us to return to our Soviet port.

Should the price of foodstuffs bought with foreign currency abroad exceed the authorised sum, or if the purchased goods are not considered to be perishable, a sum ten times that amount in rubles is deducted from the captain's salary (a good indication of the ruble's real worth on the domestic market). For having once bought 28 rubles' worth of tinned pineapples I myself had 280 rubles docked from my salary.

When a ship makes a long voyage it often happens that the foodstuffs taken on in its home port run out. One is then supposed to renew one's supplies from another Soviet vessel. Such barter deals often take place in Cuba, where ships sometimes have to wait for long periods to be unloaded. Only when there is no way of being resupplied from another Soviet ship may one use the sums allocated for daily sustenance – and even then only with a special authorisation from the shipping company's director, an authorisation valid for the number of days it takes one to reach the nearest Soviet port or one where Soviet ships dock.

In the Soviet fishing fleet, and particularly for 'non-foreign currency' voyages, the situation is even worse. For a voyage that may last six months, as many food-stuffs as possible are loaded on board before leaving port, so as to reduce the precious time lost sailing to and from floating supply ships. The already skimpy rations are further reduced through the spoiling of perishable foods like potatoes and vegetables. On fishing trawlers, of course, the caught fish forms an important addition to the usual meagre fare, served up on the mess tables in one form or another every day. But because of the shortage of fat products, such fish dishes are fried in cod liver oil. This is the only form of food served in unrationed portions.

Realising full well that the official ration levels do not assure a sufficient number of calories per day, shipping companies have organised 'shipboard shops' where seamen can use their earnings to buy sugar, butter, condensed milk, canned meat or fish, cheese, and cigarettes – at the usual on-shore prices. But such shops sell neither beer nor any other alcoholic beverages.

Seamen employed on passenger ships, and particularly international routes, are somewhat better fed. Such ships are automatically supplied by the *Intourist* organisation, which caters to foreigners – that is to say persons of a 'superior' category, who are entitled to more and better food. Although the official food rations for crewmen on such ships are the same as on other Soviet vessels, part of the food destined for foreign passengers finds its way, through all sorts of devious channels, to the seamen's tables. Even higher are the rations prescribed for certain specialised ships involved in research, particularly those carrying members of the Academy of Sciences or which are used in connection with space programmes.

One area where crew conditions are notably in excess of the norm for the Soviet fleet is in the field of scientific research and military surviellance. This vessel, the *Kosmonavt Vladimir Komarov* is used for tracking space flight, ballistic missiles and specialist intelligence gathering. (*FotoFlite, Ashford*)

Soviet cargo vessels can usually be seen at most French ports where a considerable amount of traffic handling takes place. Here *Petrovsky,* a 'Perm' class break/bulk vessel is seen handling a cargo of timber at St. Malo. There are nearly 1,000 ships of this general cargo type in service with the Soviet Merchant Marine. (*A J Ambrose*)

Food ration levels also vary greatly in the Soviet Navy. Here too officers can fill out their daily diet by paying for extra foodstuffs out of their own pockets. On submarines food allocations are considerably better than on surface vessels, for in the Soviet Navy, as in the army and in all areas of civilian life, there exists an entire gradation of food norms.

Once, when I was in a seamen's hospital in Riga, Latvian Soviet Republic, I discovered that the daily food ration for an invalid was exactly 52 kopeks! By the doctors' own admission this was barely enough to assure one a daily diet of 1,200 calories. Virtually everybody employed in the hospital – cooks, serving women, nurses and doctors – were surreptitiously helping themselves to food officially destined for the patients. To say nothing of the food supplies that were simply being stolen and taken home.

At the time I was hospitalised, my father-in-law, a KGB officer, was admitted to a special hospital in Riga reserved for persons working for the Ministry of State Security. In *that* hospital each invalid was assigned a daily ration of 3 rubles: six times more than that offered in the ordinary seamen's hospital.

For the past half a dozen years I have been serving with the Swedish merchant marine, and the question I keep asking myself is whether Soviet seamen will ever be able to be fed like their Swedish colleagues. In the Swedish merchant marine there are neither norms nor restrictions, and the food is of the finest quality and of a wide variety. In addition to regularly served breakfasts, lunches, and suppers, anyone who feels hungry can at any hour of the day go to one of the refrigerators in the mess-room and help himself to cheese, sausage, milk, fruit, butter, and salad dishes carefully prepared by the ship's cook. Swedish seamen have not the faintest idea what it feels like to have to go without fresh vegetables and fruit. When a fish dish is scheduled for a meal, a meat dish is automatically offered as an alternative for those who don't like fish. Everywhere, from bridge to engine-room, there are hot-coffee dispensing machines. In addition – something quite inconceivable to a Soviet seaman – there are frequent on-board parties.

Recently I paid a call on my company's administrative offices in Stockholm and asked one of the managers concerned with supply problems what was the daily sum allocated for the feeding of a Swedish seaman. 'We have neither norms nor limits,' he replied. 'We spend whatever is needed. We can't make allowance for price variations in different countries.'

Inasmuch as Swedish merchant ships are supplied on basis of wholesale duty-free food prices, one can say that the average Swedish seaman receives between six and seven times more food than his Soviet counterpart.

On Swedish merchantmen there is no captain's assistant for political indoctrination and control. On the other hand there is an assistant, with the rank of second mate, who is responsible for the feeding of the crew; he has to deal with the unions, which are quite independent and which keep a close eye on such matters.

One of the most difficult things for a Soviet seaman to understand is the role that a union plays in the life of seamen in the West. For the Soviet seaman the *profsoyuz* (union) is no more than a governmental bludgeon used to mete out punishment according to the dictates of the Party or the KGB; it is a fig leaf both concealing and helping to organise the pitiless exploitation of the seamen. The very statutes of a Soviet *profsoyuz* define its first task as that of achieving 'socialist emulation' – a sweat-shop system aimed at increasing output according to unchanging norms and set prices.

Here, for example, is an article in a collective bargaining agreement between maritime unions and a

shore leave; 24 hours of watch duty while in port are matched by three days of shore leave. When a seaman is sent to serve on a ship or is put ashore on duty, he receives travel and food allowances, a 1st-class railway ticket (tourist class for air flights), individual hotel accommodation, and all his taxi and luggage transport expenses are reimbursed. These are unheard of luxuries in the USSR.

I have in front of me, as I write these lines, my salary earnings sheet for December 1980, when I was second mate on the Swedish tanker *Oceanus*. My basic salary was 6,759 Swedish crowns. To this were added 669 crowns as compensation for my captain's diploma (the rank I held in the Soviet merchant marine), as well as 92 crowns for uniform expenses. That made a total of 7,520 crowns.

Swedish shipping company: 'When a navigational officer with at least two years of service is transferred from a ship of a larger category to one of a smaller category, he retains the salary paid to him for the larger category.' Such a stipulation is unknown to Soviet seamen and officers.

In the Swedish merchant marine a navigational officer's salary is based on a working week of 35 hours, the rest being considered as overtime. For five extra hours of night watch one is granted eight hours of

I am entitled by collective bargaining to 2.33 days of leave per month. The compensations earned for night watch duty, service on Saturdays, Sundays, and holidays represented 45.23 days. Altogether I was entitled to 45.5 days of shore leave for each month of service at sea.

Soviet seamen with whom I have discussed these matters listen with incredulity. They simply refuse to believe that while on shore I could receive, in addition to my regular salary, a tax-free allowance of 53 crowns (8 rubles at the official rate of exchange) a day for food. After all deductions have been made, I receive 6,500 crowns a month while on shore – enough the cover my normal living costs. I am not obliged to indulge in any sordid *bizness* deals. My legally earned salary is enough to cover the upkeep and running expenses of my Mercedes, the rent of my three-room apartment (with its fine balcony view over the Swedish countryside), the purchase of furniture, a colour TV set, video, trips to Greece, France, Spain, etc. And I am not tormented by the prospect of an impecunious retirement.

This last point is worth dwelling on, for little about the scandalously low levels of Soviet retirement benefits and disability pensions is known in the West. I myself, at a time when I was still relatively young and serving on fishing trawlers in the northern seas above Murmansk, did not look closely into pension matters. But I noticed that as a general rule the sailors among us who were getting on in years awaited their pensioned retirement with anxiety and joylessness. They began saving up and tightened their belts, limiting their purchases of many things they could have bought or wished to buy. They were preparing themselves for retirement, as though for personal poverty. For that is the stark, simple truth: in the USSR the retirement pay system for the ordinary mortal amounts to a transformation of one's social status down to the level of a desperate absence of civil rights, and persistent, dire want.

Two basic factors are involved here: (1) Retirement pay totals 60 per cent of the wages earned after 25 years of work. (2) An old-age pension cannot exceed 120 rubles a month. To reach this 'ceiling' in pension payments a retiring seaman must have earned an average wage of not less than 200 rubles a month for a period of ten years. But three quarters of the seamen do not earn that much, and their pension payments average 60 to 80 rubles per month – which is to say, somewhat below subsistence level. In conditions characterised by permanent production bottlenecks and by chronic shortages of commodities in State-run stores, and of high prices in the parallel (not State-controlled) 'market', such pension payments assure an existence on the very verge of famine.

The situation as regards invalidity payments is, if anything, even more pernicious. In 1972 a seafarer who had a record of 30 years at sea (17 of them as a sea captain) was granted an invalidity status in the so-called 'Group III' after suffering a heart attack. According to Soviet law he lost the right and the possibility to work in his speciality – which meant that in effect he lost his professional capability.

A disability pension was accorded to him – amounting to exactly 27 rubles and 40 kopeks a month! This seafarer had two children of school age and an apartment that cost him 36 rubles a month. This kind of 'care for the welfare of the simple Soviet man' surpasses the bounds of sadistic mockery. For in strict fact there is no such thing as an on-shore profession for someone who has no experience of shore employment. There are only various form of labour, all of them requiring physical exertion. But physical exertion for somebody suffering from heart trouble means death.

By way of comparison, let me cite the conditions that prevail in non-communist Sweden. As a captain's assistant – not as captain – I had to go into retirement for reasons of health. I passed over in to what in Sweden is called a 'privileged class'. By way of insurance covering my material needs I am paid (1) 4,469 Swedish crowns of state pension, (2) 1,404 crowns from the seamen's pension fund, and (3) 3,803 crowns of non-taxable relief income to cover apartment rental costs. After the payment of all taxes I am left with 5,250 crowns (about $700) a month to live on, and the assurance that if prices rise, my pension payments will increase correspondingly.

The social security benefits enjoyed by Swedish seamen are among the most generous in the world. They pay nothing for medical examinations and medicines. The first five months in hospital are paid at the same rate as shore leave. Soviet seamen simply cannot imagine that the State (in this case the Swedish state) should provide retired sailors with rent allowances for a two-room apartment, a 50 per cent reduction on all forms of public transportation, half-price tickets for most museums, cinemas, and theatres, and even free meals in schools. Nothing remotely comparable exists in the USSR.

Soviet seamen find it equally hard to believe that in the Swedish merchant marine one can buy a duty-free packet of cigarettes for half a crown, and a bottle of whisky for 10 to 12 crowns. In the Soviet merchant marine not only is one not allowed to drink on board; one cannot even take any form of alcohol on to a ship. (Alcoholism, be it remarked in passing, is a major blight in the USSR, undermining work discipline, causing work accidents, poor productivity and other evils).

Generally speaking, in the West Saturdays and Sundays are regarded as holidays. In Sweden there are, in addition, close to 30 other religious or national holidays in the course of the year. On such days beer and alcoholic drinks are served free of charge on board. Nobody tries to get roaring drunk. On our ship one of the refrigerators in the mess-room is always filled with liquor, beer, Coca-Cola, or other beverages.

Only on a minority of 'trusted' vessels are Soviet seamen allowed ashore in a western port. Usually they must go ashore in groups of five. If one member of the party defects, then all the remainder are held responsible. Here *Khudozhnik Pakhimov* is seen docked at Tilbury. (*A J Ambrose*)

We even have a saloon bar. It is a very comfortable place with well upholstered armchairs and sofas, a TV set, and a hi-fi stereo hook-up. There is a bar, complete with tall stools and the rest, as on land. On its shelves, there are alcoholic drinks, including Stolichnaya and Kubanskaya vodka. Needless to say, there is no barman. Each seaman helps himself, mixes his cocktails, inscribing a cross for each drink opposite his name in the register.

Here a bottle of beer costs less than half a Swedish crown, and a bottle of whisky from 10 to 12 crowns only. All proceeds quietly – without fuss or feathers, and above all without lectures of indoctrination from snooping political commissars, who on Swedish merchantmen, as on others in the West, are neither needed, nor wanted.

Developments in BASH (Barge Aboard SHip) Vessels

by A J Ambrose

If there is one thing that most of the unusual modern ship types do not possess, it is cosmetic beauty. As compared to the designs of the past, gracefulness and appeal to the eye do not apparently figure very highly in a ship designer's order of priorities. Nevertheless, many of these modern high-utility and cost-efficient vessels do indeed have a character all of their own and an appeal which is, admitedly, sometimes difficult to justify. From an enthusiast's point of view, it is common to hear such comments as 'why don't they make them like that anymore?' when a particularly attractive *ex*-liner cruise ship or a three-island cargo vessel sails by. Perhaps, one day, our descendants may make exactly the same statement when a LASH ship appears over the horizon, breaking the monotony created by the 100-knot semi-submersible hyper-conductor-powered tankers which may well be the ships of the day? Or will all oil transport be by pipeline then? A growing tendency, even today.

Tillie Lykes at sea with only two of her Seabee barges visible aft. The remainder of her upper deck cargo are containers. She can carry 824 conventional containers on her upper deck while still having space for 24 fully-laden barges on her two lower decks. (*Lykes Lines*)

LYKES LINES

First of the Seabee variants, Lykes Lines own *Almeria Lykes*. They are of 21,677 grt, 39,026 dwt, 266.99 m length overall and are powered by a 36,000 shp twin geared steam turbine giving them a service speed of 19½ knots. All three of this class were completed by General Dynamics between 1971 and 1973. (*Drawing: A J Ambrose/NAVY International*)

One aspect of the present maritime environment which the enthusiast, seaman or marginally interested observer can console themselves with however, is variety. Even with the modern trends of standard design and construction, the seas and oceans of 1983 still provide more than their fair share of unusual and varied ship types to be seen. One of these unusual ship types not noted for its beauty is the barge carrying vessel which, in 1983, appears to be commencing a new period of development and popularity, with no less than seven new examples either completing or under construction this year alone.

Variations on a single theme

About 13 years ago, a radical new type of ship emerged. This was the LASH ship, of which today there are three primary types. The first two variations appeared around the same time in the early 1970s. These have been termed the LASH vessel and the Seabee vessel, although the former term is often used to cover the entire spectrum of the 'Lighter or Barge Aboard Ship' concept, including also the third type commonly known as the BACO or BACAT system. All three configurations have many similarities in that they are designed not for the carriage of cargoes in break/bulk or conventional containers, but in large barge units which are lifted or floated aboard the mother-ship or 'ocean carrier' for the deep-sea voyage.

The first of these, which appeared in 1969, was the American *Acadia Forest*. She was designed to operate as a barge carrier following the LASH formulae, wherein the barge is lifted and positioned aboard the mother ship with the aid of a travelling gantry-crane which moves forward and aft along most of the vessel's length.

Two years later, the first of three Seabee vessels put to sea. These vessels adopted a totally different cargo handling form to the *Acadia Forest* type. Instead of a gantry-crane, the Seabee uses a submersible stern-lift as an integral part of the ship. This offers a number of advantages over the *Acadia Forest*'s system, as larger and heavier lighters and single-unit loads of up to 2,000 tons can be handled.

Evolved by Lykes Lines and the New York naval architects J J Henry, Seabee was developed principally to act as a liner service able to handle containers, bulk commodities and domestic goods packed in barges, heavy and outsize loads, and especially those cargoes which could not use the conventional 40 ft container unit. However, the Seabee, LASH and BACO concepts went much farther than that.

Unlike most conventional ships, these barge carriers do not need to enter port to load and unload, and consequently can save time and money, as expensive alongside berths can be dispensed with altogether. With the Seabee, barges are loaded by means of a ramp mounted between the ship's catamaran-like stern, where small tugs push the loaded barge between the ship's siderails, over the ramp, and then the complete ramp section lifts the barge and contents up level to one of the decks. The barge is then moved forward along rails to its resting place on the ship, where it is held in position by pneumatic jacks. Unloading is just as simple, using the reverse procedure.

One non-American LASH ship of the first generation was the Dutch vessel *Bilderdyk*, seen here with a full load of the smaller LASH barges. She has since been sold to US owners. (*FotoFlite, Ashford*)

(1) The stern of *Doctor Lykes,* showing the barge lift platform partially lowered. The lift submerges to about 12 ft under water level and (2) small handling tugs push the barges in over the lift platform, two abreast. (3) The platform is then raised underneath the two barges and lifts them to the required deck level (*NB* An idea of size can be gained from the fact that the two barges shown are each loaded with 8 × 40 ft containers on their upper surfaces alone, while up to 850 tons of other cargo is packed inside the barge itself). (4) This view of *Almeria Lykes* shows the barge lift at its upper level, the barge on it about to be moved forward along the deck rails into position on the upper deck. This particular view is interesting, as the barge shown on the lift platform is not one of the standard 90 ft Seabee barges but a special heavy-lift flatbed unit of 112 ft length, upon which are stacked 14 conventional 40 ft containers. These special barges are built to withstand deck loadings of up to 8,000 lb per square foot. (*Lykes Lines*)

Although the LASH and BACO concepts use a different loading system, the same general rules apply. Loading and unloading can be performed in any sheltered waters, and can be an extremely fast procedure with a complete load of barges capable of being loaded or discharged in a matter of a few hours. Inherent advantages are: virtually no port dues, quick turnaround, no worries about dock strikes holding up vessels, and no waiting for berths at docks. Another advantage is that the vessel need only make one stop in each region, as the barges can then be towed to any number of ports/wharves in the given area without the ship having had to call at each one. Having discharged the barges, the ship is then free to make another journey.

In the meantime the barges are taken inland from the discharge point by small tugs up a variety of canals, rivers and waterway systems to their eventual destinations, which can be anywhere capable of accepting the Seabee barge's 35 ft beam and maximum 8 ft 6in draught. For LASH barges which are smaller an even greater range of ports, wharves and river banks are available for use. As a result, numerous small river and canal wharves can then effectively become international sea ports. In this way, cargoes can be loaded at an inland port such as Basel in Switzerland, for through transport to another inland port such as Kansas City in the United States, without the cargo being touched once between these points. The advantages of this system are obvious when one considers that waterborne transport is about one fifth of the cost of equivalent road transport, and that the multiple handling of general freight at transhipment points (eg from road or rail to ship etc) is often the most expensive, most unpredictable, and most time consuming part of any journey.

A further advantage which is now being appreciated (especially by environmentalists) is that consigning much inland transport to the rivers and canals helps reduce the flow of heavy lorries on overcrowded road networks, hence alleviating some of the anxieties created by the appearance of the larger and larger

The Seabee *Ocean Carrier*.

trucks with their inherent environmental problems.

The backbone of the concept is of course the ocean-carrier or Seabee/LASH/BACO ship itself. The most flexible of these are the Lykes Lines ships *Almeria Lykes*, *Doctor Lykes*, and *Tillie Lykes*. They can carry up to 38 of the standard Seabee barges, or alternatively, any combination of standard barges, specials, or containers, the maximum single unit weight of any item being 2,000 tons (more if external cranes are available), and virtually any type of cargo. Prefabricated oil-rigs, powerplants, tractors, containers, timber, rice, grain, even other ships have been loaded aboard on occasions. Each ship has three decks, and can carry 12 barges on the lower deck, 12 barges on the middle deck and either 14 barges or 824 conventional containers or a combination of both, on the upper deck.

The LASH and BACO concepts, while not having the same heavy-lift capability of the Seabee, do however have advantages of their own. While the LASH type do not have a float-on ability, their gantry-cranes usually have intrinsic container handling

facilities which the Seabee ships do not possess. As for the BACO, they have both float-on and intrinsic container gantries and although not able to lift-on 2,000 tonne single unit loads like the Seabee, it can nevertheless be argued that they are in fact equally as flexible.

A new generation
The first BACO LINER was completed in 1979 by Thyssen Nordseewerke, Emden, West Germany. In 1982, *Baco Liner 2* was completed by the same yard, and in late 1982 a third BACO Liner was ordered from Thyssen. The German BACO vessels are smaller than the US ships, having a capacity for only 12 lighters and 501 TEU as a combined load, as compared to the 80 lighter capacity of most first-generation US LASH vessels such as the *Acadia Forest*.

Following the initial impetus in building barge carriers in the late 1960s/early 1970s, new constructions

---

Outside of the USA, barge carriers did not really catch on until the late 1970s when a new spate of ordering developed which included *Baco Liner 2* and her earlier sister *Baco Liner 1*. Note the barge-loading door's unusual position in the bows. (*Skyfotos*)

135

Scale: 1:1200

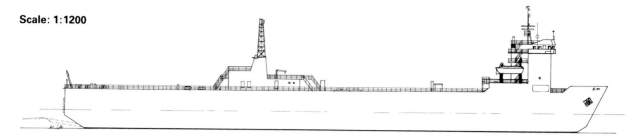

The new Valmet-built feeder barge carriers for the Soviet Union possess ro-ro and dock facilities. They are powered by two 9-cylinder Wärtsilä Vasa 9R32 turbocharged four-stroke medium speed diesels developing 7,560 bhp (5,560 kW) at 750 rpm, giving a service speed of 13½ knots. (*Drawing: Michael J Ambrose*)

thinned out and enthusiasm waned. Towards the end of the 1970s however, new interest developed as the USSR ordered two 36,000 grt barge carriers from the Finnish Valmet yards of Helsinki. These two ships, the *Julius Fucik* and *Tibor Szamuely*, were built to the USA's Seabee design which was licensed to Valmet and was to bring with it more than a little controversy due to the military utility of these designs. These two Soviet vessels were completed in 1978 and 1980, and have a capacity for 54 barges or 1,552 TEUs.

Also building at that time were two variations on the float-on theme, under construction at Hollming's Rauma shipyard. While considerably smaller than *Julius Fucik* and her sister, and not exactly of the same

barge-carrying ilk, these two 4,026 grt ro-ro cargo/dock/heavy-lift ships with float-on facilities followed a similar of development to the Seabee. It was one of these sisters, the *Stakhanovets Yermolenko*, which made the news in 1983 when she collected turbine machinery from Britain's former shipbuilders John Brown of Clydebank for use in the Soviet Siberian gas pipeline project. Examples of other cargo she carried in 1983 are shown in the accompanying illustration.

Following these vessels from the slips were the

The LASH, BACO and Seabee concept has obvious uses for naval duties in the amphibious assault role among others. Two LASH vessels, *Austral Rainbow* and *Austral Lightning* are presently chartered to the US Navy. *Austral Rainbow* is seen here lying at Diego Garcia in the Indian Ocean where both ships contain 17,146 tons of ammunition, and wait prepositioned in readiness to support the activities of the new US Central Command. Further details on the large USCENTCOM 'merchant' fleet participation can be found in our sister publication *Jane's Naval Review*. (*Military Sealift Command*)

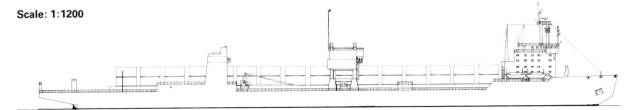

The *Aleksey Kosygin* must surely be the most significant vessel of the year in representing the return to nuclear power for Soviet merchant ships. (*Drawing: Michael J Ambrose/NAVY International*)

315, were originally due for completion in 1983 and 1984 but at time of writing the first has not yet been delivered. They are 8,800 dwt ships with a capacity

German-built and owned BACO Liners. Then came further orders from the Soviet Union, placed with Valmet in late 1981, for another two Seabee ships of a new design. These two ships, hull numbers 314 and

The Soviet *Stakhanovets Yermolenko*, passing through the English Channel with a cargo of Fast Attack Craft en-route for Cuba. This ship type was an enhanced development along the lines of the earlier Seabee vessel. (*FotoFlite, Ashford*)

for 12 barges or 513 TEUs, and although having an 8,000 nautical mile or 60 day range, they were designed principally as feeder ships for the ends of the ocean routes, and for operations in the Baltic and/or southeast Asian archipelago. Another enhancement on these vessels is the fitment of a stern-ramp so that they can handle ro-ro traffic as well as barges and containers.

Also due for completion in 1983 is the first Spanish-built barge carrier. Under construction at Astilleros Espanoles' Sestao yard, she is larger than the Valmet ships, with an 11,100 dwt, and is powered by two AESA-Pielstick 6PC25L engines developing only 3,900 bhp each, which would give her a service speed of 12 knots. Slow speed appears to be a developing feature of these barge feeder vessels, and two other vessels ordered in Italy this year are also to have a service speed of not more than 12½ knots. These two Italian builds are under construction at Cantiere Navale Breda at Venice, and are due for delivery in July and October of 1984. They are 7,200 dwt capacity vessels, and although ordered by a company named Shipcraft Sea Barges Inc, it is not immediately clear just whose ocean-carrier services these vessels will be

'feeding', as some reports have emerged suggesting it will be a new USSR service.

In the final analysis, it must be the USSR who have stolen a march on the USA with regard to the state-of-the-art barge carrier with the completion this year of the largest and most sophisticated ocean-carrier to date, the *Aleksey Kosygin*. Completing at Leningrad, this 260 m length, 61,000-ton displacement vessel can accommodate 70 barges, or 1,300 TEU, and is built to the LASH concept rather than Seabee; she is fitted with a 500-ton gantry-crane handling her barges over the stern rather than with float-on facilities.

Aleksey Kosygin's power plant is perhaps her most significant feature however, consisting of a single 135,000 kW nuclear reactor feeding two double-reduction turbines developing a total of 40,000 shp (29,420 kW) which drive a single controllable-pitch propeller giving a service speed of around 20 knots. Should she perchance stumble on a sea of ice, this is no problem: the vessel is designed to operate unaided in ice of up to one metre thick, and with her specially designed stern can accommodate an assisting icebreaker, should the going get *really* tough . . . !

The Grey Funnel Line
The Royal Fleet Auxiliary in 1983

by Thomas A Adams

Tom Adams is a professional journalist who will need no introduction to those whom have followed the fortunes of the Royal Fleet Auxiliary. He is the World Ship Society's 'RFA Person' and has completed many excellent articles covering the activities of this unusual shipping line, both historical and present day.

When the embryo of Britain's Royal Fleet Auxiliary Service was germinated some 78 years ago, little thought would have been given by those 1905 planners as to how their fleet would develop and mature in the latter half of the century. Develop and mature it did, until in the 1950s it was operating some 100 ships – one of Britain's largest merchant fleets. Today there are 26 ships crewed by 4,267 men of the Merchant Navy – 1,483 officers, 2,488 rating and 296 Hong Kong Chinese. Virtually all of the officers and over 60 per cent of ratings are serving under Company Service Contracts, the remainder being drawn from the Merchant Navy pool as and when required.

Roll and Resources
The RFA is a civilian-manned shipping company owned and operated by the Ministry of Defence (Navy Department). It is a fleet that has become an integral part of all naval operations with its task of supplying Royal Navy ships when underway at sea, with fuel, food, stores, spares and ammunition. Secondly, the RFA is tasked with the ocean-going sea transport of the Army and its heavy equipment.

HMS *Hermes* receives a transfer of fuel from the RFA *Olwen*. (*MoD Navy*)

RASing (Refueling At Sea) is an extremely difficult process to master, requiring great skill on the part of the ships' crews due to a number of factors, not least of which is the hydrodynamic interaction between the hulls of the two vessels participating. RASing on the move also requires some fairly sophisticated ships' too. In this view, HMS *Fearless* is taking fuel from RFA *Tidespring* and general stores from RFA *Stromness*. *Stromness* was sold to the US Navy in 1983, following her return from the Falklands. (*Don Sidebottom, HMS Fearless*)

The merchant ships required to meet these tasks are basically similar to those employed in commercial service – product tankers, refrigerated ships and roll-on-roll-off vessels. However, there cannot be a direct comparison. RFAs, in order to perform their specialised functions, are fitted with sophisticated cargo handling equipment not normally associated with merchant ships, to enable them to replenish-at-sea in all sorts of weather conditions, with maximum efficiency and safety. They are also equipped for vertical replenishment in the form of helicopter landing platforms with special stores lifts, flight decks and full hangar and maintenance facilities to support large naval helicopters. These ships are designed to work for the Navy and alongside the Navy, therefore NBCD arrangements involving remote control facilities enable ships to be closed-down and operated from secure command shelters. There is deck stiffening for mounting defensive weapons, degaussing arrangements, darken ship facilities and pre-wetting and washdown installations. They carry up-to-date navigational aids, radar configurations with helicopter control facilities, satellite communications systems and specialised naval radio outfits. Finally, they have that distinctive grey colour scheme accented with large black pennant numbers. However, they sail under the Blue Ensign, display their port of registry, conform to Department of Trade and MoD standards and remain merchant ships classed to Lloyd's Register of Shipping requirements.

The management of the Royal Fleet Auxiliary differs somewhat from that of a commercial company. It is a component of the Royal Naval Supply and Transport Service – the huge fleet support organisation responsible for the purchase and distribution of naval armament and victualling stores, together with the numerous and various grades of fuel and lubricant. This Service is the responsibility of the Admiralty Board member – Chief of Fleet Support, but is headed by a Director General – senior civil servant with a rank equivalent to a rear-admiral. He delegates the day-to-day management of the RFA to the Director of Supplies and Transport (Fuel, Movements and Victualling) who in turn is supported by a head office staff of civil servants and a team of marine and technical superintendents – RFA deck and marine engineering officers drawn from the sea-going personnel.

One of the more recent acquisitions is the RFA *Brambleleaf* (ex-*Hudson Cavalier*), a Stat 32 standard design tanker under long-term bareboat charter and operating as a support oiler. (*T A Adams collection*)

RFA *Resource,* a fleet replenishment ship which together with her sister RFA *Regent,* were the first British ships specially designed for supporting warships with ammunition, missiles and other dry stores. They were the first RFA ships to permanently carry a helicopter flight. (*T A Adams collection*)

Legally, Royal Fleet Auxiliaries occupy an unusual position: registered under the Merchant Shipping Acts, they are Crown vessels on non-commercial work. They enjoy many of the privileges of warships, such as non-payment of light and harbour dues, but being civilian-manned they are free to enter and leave foreign ports without the complications involved in a warship visit.

A busy year

The Royal Fleet Auxiliary and its functions came to the fore during the Falklands conflict and due to the circumstances off Bluff Cove, two of its landing ships – RFA *Sir Galahad* and RFA *Sir Tristram* tragically became household names. But the conflict is over and the fleet has had to re-adapt itself to defence cutbacks and additional tasks.

Its normal roles of home support and NATO support have been enlarged by the need for Falklands support. However, 1983 commenced with a number of ships down – RFA *Sir Galahad* lost, RFA *Sir Tristram* badly damaged, and the fleet oiler RFA *Tidepool* sold to the Chilean Navy under earlier defence cuts. RFA *Stromness*, up for disposal in cutbacks before the Falklands conflict, has unfortunately not been reprieved and is currently in the United States following her sisters *Lyness* and *Tarbatness* in transferring to the US Military Sealift Command. One cannot help feeling that Britain should have retained this valuable ship, even on a care and maintenance basis.

In an attempt to stem reductions, the charters of the support oilers RFA *Pearleaf* and RFA *Plumleaf* have been extended into 1984. RFA *Tidespring* has not gone

RFA *Fort Grange*, in refit when the Falklands conflict materialised, was rapidly completed and headed south to join her sister fleet replenishment ship *Fort Austin*. The latter was the first British surface ship to deploy into the South Atlantic following the outbreak of hostilities. The RFAs were forced to deploy early (they started moving on 24 March 1982), as their speed does not match that of the Naval units they were to supply. (*T A Adams collection*)

the way of her sister and after several arduous months in the South Atlantic has just undergone a major refit.

With her speed of just over 28 knots, the US Navy's fast combat support ship *Seattle* can keep up with a nuclear-powered carrier battle group. There has long been a case for the RFA to possess two fast supply ships of this nature to support the two operational ASW groups formed on the *Invincible/Illustrious/Hermes*. (*Michael J Ambrose*)

RFA *Blue Rover*, Naval-designed small fleet oiler. She can replenish three ships simultaneously – one on either beam and one astern – with various grades of fuel, fresh water and limited quantities of dry stores. The tankers of this class are equipped with large helicopter decks served by a large stores lift. (*T A Adams collection*)

Reports that one of the fleet replenishment ships (*Regent* or *Resource*) would go into reserve have proved unfounded and both vessels remain fully operational.

A further interpretation of the RFA's normal role is her support of naval forces participating in major exercises. One example was 'Springtrain 83', held to the East and West of Gibraltar, and led by HMS *Invincible*. In this exercise, 12 HM Ships, two submarines and a number of other ships and shore-based aircraft took part. RFA *Resource*, RFA *Olwen* and RFA *Black Rover* were in support. 'United Effort 83' in late May followed immediately by the NATO striking fleet's North Atlantic exercise – 'Ocean Safari 83' – were both supported by RFA *Regent*, RFA *Olwen* and RFA *Appleleaf*. 'Orient Express' – the major seven month out of NATO area deployment by the Royal Navy commenced in September. Led by

HMS *Invincible* it was supported by RFA *Regent*, RFA *Olmeda*, RFA *Appleleaf* and later joined by RFA *Grey Rover* which was later relieved by RFA *Blue Rover*. In late September various units became involved in the Mediterranean exercise 'Display Determination 83'. Here RFA ships were busy supporting HMS *Hermes* and HMS *Illustrious*.

New ships

In march two small commercial roll-on roll-off ships, *Lakespan Ontario* (1,566 grt, built 1972) and *Grey Master* (1,899 grt, built 1973) were chartered for 1½ and 5 years respectively. Renamed RFA *Sir Lamorak* and RFA *Sir Caradoc*, these ships have replaced the landing ship casualties from the Falklands. Both are now fulfilling a NATO role on the regular Marchwood/ Antwerp route.

Early in the year the Harrison Line container ship MV *Astronomer* (27,867 grt, built 1977) was chartered by MoD for two years. Originally chartered in 1982 to replace the *Atlantic Conveyor* as an aircraft ferry, she was eventually used as a helicopter support ship. It was reported that in South Atlantic conditions she was a 'wet' ship and somewhat unsatisfactory. However, in April she entered Cammell Laird's at Birkenhead for a multi-million pound conversion to a forward support ship primarily for South Atlantic operations. She has been fitted with the ARAPAHO System leased from the United States, a modular containerised system which converts container ships into helicopter carriers. It consists of a flight deck, aircraft hangar, maintenance and fuelling facilities, accommodation containers and defence armament support units.

RFA *Sir Lancelot*, Landing Ship Logistics. She was the proto-type of the class of roll on/roll off ships with beaching capability, designed for the Army and operated under the management of British India. In 1970 they were transferred to RFA management and manning. (*T A Adams collection*)

Her flight deck has been designed to operate two Sea King ASW helicopters and the hangar, at the forward end of the flight deck, can house up to four Sea Kings. The ship has also been modified to provide solid stores support with one hold converted for this purpose and a 2-tonne stores-handling lift installed. Naval communications facilities have been fitted along with a sophisticated radar and flight control system. Accommodation has been provided for 61 RFA crew, 150 RN flight personnel, an RNSTS stores party and a small number of 'advisory' crew members from the owners Harrisons. Thus modified, the vessel entered RFA service in late '83 as RFA *Reliant*. She is defensively armed with four 20 mm AA guns, a passive ESM installation and a Chaff-dispensing mortar system.

RFA *Reliant* has obviously been converted based on experiences from 1982. However, she must still be considered an experimental fit and her operation will be closely observed by both the Navy and industry. With so many large container ships under-used in the current commercial market it may be a premium time for Navies to undertake long-term charters for 'ARAPAHO conversions'.

A changing role
Currently no ships are being constructed for the Royal Fleet Auxiliary and no plans openly exist to replace the 23-year-old *Pearleaf* and *Plumleaf* support oilers. The 'Sir' class landing ships are a 20-year-old design and replacement must be under consideration. A

The problems of operating unarmed RFAs in the front lines during any form of conflict were manifest in a tragic way during the Falklands conflict. RFA *Sir Tristram* and *Sir Galahad* had no protection whatsoever when they were attacked. (*MoD Navy*)

replacement for *Sir Galahad*, to have been built in Australia, has not materialised. However, an improved LSL design, similar to HMAS *Tobruk*, has been ordered from British Shipbuilders.

RFA *Sir Tristram* was brought back to the UK in June. She has received a detailed survey with a view towards repairing. If this proves to be uneconomical her spares value alone will have made the bringing

RFA *Olwen,* a large fleet oiler, returns to Gosport after her participation in exercise 'Ocean Safari 83'. (*A J Ambrose*)

In addition to the loss of *Sir Galahad* and *Sir Tristram* to enemy action, and the loss of the 'Ness' class to the auctioneer's hammer, RFA *Tidepool* has now left the RFA's fleet too. She has been sold to Chile. (*HMS Osprey*)

RFA *Sir Caradoc* (ex-*Grey Master*), a commercial roll-on roll-off vessel chartered by the RFA for five years and serving in the role of a landing ship. (*Royal Fleet Auxiliary*)

Now the RFA *Reliant,* an ARAPAHO cruiser, she is seen here in her earlier days as the container ship *Astonomer* just prior to her requisition by the MoD following the loss of *Atlantic Conveyor* in 1982. (*FotoFlite, Ashford*)

home worthwhile.

The design contract awarded some years ago to Swan Hunter for a new combined oiler/stores ship is still reportedly under consideration, but covered by a blanket of 'no comment'. This 'one-stop ship' concept is very successful and is used, for example, by the Dutch and Canadian Navies. However, for the RFA it poses problems. RFAs are merchant ships and as the

Merchant Shipping Acts now stand, the carrying of oil and ammunition together is illegal. If the concept is adopted the RFA or the Merchant Shipping Acts will have to be changed.

Since the Falklands conflict there has been much talk and discussion on the RFA and its role, not least on the fact that these valuable and vital ships are unprotected merchant ships. Indeed, a retired senior

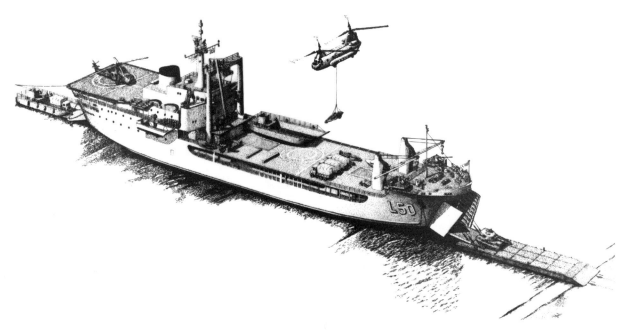

▼ RFA *Sir Tristram* is brought home on the heavy-lift semi-submersible *Dan Lifter* in June 1983. (*FotoFlite, Ashford*)

A new improved 'Sir Lancelot' class LSL is to be built to replace the *Sir Galahad*. It is expected that she will follow the design of the uprated LSL HMAS *Tobruk* as shown in this artist's impression. (*Royal Australian Navy*)

RFA officer has called for the ships to be placed under the White Ensign. The protagonists of this line seem to forget a number of vital facts: first, the shortages of skilled manpower in the Royal Navy – they would not be able to man these ships; and second, the career RFA officers and senior rates are Merchant Navy personnel with Department of Trade qualifications, men proud of their RFA/Merchant Navy traditions. It

should not be assumed that they would automatically transfer to the disciplines of the Royal Navy.

Royal Fleet Auxiliaries are by necessity changing. Increasingly they are carrying defensive weapons, passive ESM systems and Chaff radar-decoy mortars. Currently, £1m is being spent fitting 11 RFAs with the *Shield* Chaff-dispensing mortar system. If these defensive weapons expand to take in missile systems such as the Sea Wolf then the time must be close when a foreign port authority will question their civilian status, and may be even refuse them entry.

Short of becoming White Ensign, it would nevertheless appear that a change in RFA management and/ or civilian status is inevitable.

SHIPS OF THE ROYAL FLEET AUXILIARY (1983)

	Initial operating capability	Displacement (full load)	GRT	DWT	Main engines	Service speed (knots)	Complement (RFA)	Notes
Large fleet oilers (AO)								
Olna	1966				Double reduc-			Admiralty
Olwen (ex-Olynthus)	1965	36,000	18,600	25,000	tion steam	19	94	designed
Olmeda (ex-Oleander)	1965				turbines			
Tidespring	1963	27,500	14,130	18,900	Double reduc- tion steam	18	110	Admiralty designed
Small fleet oilers (AOL)								
Black Rover	1974							
Blue Rover	1970							
Gold Rover	1974	11,500	7,510	6,700	Diesel	18	48–50	Admiralty designed
Green Rover	1969							
Grey Rover	1970							
Support oilers (AOT)								
Pearleaf	1960	25,700	12,352	18,700	Diesel	16	55–60	see Note 1
Plumleaf	1960	26,400	12,450	19,400	Diesel	15½	55–60	see Note 1
Appleleaf (ex-Hudson Deep)	1979							
Bayleaf	1982	40,200	19,976	33,000	Diesel	15½	55–60	see Note 2
Brambleleaf (ex-Hudson Cavalier)	1979							
Fleet replenishment ships (AFS(H))								
Fort Austin	1979	22,890	16,054	8,165	Diesel	20	133	Admiralty designed
Fort Grange	1978							
Regent	1967	22,890	18,029	—	Steam turbines	20	123	Admiralty designed
Resource	1967							
Helicopter support ship (AG(H))								
Engadine	1967	9,000	6,384	—	Diesel	14½	73	Admiralty designed
Landing Ship Logistics (LSL)								
Sir Lancelot	1964	5,500	6,390	2,215	Diesel	17	69	see Note 3
Sir Percivale	1968							
Sir Geraint	1967	5,674	4,473	2,443	Diesel	17	69	see Note 3
Sir Bedivere	1967							
Sir Caradoc (ex-Grey Master)	1983	—	1,899	3,362	Diesel	16	24	Built 1973
Sir Lamorak	1983	—	1,566	2,677	Diesel	18	24	see Note 4
Fleet support ship								
Reliant (ex-Astronomer)	1983	—	27,867	23,491	Diesel	20	61	Built 1977

Notes:

1 *Pearleaf* and *Plumleaf* were originally on long-term bareboat charter, currently extended into 1984.

2 These are Stat 32 standard tankers, altered to suit RFA requirements and operated on long-term bareboat charter. Long-term charter costs for the RFA in 1983 were estimated at £6.5m.

3 The 'Sir' class LSL were originally designed for the Army and only transferred to RFA management in 1970.

4 *Sir Lamorak* (ex-*Lakespan Ontario*) (83); *Lady Catherine* (81); *Lune Bridge* (80); *Anu* (80); *Northcliffe* (74); *Anu* (73); built 1973.

RFA *Black Rover,* outward bound from Portland. With more ships to support over greater ranges, the RFA today could certainly not cope with another Falklands conflict in 1983 without widespread use of requistioned or chartered merchant tonnage. More merchant vessels would be needed than the 80-plus called-up in 1982. Moreover, a number of the '82 STUFT (Ships Taken Up From Trade) are no longer sailing under the British merchant flag, and consequently the pressures on the RFA would be even more intense. (*Royal Fleet Auxiliary*)

. . . continued Falklands activity

A photo feature by A J Ambrose

Following on directly from the feature in last years' Review, the Falklands Islands and the establishment of a major British Garrison thereon, have continued to provide many unusual and varied ship movements within both the British and other European merchant fleets. Among the most dramatic of these developments were the so-called hijacking of the roll-on roll-off ferry *Keren* (ex-*HMS Kerenm*, ex-*St Edmund*) by a naval crew; the controversial Maltese incident concerning the refitting of *Cunard Countess*, and the charter and subsequent conversion of the container ship *Astronomer* into its new guise as the ARAPAHO ASW cruiser *RFA Reliant*. Nevertheless, while these three incidents drew most of the publicity during 1983, there have been a number of other charters and shipping moves in the South Atlantic, equally deserving of mention.

HMS *Keren,* now the mv *Keren,* heads south from Wallsend after her 'hijacking' by a naval crew during the Easter holiday weekend. Originally planned to be operated by a merchant crew, trade union deadlocks forced the Navy to remove the vessel from the builders yards. By the end of April however, the matter had been resolved and *Keren* sailed south to Ascension Island with a merchant crew after all. She was purchased outright by the British Ministry of Defence for a figure believed to be around £7½ million, and now operates as a troopship between Ascension and Port Stanley. (*FotoFlite, Ashford*)

The small coastal tanker *Northgate* was also chartered for a fuel run.

The newly completed *Norbrit Faith,* termed a 'mini-bunker', has a particularly trying maiden voyage, not in the European coastal trades for which she was designed, but a 16,000 mile round trip to Port Stanley. (*Skyfotos*)

Following the fall of Port Stanley in June 1982, a number of merchant ships were hastily called up to provide the necessary support to the British garrison which was rapidly running short of supplies. Among these was the *Mermydon* which returned to commercial service early this year. She carried a variety of stores including a large number of portacabins. (*FotoFlite, Ashford*)

The Argentine merchant marine put in an appearance near the TEZ in early 1983 in the shape of the cargo vessel *Lago Lacar,* a sistership to the *Lago Traful* (shown). She had embarked a party of relatives of Argentine servicemen who had been killed in action. As with the *Bahia Paraiso* on 19 March 1982 however, she did not request permission to visit the islands in the appropriate form and was therefore turned away at the edge of the TEZ. (*Skyfotos*)

When Blue Star's *Rangatira* returned home to the UK in October 1983, she bought with her a number of embarassing problems, namely irate merchant seamen whom were angry that the ship's arrival back in UK waters would put them on the unemployment register. (*Skyfotos*)

Safe Esperia had insufficient space for the whole garrison however, and so another accommodation block was barge-mounted and loaded aboard the (19,216 grt/33,200 dwt) *Dyvi Swan* for transit south. This second unit, the *Pursuivant*, had space for about 900 men. (*FotoFlite, Ashford*)

One of the most pressing problems following the cessation of hostilities was accommodation for the troops. As a result, the accommodation barge *Safe Esperia* was hastily chartered and shipped south to Port Stanley on the (10,281 grt/ 13,282 dwt) heavy-lift ship *Dan Lifter*. (*FotoFlite, Ashford*)

Cunard Countess was withdrawn from her cruise activities in the USA in 1982 to take up duties as the 'Falklands Ferry' between Ascension and Port Stanley. When returned to commercial service (see chronology) she became the centre of a large controversy surrounding her refitting in a Maltese shipyard. She is seen here leaving Malta in mid-1983. (*Skyfotos*)

While British trade unions were quick to complain about the volume of foreign tonnage chartered, prior to the conflict the island's only service from Europe had been operated by Denmark with the 499 grt/1,290 dwt *A.E.S.* When Argentina started the war the *A.E.S.* was heading towards Port Stanley but was turned round and made for Ascension. On arrival there, she was told to go back to Las Palmas where she waited for fighting to cease. She is now back on her regular run from Gravesend to Port Stanley. (*Skyfotos*)

The Norwegian ro-ro *Sand Shore* was one of three foreign flag vessels term-chartered for duties in and around the Falkland dependencies. Most of the other foreign flag vessels used were trip-chartered. (*Skyfotos*)

Also chartered was the *Cable Ship Monarch*, used for various duties in the 'physical' communications mode. (*Skyfotos*)

The latest Royal Navy 'warships' to enter service in the Falklands are three offshore supply vessels including the *Seaforth Saga.* Now renamed HMS *Protector,* she is used as a patrol vessel and for general communications and mooring duties. (*Skyfotos*)

Purchased by Cunard to carry construction workers between Cape Town and Port Stanley, the ex-Danish North Sea ferry *England* is now operating under a temporary British flag. She is seen here following her departure for the South Atlantic in mid-1983. Her duties are not primarily military as with the *Keren,* but associated with the airport construction project. (*Skyfotos*)

Having been a member of the original logistics train for the military authorities, China Mutual Steam Navigation's *Lycaon,* incorrectly donated to Cunard in last year's Review, was re-chartered in 1983 to carry materials for various construction projects now underway in the islands. (*Skyfotos*)

The Defence of Merchant Shipping

by Andrew J Ambrose

The strategic importance of merchant shipping during a period of tension or open conflict is an aspect of national and international debate which rarely receives the publicity and support it deserves and needs.

Merchant shipping is all too often at the back end of defence priorities, its importance often overlooked. It lacks the glamour of the dashing destroyers, powerful aircraft carriers, and the pomp and regalia normally associated with the fighting ships of the free world's naval forces. Yet, in the final analysis, it is the merchant ship's ability to deliver its cargoes in a safe and timely manner that is the ultimate manifestation of the oft-quoted term 'Sea Power'.

Strategic significance

During the Second World War there was no doubt in the minds of both Winston Churchill and Admiral Doenitz, that shipping logistics were the pivot point upon which the war would be won or lost. As Winston

---

. . . 'At 1930 we were told that an Air Raid was imminent and two minutes later, just as we got to "Emergency Stations", we were hit by two Exocet missiles low down in the port quarter' . . . (Captain M H G Layard, CBE, RN, Senior Naval Officer, *Atlantic Conveyor*). (*Courtesy Flag Officer Naval Air Command*)

The loss of *Atlantic Conveyor* off Falkland Sound on 25 May 1982 was to demonstrate the vulnerability of a modern merchant ship in a most tragic manner. In retrospect, there appear to be two areas worthy of greater study and effective action – these are the provision of a more effective form of evacuation in poor sea state conditions and, of course, the provision of some form of defensive armament. (*Courtesy Flag Officer Naval Air Command*)

Churchill said *'The Battle of the Atlantic was the dominating factor all through the war. Never for one moment could we forget that everything elsewhere depended on its outcome.'*

Today, this position would be no different. The European partners of NATO would be totally reliant on the arrival of US military units and various domestic, industrial and general logistic support from across the Atlantic, as well as fuels and general cargoes from a number of other diverse points in the world. At least 95 per cent of these cargoes would need to enter Europe by sea. In short, the outcome of a modern East-West conflict of almost any sort would be dependant on the free world's ability to maintain free passage on the world's oceans, particularly of course the North Atlantic.

There can be no doubt that NATO's determination to keep the 'Atlantic Bridge' open is a precondition of *any* credible military plan to defend Europe from a Soviet advance. There can also be no doubt that such NATO determination is mirrored by a Soviet naval build-up whose protagonists are dedicated to constricting, or blocking altogether, any North American reinforcement of Europe. However, while history has proven quite conclusively that the odds of the Second World War Battle of the Atlantic achieved some form of balance, it is not at all clear that a similar view of a present day conflict would reflect such optimistic odds for NATO, much less any form of parity in relationship between the sizes of the two opposing forces.

Changes in the balance

Reflection on the Second World War deployment abilities show that at outbreak of war in 1939 Hitler had only 46 U-boats in operational order. This rose to 91 boats in January 1942, 212 in December 1942 and eventually to a peak of 240 in April 1943. In fact, however, the maximum number ever deployed in the North Atlantic was only 112 boats.

Between them, the U-boats accounted for around 430 ships of more than *two million* tons in 1941 alone. In 1942 they *doubled* that figure. Added to the losses from air attack and mines, a total of 1,299 ships totalling 4,328,558 tons were lost in 1941, followed by 1,646 ships of 7,790,697 tons in 1942. It is clear from these figures that there was no obvious balance between U-boats and Allied anti submarine warfare (ASW) forces. In fact, the balance was not reached until 1943 when the Allies were able to deploy 25 carriers of various types, 800 surface escorts and around 1,100 maritime aircraft. By this time, Admiral Doenitz had only 50 U-boats permanently deployed in the area,

A Soviet 'Juliet' class SSG cruises off Britain's south coast ports in the summer of 1983. In addition to her 18 nuclear/high explosive-armed torpedoes, she carries four SSN-3A (Shaddock) cruise missiles with a range of 250 n.miles. What weapons can NATO use to destroy this threat before it has launched its 350 kiloton warheads against a convoy? (*FotoFlite, Ashford*)

'There are two types of vessel at sea today: Submarines, and Targets.' (*HMS Drake*)

and the Luftwaffe's air threat had been diminished by the build-up of Allied air power over Europe.

Unfortunately for the West, the position today is one of complete contrast. There are not 25 carriers of various types, there are not 800 escorts and there are not 1,100 maritime aircraft in the NATO armoury, let alone such a number available for North Atlantic deployment. Yet, the numbers of opposing forces are proportionately even higher!

In today's scenario, the USSR alone can deploy twice the number of submarines that Doenitz ever deployed. And not only that: many of these units *can launch attacks from beyond the range of Western surface-launched ASW weapons.* Furthermore, the modern submarine's speed advantage over its Second World War counterpart, coupled with the vast advances in weapons and sensor-systems technology, has provided the USSR with massive advantages if intent on a path of aggressive hit-and-run commerce raiding.

Even the shape of modern commercial ship development has enhanced the submarines potency by providing larger, more cheaply built vessels to act as targets. And, due to the increase in traffic carried nowadays, *more* of them too! Indeed, targets are just what merchant ships are seen as in many naval circles today, hence the Royal Navy Submarine Service's oft-quoted catch phrase/motto: *'There are two types of vessel today: Submarines and Targets'.*

By extension, the present situation paints a gloomy picture for the merchant seaman too, as the loss of life in the merchant service during such a scenario would be very, very extensive and severe. Although, having said that, these losses would not be likely to exceed those of the Second World War numerically due to the smaller crews manning the merchant ship of today. Nevertheless, proportionately they would still likely be higher than those of any of the armed forces, as was the case during the Second World War. Nevertheless,

even with such a gloomy picture of merchant shipping survivability, short of surrender or defeat the West must keep the sea lanes open.

Apart from the commercial and industrial trade-flows which would largely need to be maintained, there is the additional requirement for the sudden NATO reinforcement sealift from the United States to Europe. This reinforcement would require a rapid shipment of more than 17 million tons of fuel and 11 million tons of supplies, not counting the actual troop movements. This lifting would be carried out by the NATO 'pool' of merchant ships, consisting of a variety of tankers, ro-ro cargo vessels, container ships and dry cargo vessels. Unfortunately however, another recent problem to have reared its head is that of ship-availability, as the West's merchant fleets have been in a process of decline over the past three–four years, whereas, the Soviet fleet has continued to expand!

Thus, the picture of the Atlantic Bridge philosophy, its survivability, and by extension, the survival of Western Europe, is not a happy one to view. Its survival is vital nonetheless. It is of primary importance that the continuity of the economic lifelines be maintained. But, how can this be done?

Turning the tide of thought

The first stage of course is the requirement for a widespread recognition of the strategic importance of merchant shipping, and in this area, three tragic developments in recent years have had marked effect in bringing this point to the fore. These developments were the Iranian Revolution and subsequent invasion

The Rapid Deployment Force initiated a revitalisation for the US Navy's Military Sealift Command. This artist's impression shows (top) the five 'Maersk' class TAKX vessels now under conversion, and (bottom) the five new TAKX ships under construction at the Quincy yards of General Dynamics.

Various forms of ro-ro vessels would be used to lift cargoes into Europe. These would be the most sought-after type of ship afloat during a conflict, as indeed they were during the Falklands conflict. The *Opal Bounty* and her sisters may be ugly looking vessels, but are most useful as they can turn their wheeled cargo around in as little as an hour given a clear length of quayside. (*A J Ambrose*)

---

of Afghanistan, and the Falklands conflict. The former items hastened the establishment of the US Rapid Deployment Joint Task Force (RDJTF), now unified and established with the new title US Central Command (USCENTCOM).

The establishment of USCENTCOM on 1 January 1983 posed some major problems for the US forces, primarily in the field of logistics. The new force is unique in that almost all of its 300,000 personnel and their equipment are based in the USA and, therefore, before entering combat must be shipped several thousand miles just to get in position. It must then be supported.

As such, the new force had the effect of concentrating much thought onto the problem of shipping logistics and, as a result, after many years of decline in the US merchant fleet, 1982/83 saw the framework laid for a revitalised merchant ship building programme and the adoption of a modernisation and improvement plan for many of the obsolete units forming the US Strategic Fleet Reserve. In addition, such developments in the military sphere were also instrumental in providing the conditions for improvement in the merchant sphere proper, one example being the 1983 order by United States Lines for their twelve 4,000-plus TEU container ships.

Consequently, from a fleet which had diminished by more than ten million tons since 1947 it was refreshing to see the latter parts of 1982 heralding the first increase in size of the US fleet for some 35 years. In 1983 this upward trend continued, and improved.

Unfortunately however, no such trends could be witnessed in the British merchant fleet. While the Falklands conflict suddenly and effectively emphasised the importance and significance of the strategic value of merchant ships, those lessons appeared to have been largely ignored in certain circles – specifically political circles – and now, two years on from the sailing of the largest single merchant task force since the close of the Second World War, the strategic significance of the merchant vessel seems to be fading into the background once again. The British fleet has continued on its downward path, and even after *promises* of a major inquiry to establish that there are always sufficient merchant ships available the British Government has taken *no* obvious steps in this direction. In fact (if emphasis of this point were needed) a number of the vessels used for the Falklands Logistic Train have now been sold abroad. Furthermore, it should be noted that the British Government used a large number of foreign company vessels in the Falklands fleet in the first place.

One or two lessons of the Falklands did appear to make their mark on the powers-that-be, such as the vulnerability of the merchant vessel when under attack. However, even the proposals which materialised on this score seem to have lost their impetus in the corridors of power in recent months, and original post-Falkland plans for defensively-armed merchant ships, including Sea Harrier-equipped container ships and the like, now appear to have fallen by the wayside as the British Treasury trims its budgets once again.

Presumably, some Western governments such as Britain's do not see the values of supporting merchant shipping in a state of strategic readiness. Perhaps if they were to pay a little more attention to the duties of a merchant vessel during wartime (and during peace-time too, for that matter) then maybe, just maybe, they would see things in a different light.

Varied roles and requirements

In addition to the merchant vessel's normal peace time duties of earning foreign currency, supporting the imports and exports of raw materials, manufactured goods, energy requirements, food supplies and domestic goods, a period of tension or conflict will impose considerable additional demands on a nation's maritime commitments. Although there are a multitude of varied roles for the fleet during a conflict, broadly speaking these roles can be divided into five categories:

1. The maintenance of the continued traffic of socio-economic imports/exports, with such additional demands as may be imposed, to support life and the domestic industry of a nation at war.

    This category will be of more importance to Island nations such as Britain, and the nations where self-sufficiency in fuel/energy or other natural resources is of a low level. For example, the USA has not been self-sufficient in oil since the 1950s, and Europe needs to import more than 50 per cent of its annual oil requirement. On the other hand, the USSR is a net exporter of oil and thus has little need to maintain imports of this nature during a period of conflict.

2. The adaption of merchant ships for naval duties. This category would include container ships converted to act as aircraft carriers as in the US ARAPAHO project and the British SCADS project, trawlers, etc converted for roles as minesweepers and patrol vessels, and various one-off conversions for a multitude of coastal defence duties, and the like.

3. The adaption of merchant vessels for military logistics roles. In this category would fall a large number of roll-on roll-off vessels, etc which would be used as landing ships to put forces ashore in Europe and elsewhere in similar fashion to the adopted use of many ships during the San Carlos landings of 1982. Most passenger/vehicle ferries and liners/cruise ships would be used in this category of operation. Crews would be mainly civilian, with heavy naval representation.

4. Supportive logistics for naval operations. Under this category fall the bulk of present day fleet auxiliary units, which would need to be supplemented with a large proportion of called-up trade vessels. Converted to supply ships and RASing tankers to enable naval units to remain at sea and on-station, these vessels would be very important because in a hot-war situation no naval vessel of any size could safely enter port to crew change and re-supply. In doing so it would present itself as too vulnerable a target in a position where its co-ordinates would already be known to the enemy, thus inviting attack from long-range land-based or submarine cruise missiles and their derivatives. Crews would be mainly civilian, with a large proportion of naval officers.

5. Special categories, including Hospital Ships, Prison Ships, Salvage and Rescue vessels, Fleet maintenance vessels, etc. This category would utilise converted passenger vessels for the former roles, salvage tugs and oilfield supply vessels

with towage abilities for the second duties and called-up specialist offshore support vessels for the latter tasks.

As regards ship requirements therefore, with the exception of category one which, theoretically at least, should be fairly well supported by the exigencies of commercial justification, one can draw up a list of ship-types most necessary for the contingencies of war:

(a) Trawlers for categories 2 and 5
(b) Container vessels for category 2 and possibly 3
(c) Roll-on Roll-off vessels for categories 2 and 3
(d) Passenger/Vehicle ferries for categories 3 and 5
(e) Passenger liners, cruise ships for categories 3 and 5
(f) Lighter carriers for category 3
(g) General cargo vessels for categories 3 and 4
(h) Tugs and other specialist vessels for category 5
(i) Smaller parcels tankers for categories 3 and 4

It will be noted that the larger vessels such as bulk carriers and crude oil tankers do not lend themselves readily to any of the latter four categories. With the absence of geared port terminals reducing their flexibility, the uses for the present generation of gearless container ships will also be of little practical use outside category 1, with the possible exception of their use as SCADS or ARAPAHO cruisers in category 2. Even then, a far better combination for this duty is apparent in the container ship with roll-on roll-off capacity such as the RFA *Reliant* (ex-*Astronomer*), or ships of similar nature.

With the possible exception of item 'b' therefore, all the other eight types mentioned above qualify for some level of Governmental interest for wartime duties. It is therefore interesting to look at some statistics drawn from Lloyds Register of Shipping, showing a breakdown of specific ship types of the UK, USA and USSR fleets:

	UK	USA	USSR
General cargo and ro-ro	659**	447*	1,805*
Lighter carriers	Nil	21	2*
Passenger/cargo ships	1	8	16
Tankers††	299**	286	483*
Fishing vessels†	32**	197	1,927*
Ferries and passenger ships	145	60	254*

* Number increasing.
** Number reducing.
† Excluding coastal and inshore types.
†† Only tankers of below 40,000 grt are listed as larger units would, for all practicable purposes, be of little use outside category 1.

General cargo and reefer vessels such as the *Geestport* (shown), *Avelona Star* and a number of others were called up for Auxiliary support tasks in 1982. Royal Navy teams using these vessels alongside their civilian crewmates were highly impressed with these ships' capabilities and performance. (*Drawing: Michael J Ambrose*)

Scale: 1:1200

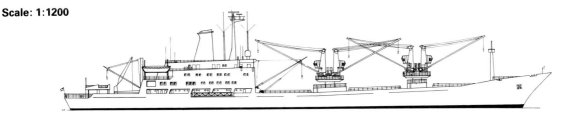

Virtually all of NATO's big roll-on roll-off vessels will be needed to leave their commercial trades and help to lift US and Canadian reinforcements to Europe. This large Dutch ro-ro can lift about one quarter of a mechanized division in one sailing. Unfortunately however, her size makes her a big target, and the fateful free-surface-effect of a ro-ro with its watertight integrity removed eliminates much of the attraction of these large examples. (*Nedloyd/Pim Korver*)

their navy and, as Admiral Gorshkov (CinC Soviet Navy) has stated, 'represents a standing naval force, worldwide . . .' Additional evidence supporting this policy is often cited: for example, the Soviet Merchant Marine is largely manned by naval reservists and has many quasi-naval duties not ordinarily carried out by Western merchant vessels.

However, close scrutiny of the pattern of development of the Soviet merchant fleet does not in practice bear this out. If used primarily for military purposes, the Soviet fleet is not so useful to the USSR as it would be to the West. Firstly, the Soviet Union does not need to maintain commercial seatrade during a conflict. Secondly, the Soviet Navy, while having expanded its Blue Water activities in recent years, does not yet have a need for such an enormous auxiliary network. Thirdly, while there is no doubt that such a merchant fleet would be extremely useful in amphibious and long-range force-projection operations, in practice it has only been relatively recently that the Soviet 'over-the-beach' capability has improved to such a degree that it can be considered credible outside the Baltic, etc. As such, the development of the Soviet merchant fleet has borne no relationship either realistically or chronologically to the non parallel development of the Soviet amphibious capability. In fact, it has only been in recent years that these two factors have become more and more interdependant.

These factors, along with many others, are more indicative of the Soviet Merchant Marine being considered more as a peacetime force rather than an implement of war. Certainly, the Soviet fleet does have several strategic reasons for existance. But, in the main these reasons have not, until recently, been concerned with the projection of force, but rather a policy of frustrating the West's ability to project its logistic train from the USA to Europe. And as such, the main plan appeared to be one of frustrating the

Small tankers such as the *British Esk* would be automatic requisitions for fleet replenishment and for moving the vast military fuel requirement from North America to Europe. (*FotoFlite, Ashford*)

From these statistics it can be seen that a rather troublesome pattern of fleet development has emerged. As already stated above, the Soviet Union does not have a fundamental need for a shipping fleet of this nature because unlike the West, the USSR is largely self-supporting in almost all areas. Why then has the USSR decided to make its mark on precisely the types of ships of strategic military value when the ships which have usually provided the best commercial prospects are almost totally absent from the Soviet register? Note for example, that there is not one ULCC, or even VLCC, in the entire Soviet fleet!

The easy answer to this question, and one which has frequently been put forward in the past, is that the entire Soviet merchant fleet is just an extension of

It is worthy of much concern in western naval circles, that the USSR has the use of greater numbers of general cargo types than are available to the USA's Military Sealift Command. This vessel, the *Kapitan Markov*, is a typical specimen. Ice-strengthened, 7,684 grt, 8,842 dwt, a speed of 15 knots and not too large a target. (*FotoFlite, Ashford*)

The USSR operates a large fleet of both purpose-built AGIs such as the 'Balzam' class, and converted trawlers such as the *Kose*. (*FotoFlite, Ashford*)

West's ability rather than improving the East's. One can imagine that the orders given to the bulk of the Soviet fleet during time of war would simply state 'stay in port'.

To itemise the strategic thought behind the Soviet fleet, their priorities might be considered as:

1. To capitalise on the ship types and hulls, which would prove most useful to the West during a period of conflict
2. To earn valuable foreign currency during peace time
3. To advance the position of the USSR in the Third World
4. To provide a level of supplementary auxiliary support to naval forces should this be necessary
5. To provide additional amphibious and force-projection capability when necessary

6. To provide employment for the populous
7. To gain intelligence both in the military sense and in the socio-economic sense with a wide range of oceanographic research programmes and the like
8. To provide a cheap input of foodstuffs from the fishing fleet, while at the same time gathering intelligence on Western movements and retaining a large fleet of vessels suitable to undertake patrol and minesweeping duties following the outbreak of conflict.

Traditionally, categories 2, 4 and 5 have been considered the priorities, but today, with the massive

The container ship *Jervis Bay* has an evocative name bringing back memories of her last war namesake. However, for uses outside the SCADS or ARAPAHO concept she would need ports with full container handling facilities and therefore, has few attractions for use in modern warfare. (*Drawing: Michael J Ambrose*)

Scale: 1:1200

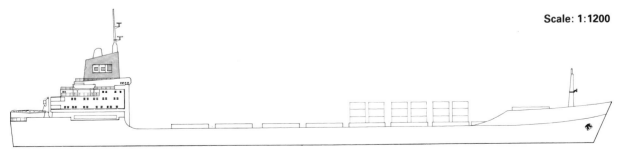

The Soviet tanker *Sheksna,* one of a class of six, has facilities to transfer fuel to two naval vessels simultaneously. She is one of a large fleet of naval auxiliaries which support the Soviet Navy. Short of a plan to invade the USA or something similar, they would have little need to call up their merchant fleet for support. (*FotoFlite, Ashford*)

declines in the merchant fleets of the West, category 1 has assumed a far greater significance and may well have always been the one the Soviets would have put at the top of their own lists.

In the West, shipping largely takes place on a free trade basis. If the work is not available for certain types of ship, then normal commercial considerations will usually assure that such types of ship are simply not built. If the USSR therefore constructs and operates large numbers of the ship types of greatest value to the West, and subsequently offers these in subsidised form to the world's open shipping markets (notably while reserving all Soviet cargoes for their own hulls) then, by the simple extension of free market influences, the West will cease to build these ship types. As a result, the USSR will then have a monopoly on them, and in the event of a major conflict NATO will, to put it in the simplest terms, not have sufficient tonnage (of the right type) available to move the requisite cargoes for the European reinforcement. Add to this lack of suitable ships the likely attrition rate the Soviet submarine and naval aviation forces will inflict – estimated in some NATO circles to be around 30 per cent – and one will quickly realise that this Soviet frustration policy could well starve Europe into submission or, more likely, the earlier use of nuclear weapons.

Bear in mind when thinking about this reinforcement that in a recent NATO exercise 'Wintex 83', General Bernard Rogers (Supreme Allied Commander

Europe) became increasingly concerned that if the reinforcement convoys did not arrive by about the fourth day of conflict materialisation, then he would have to escalate to use of theatre nuclear weapons almost immediately! This in turn means that the reinforcements must have been ordered long before the first Soviet tank divisions started rolling over the border. By natural extension, if the Soviets do not want this reinforcement to take place, then they will attack the convoys before war has actually broken out in Europe. Following this line of thought further, this

The Soviet SA-15 type ro-ro icebreaker *Igarka* leaves her Turku builders in February 1983 bound for the Soviet Union. While these capable vessels emphasise an amphibious assault role for the Soviet merchant fleet, it must be noted that it is only relatively recently that this emphasis has formed such a major part of Soviet new-building plans. (*K Brzoza*)

Igarka's sister and   th completion in the SA-15 'Norilsk' class, the Finnish-built *Monchegorsk* on trials under the Finnish flag in May 1983. These sophisticated vessels are capable of working in temperatures of as low as −50°C and can break ice up to 1 metre thick. In worse conditions, they have an unusual stern arrangement which allows a pusher icebreaker to prove extra assistance. (*K Brzoza*)

means that the Soviet submarine fleets will have deployed out from their bases prior to the outbreak of hostilities, and thus NATO's advantage of being able to block the Iceland-UK gap with ASW forces is to a certain degree negated. The alternative being of course, for the West to start the war by attacking the Soviet submarines as they initially try to deploy out into the Atlantic from their Northern bases.

Either way, the prospects are not particularly heartwarming, although the requirement that the Soviets must presage their invasion by deploying their Northern fleet will at least give the West some advance warning of their intentions. But, unfortunately, they would not in practice need to do this until after they had initiated hostilities in Europe and, if based upon this warning alone, the reinforcement convoy would be late. Too late.

In the final analysis therefore the West must not only be politically prepared to make the first move, but must also have contingency plans to fight the European reinforcement through a pre-deployed Soviet fleet, remembering that any losses have already been exacerbated by a lack of sufficient ships of the right type. The defence of those remaining and still reducing maritime assets the West possesses therefore assumes an altogether more important significance.

Defending diminished assets

From the point of view of the merchantman there are two primary means of increasing defence potential. These are improved organisation of sailings to maximise the defence potential of the numerically reduced naval units and, secondly, the obvious route of increasing the provision of defence systems by increasing the quality and quantity of escort vessels and/or by providing the merchant vessels with their own intrinsic self defence systems. Of the second path, the requirement for additional escorts, AEW and maritime aviation, is well documented in just about every free-world naval publication and, although highly relevant to the survival of merchant shipping, we shall not concentrate on that aspect here.

General cargo or break/bulk, dry bulk vessels such as the *Zak* (formerly P&O's *Strathtay*) are no longer being built in sufficient numbers to support NATO's future commitments. (*A J Ambrose*)

Gone nowadays is the theory that NATO would hold up all Atlantic shipping in the early stages, thereby prompting a confrontation of opposing naval forces prior to the sailing of any convoys. The urgency of the European reinforcement would dictate otherwise. That being the case, one must proceed on the premise that the reinforcement sailings must fight themselves across in an extremely hostile environment. All the way.

As for the organisation of sailings, recent years have shown a marked tendency to swing away from the almost traditional convoy system for a number of reasons, in order to try to offer better protection for the merchant ships with the limited naval resources available. One of the problems associated with the concept of large convoys nowadays is the prospect of a centre-convoy strike with a large nuclear weapon possibly approaching the Megaton range. However, the convoy as such is very far from dead, the concept has simply been readjusted to take modern conditions into account.

Of the options available to the naval planners, there

Deep-sea ro-ro vessels such as P&O's *Norsea* typically operate at speeds averaging 17 knots. While these types represent some of NATO's most useful sealift assets, their speed advantage over earlier types means that they must slow down when working in convoy, to allow the ASW escort's sonars to be operated to their best effect. (*Drawing: Michael J Ambrose*)

Scale: 1:1200

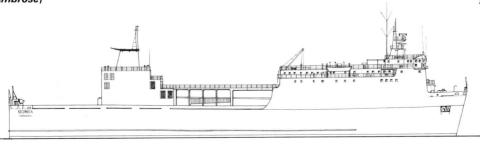

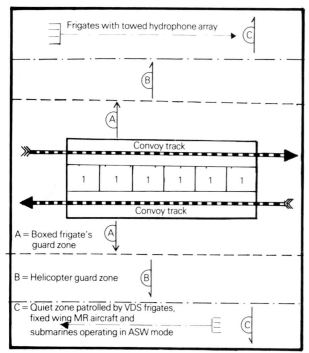

Fig 1. Defended lane concept.

Firstly, it will limit the overall size of the convoy thus reducing the size of the target. Secondly, even the smaller convoy must spread out a lot more to nullify the effects of even the smaller kiloton-range warheads of the Soviet anti-ship missiles. As for the speed disadvantage, ships with speeds in excess of 15 knots for example may be forced to either slow down to convoy speed, or sail independently.

Unprotected independent sailings are unlikely to arrive.

In an attempt to remove some of these problems, the patrolled sea lane was re-adopted. Its failure was primarily due to the fact that the 'enemy' can choose his own position to enter conflict when engaged in hit and run activity, whereas the limited number of escorts must be spread over a vast area thus reducing their likelihood of being in the right place at the right time. A further improvement later materialised however, known as the defended sea lane. This concept which is fairly new, embodies all the advantages of the patrolled sea lane yet has few of the disadvantages, and allows forms of convoy and high speed lone sailings to be retained, albeit in a modified form.

The basic principal of the defended sea lane is shown in the adjacent Fig 1. It consists of the establishment of two sea lanes, each approximately five miles wide, running parallel to each other, but separated by a further five mile wide corridor. Thus, the area is 15 miles across in total. In one outside lane the merchant ships travel east–west while in the other outside lane they travel west–east. The centre lane is divided into boxes, each five miles wide by five miles long. In each of these boxes sits one ASW frigate such as a USN 'Knox' class ocean escort, or an RN Type 22 frigate for example. These frigates are responsible for ASW effort in an area approx 35 miles wide from the centre-point of their respective boxes. Using listening devices, including active sonars, they would sweep out as far as ten miles either side of the two defended lanes, and would usually be assisted by their organic ASW helicopter(s) in these duties.

The ASW frigates would patrol their own boxes at cruise speed (around 8/14 knots) and would not move

The 'boxed' frigates would be units such as the US Navy's USS *Alwyn*, a 'Knox' class ocean escort which participated in 'Ocean Safari'. (*A J Ambrose*)

are five primary sailing organisation concepts to choose from. They are:

1. Conventional convoys
2. Independant sailing
3. Patrolled sea lane
4. Defended sea lane
5. Generated chaos.

Of these systems, all have their advantages and all have their disadvantages. Probably the system with the most of the latter is item 3, the patrolled sea lane. This has been tried on a number of occasions, both recent and historical, and has largely been regarded as a failure.

As already stated, the large conventional convoy has many inherent problems, not least of which is its speed. Modern merchant vessels typically travel faster than equivalent Second World War types, an average speed today being somewhere between 16 and 17 knots. This represents an advantage over Second World War vessels but, unfortunately, it also detracts from the value of the convoy, as at this speed the convoy escort's principal passive sonar devices are in a marginal area of usefulness due to turbulence and noise created by the ships themselves. Furthermore, the sight of a big convoy could well act as an invitation to the Soviets to hit this extremely valuable target with strategic nuclear weapons rather than with tactical ones. Thus the convoy's existence on a large scale could incite the lowering of the nuclear threshold.

These two factors, therefore, regulate the convoy to some extent. The nuclear factor will have two effects.

Royal Navy 'boxed' frigates could include Type 22 ASW frigates such as HMS *Battleaxe*. However, the capability of these particular vessels is such that they might prove to be more usefully employed further north in the Iceland-UK gap. (*FotoFlite, Ashford*)

Hopefully, US Navy carrier battle groups would be moving in and out of the lane system from time to time, bringing with them their surface escorts and air wings which would ensure that few, if any, enemy aircraft were able to penetrate the convoy's defence screen. In this view, an RA-5C Vigilante is launched from the waist catapult of the USS *Nimitz* while the cruiser USS *California* cruises off to port. (*United States Navy*)

along with the convoy. Like this, they are able to maintain their ASW detection gear in operation at all times which would not be the case if they were moving

Alternate boxes could contain ASW units with some measure of area air-defence against high-flying reconaissance aircraft. The Type 42 DDGs such as HMS *Glasgow* were designed for this task and have ideal reactive abilities to counter threatening submarines too. Use in this area of operations rather than in the Choke-gap further north, would also reduce this types vulnerability to close air attack occasioned by their lack of effective point-defence systems. (*FotoFlite, Ashford*)

at convoy speed. These vessels would also provide some level of area or point-defence against air or missile attack on both themselves and the convoys, depending upon both the type and sophistication of their equipment and, of course, the direction of threat materialisation. Alternate boxes would probably deploy frigates with area air-defence missile systems – assuming their availability of course.

Moving further out from the centre of the lane system, the various ASW helicopters and some types of MR aircraft would be working. They would provide a further screen to the convoy and be assisted by any available close-in screen of surface ASW vessels.

Outside this area, a further zone of approx 60 miles width is created (dependant upon water conditions). This is known as the 'Quiet Zone'. In this zone friendly submarines, fixed wing ASW aircraft and frigates towing trailed hydrophone arrays would maintain an almost silent listening watch using entirely passive devices, until a contact is established whereafter active systems would be switched on. In this area, unfriendly submarines would need to make noise while working into their attack positions and are thus at the most vulnerable position in their attack-cycle.

Inside this zone, closer to the convoys, would be the other surface units including base vessels for the aircraft, such as the British 'Invincible' class ASW cruisers and, hopefully, US and French carrier battle groups. The former units would probably stay with the screen at all times, but the carrier strike forces would likely work in and out of the screen as required, providing (when they are there) a good measure of

It is conceivable that certain of the US Navy's amphibious assault units could be used in the 'Sea control Ship' role. In the early 1970s the USS *Guam,* sister to the *Inchon* (shown), was converted for sea control escort duties, but reverted to an LPH in 1974. Several of this class have also operated RH-53 Sea Stallion minesweeping helicopters – another aspect of merchant ship defence which needs greater study. (*SkyFotos*)

area air defence.

Along with the 'sea control ships' such as *Invincible* would be the area air defence frigates, cruisers, and destroyers attached to the force, aided from time to time by the appearance of a carrier strike group with its own screen vessels.

All told, this defended lane concept removes some of the disadvantages of the traditional convoy in that the escorts can work at speed which suits them best, while the merchant ships are free to be grouped into their own convoys relative to the ship's individual speeds and, if necessary, can even be sailed independently along the protected lane. Nevertheless, there are still disadvantages. The biggest of these is that defended sea lanes cannot be provided over the total width of the Atlantic as there simply are not sufficient escorts to provide the required level of screen. Therefore, the concept while apparently most effective, can only be used over stretches of water where the traffic is heaviest, meaning that at the end of each such section, ships either revert to independant sailing in patrolled areas or to the more traditional escorted small convoys.

Ocean Safari 83

This relatively new concept was tried out between 7 and 17 June 1983 in a major multi-national exercise called 'Ocean Safari'. Sixteen merchant ships were

chartered and split into two groups of eight ships. The first group, designated *Convoy FALPDEM –01* and *PDELISM -01* was assembled at Falmouth in SW England and consisted of the mechant ships *Berge Adria* (223,900 dwt), *Resknes* (6,250 dwt) and *Korsnes* (4,542 dwt) from Norway; *Macedonian Reefer* (12,000 dwt) from Greece; *Wejadia* (7,900 dwt) from West Germany and *Ringes* (5,790 dwt), *Eastern Maid* (26,000 dwt) and *Servia* (12,182 dwt) from the United Kingdom.

The other (northbound) convoy, *LISPDEM -01* and *PDEFALM -01*, was assembled at Lisbon, Portugal, and consisted of: *Radnes* (5,750 dwt), *OBO Princess* (127,050 dwt) and *Nortranse Elma* (118,733 dwt) from Norway; *Mercandian Admiral* and *Mercandian Ambassador* (7,200 dwt) from Denmark; and *Rollnes* (5,789 dwt), *Bothia* and *Scythia* (12,182 dwt) from the United Kingdom.

All together, over 90 NATO and French vessels took part including no less than four aircraft carriers, the French *Foch*, the Royal Navy's *Hermes* and *Illustrious*, and the US Navy's *John F. Kennedy*. In addition, land-based aircraft also played a major part bringing the total of aircraft deployed during the exercise to more than 300. Included in this total were two new entrants to the scene in the shape of two of NATO's new fleet of Boeing E-3A Sentry AWACS aircraft operating from RAF St. Mawgan in South-West England.

The exercise was designed to protect merchant shipping from a variety of threats including submarine, missile, aircraft and mine warfare. Forces taking part

Fig 2. Sketch map showing 'Ocean Safari 83' tracks.

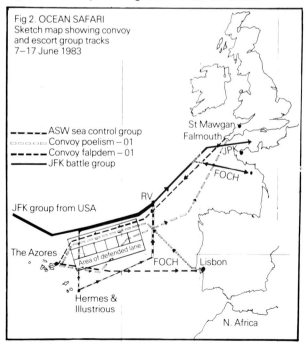

The Norwegian *Resknes* was one of 16 merchant vessels participating in 'Ocean Safari'. Worthy of note was that these two 8-ship convoys each comprised a similar total tonnage to that of a typical 20+ ship convoy of the Second World War. (*FotoFlite, Ashford*)

were drawn from Belgium, Canada, West Germany, the Netherlands, Norway, Portugal, the United Kingdom, and the United States of America. France, although not a member of NATO's military structure, also provided substantial participation.

The convoys were sailed from Falmouth and Lisbon to the Azores and then on to Lisbon and Falmouth respectively, as shown in Fig 2.

Convoy *FALPDEM -01* was escorted out of Falmouth by the multi-national NATO permanent force STANAVFORLANT (Standing Naval Force Atlantic) which consisted of eight frigates and destroyers, while the Royal Netherlands Navy and the Portuguese Navy provided the escort for convoy

Both HMS *Illustrious* (shown) and HMS *Hermes* took part in 'Ocean Safari'. It does not, however, seem likely that both these ships would be engaged in these duties during a conflict. Somebody would need to be working the ASW barrier between Greenland and the UK. (*FotoFlite, Ashford*)

The USS *John F. Kennedy* provided long-range air defence, interdiction strikes in France and Scotland, and 24-hour AEW coverage for the convoys. (*A J Ambrose*)

LISPDEM -01. These convoys were conventional in the sense that they were escorted. Between the Iberian peninsula and the Azores however, both convoys went through an established 'defended sea lane' while the carrier strike groups, approaching from the west, skirted the northern side of the zone providing area air defence and enhanced ASW screening. Simultaneously, the carrier's strike squadrons launched simulated projection attacks to areas in France and the UK.

From the interoperability point of view, the exercise was a resounding success, with all the different nations involved working well together even with the problems of language and non-standardisation of equipment. The convoys were subjected to attacks from 12 'orange' (friendly enemy) submarines, three 'orange' surface action groups, and 'orange' strike aircraft operating from Portugal, the Azores, France, and UK bases. To liven things up a little, 'red' (or not so friendly enemy)

Nimrod MR aircraft operated reconnaissance flights well out into the Atlantic during 'Ocean Safari' from their base at St. Mawgan. The Nimrod MR is among the most sophisticated MR aircraft in the world, able to detect the presence of a submarine's periscope at ranges in excess of the range of any ship's radars. (*A J Ambrose*)

forces also appeared on the screen, these including two Soviet submarines as well as the usual gathering of AGI trawlers. It was believed however, that one of these 'red' submarines stumbled into the exercise area while on a positioning shuttle from the Med to the Northern Fleet base near Murmansk. Tailing his surface escort in the shape of a Soviet merchant vessel, the Soviet submarine commander must have been quite

surprised about all the attention he received from a hawk-eyed RAF Nimrod pilot who saw his periscope emerge from behind the cargo vessel. With no further ado the Nimrod pilot turned, located the 'red' unit, and dropped a simulated depth charge on it which emits a 'pinging' sound which the submarine can hear and, for the purposes of the exercise, indicates '*if this had been for real, pal, you would be a liquidated unit!*'

Several Soviet aircraft also turned up to watch and were suitably intercepted by F-14 Tomcats from the USS *John F. Kennedy*, and on at least one occasion a Soviet reconnaissance aircraft was intercepted simultaneously by no less than three aircraft from three different carriers from three different countries, the USA, UK and France. Such multi-national determination will obviously not go un-noticed in the Kremlin where present policy is to try to split the friendship and co-operation of NATO's partners in a 'divide and conquer' plan.

Long-range air defence of the 'Ocean Safari' convoys was provided by F-14 Tomcat aircraft aboard the USS *John F. Kennedy*, and Super Etendards aboard the *Foch*. (*A J Ambrose & Dassault-Bréguet*)

During 'Ocean Safari', and indeed at most other times, Soviet Tu-20 Bear reconnaissance aircraft range far out into the Atlantic in search of western merchant and naval units. In a conflict, they would provide 'bridge guidance' for Soviet anti-ship missiles. Naturally, they must be intercepted prior to this taking place. In this view, taken during 'Ocean Safari' in June 1983, a Soviet Bear is intercepted by no less than three NATO aircraft: A Sea Harrier, a F-14 Tomcat from the *John F. Kennedy*, and the third which was taking this photograph. (*Courtesy Flag Officer Naval Air Command*)

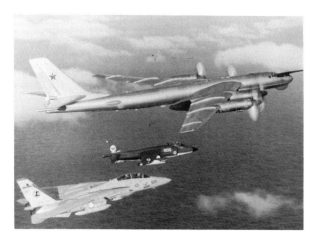

Comments on the effectiveness of the convoy's air defence screen seemed to differ depending upon which Admiral one questioned. A consensus of opinion showed however that no 'orange' (or 'red') aircraft approached within 70 miles of the major surface group without having been intercepted. In fact, most were intercepted at over 500 miles out, while some of the opposition were intercepted as far as 1,000 miles from the convoy! Good news that, for a merchant seaman. But one wonders how many convoys will be gifted with a four aircraft carrier escort screen. Probably not many.

As reported above, 'Ocean Safari' also benefitted from the appearance of an Airborne Early Warning (AEW) screen in the shape of the two NATO E-3A Sentry AWACS, and RAF Shackleton AEW aircraft. In addition, four E-2 Hawkeye AEW aircraft were deployed from USS *John F. Kennedy*, and at least one of these was airborne for the whole ten days of the exercise. It is worthy of note therefore, that the

The Royal Air Force's front line of defence in the AEW game is still the ageing Shackleton, which handled AEW for the first two days of the exercise. They are due to be replaced within the near future by the Nimrod AEW variant. (*A J Ambrose*)

On the third day of the exercise, two of NATO's six new E-3A Sentry AEW aircraft arrived on the scene, having flown into St Mawgan from their NATO base at Geilenkirchen, Germany. These six new aircraft are crewed by a multi-national team drawn from NATO member countries and are backed up by the USAF's own E-3As and RAF Shackleton/Nimrods. (*Courtesy Chris Sheppard, MoD/RAF*)

convoys suffered no major losses to aircraft as the AEW aircraft were able to provide interception vectors in good time, and that this is in strict contrast to the tragic events of the Falklands conflict as reported in the last edition of this Review.

The ASW defences gave few new answers in the conventional convoy sections of the passage, the faster speeds and sophisticated weaponry of the modern submarine still providing their problems to the convoy commander. The interoperability of multi-national units in NATO's STANAVFORLANT and the Dutch/Portuguese escort squadrons was considerably improved on previous exercises however, and if any singular point of success stands out in *Ocean Safari* as a whole, then multi-national interoperability was surely it. As Rear-Admiral Flatley (Commander of the Carrier Strike Force) put it, 'everything just dropped into place'.

From the merchant ship's point of view the defended sea lane did on this occasion prove to be extremely effective. Probably the greatest advantages are that the concept allows the ASW forces to work at their most effective speed while the merchant vessels can travel at theirs. Additionally, the concept has the effect of grouping all the potential 'targets' into one defended area, thus negating to a large degree the hostile unit's ability to choose his own point of attack. The concentration of all the friendly units means that the enemy must strike at a position chosen by NATO (ie within the sea lanes), thus removing some of the enemy's initiative while increasing NATO's.

Nevertheless, as previously stated NATO has insufficient ASW and maritime-air assets to provide a protected sea lane over all the sea lines of communication that must be kept intact, and so escorted convoys and lone unescorted sailings are still likely to be necessary.

Generated chaos

In the 'generated chaos' concept, patrolled sea lanes, defended sea lanes, lone sailings, hunter-killer groups, and convoys are all used together to provide an intricate weave of utter chaos with which to confront the enemy. An example of how this might work is shown in Fig 3.

The principle of the concept is to provide the greatest level of protection over the widest possible area with the finite resources available. This would probably involve defended sea lanes in areas where the most intensive traffic flow was apparent and where the greatest level of defence was necessary. These areas would most likely be mid-ocean and areas adjacent to South-Western Europe in the intense-traffic corridors off Gibraltar, etc. One can picture, for example, the largest of these protected lanes starting about 1,000 miles east of the USA's Eastern Seaboard, and continuing across the Atlantic skirting well north of the Azores and terminating about 500 miles north-east of Cape Finisterre. This lane would therefore handle much of the traffic between the USA, Europe and the entrance to the Mediterranean.

Once the traffic had left the defended lane other styles of defence must therefore be established. Of necessity, these defence postures would take a wide variety of forms. One of these forms of protection might initially be land-based air power but obviously the restriction that the effectiveness of land-based aircraft diminishes in proportion to the increases in distance from their bases must be applied.

The maximum effective area covered in this manner would be restricted due to the respective aircraft's loiter time ability, which in turn would indicate a screen coverage capability extending to at most 1,000

The AEW SeaKing is fitted with the Searchwater Radar which was originally designed and conceived as a maritime reconnaissance radar. In the SeaKing it has been adapted to the AEW role, and although able to provide more power than the earlier Gannet AEW radars, there is some doubt over Searchwater's ability to locate and track high-speed airborne targets such as missiles. (*Flag Officer Naval Air Command*)

miles from the coast, sufficient, perhaps, to stretch as far as the protected lane. Within this general area ships might be sailed either independently or in small groups, while both aircraft and hunter-killer surface and sub-surface groups offered a general area coverage, the diesel-electric patrol submarine figuring highly in this regard.

The idea of generated chaos is to get the Soviet submarine to expose himself 'above the layer' such as the chap has done in this view. Once forced to 'take a look', any VDS-towed-array-hydrophone frigate or any MR aircraft in the vacinity would be onto the offender in minutes. (*MoD RAF*)

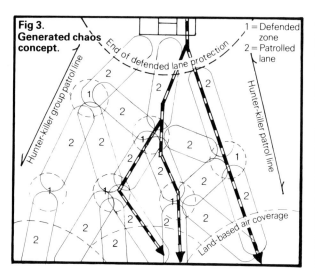

Fig 3. Generated chaos concept.

1 = Defended zone
2 = Patrolled lane

Frigates such as the 'Garcia' class escort USS *Voge* would work small protected zones. They would sweep up and down the patrolled lanes from time to time, either themselves, or with their helicopters. This particular view shows a Sikorsky Sea Lion about to refuel from the *Voge* while remaining airborne. Normally this class operate an SH-2D LAMPS (Light Airborne Multi-Purpose System) helicopter. (*Sikorsky*)

At the up-threat end of the sea lane, this patrolled area policy may not be sufficient, and thus, on leaving the protected lane, escorted convoys may again be required. One idea to improve coverage in this regard however is the adoption of a series of protected zones linked by a series of patrolled lanes (see Fig 3). The protected zones would be constantly changing position with the patrolled lanes moving across, so to speak, to keep the zones connected. In each of the protected zones an ASW frigate or group would be sited, which would provide cover to ships joining and leaving the zone, while additional ASW units, both air and surface, would provide regular sweeps up and down the lanes from one zone to another. The distance apart of the zones would vary depending on the ASW units sensors, number of helicopters, weapons and prevailing water conditions, and on the level of lane-patrol activity that can be provided by other units.

Up these patrolled lanes would travel a combination of fast independents such as the 20/25 knot container ships and passenger-type vessels, escorted convoys travelling somewhat slower and, possibly, non-escorted convoys consisting of merchant ships with similar speed characteristics, some vessels of which provided with a level of defensive armaments ranging from containerised missile systems, ARAPAHO ASW fitments and even Sea Harrier ski-jumps to just simple AA guns in the 20/40 mm range.

To enhance this system yet further, the regular appearance in these lanes of naval units working as ASW groups and occasional skirting of the lanes by surface action and carrier strike groups while in transit from one area to another would also provide the enemy with a headache or two, and the total confusion of sub-surface sound patterns, a constantly changing route network, unpredictable sailings and the generally complex nature of operations (which of course would of necessity be computer-directed to provide the greatest screen available in any given area at any one time) would combine to provide the attacker with an appearance of utter chaos. As a result, the said submariner would have to work into what he feels is his best attack position only to find that these awkward movements have forced him to either pop his head, periscope, aerial or other item above 'the layer' and create so much noise into the bargain that he has given his position away to either the ASW frigate moving quietly about his zone with his Variable Depth Towed Array passive sonar, or to a hawk-eyed MR aircraft or helicopter hovering above.

Arming the merchantmen

There seems to be little room for argument that the present round of interest in arming merchant ships was given considerable impetus by the loss of one vessel: *Atlantic Conveyor*. There is, however, a great deal of argument about the financial matters associated with merchant ship defences. And both sides have really got strong points to make.

It is unlikely that any merchant vessel could deal with the threat posed by a Soviet surface action group which managed to break-out into the Atlantic. This Soviet 'Krivak' class FFG is more heavily armed than many western naval vessels, let alone armed merchantmen! (*FotoFlite, Ashford*)

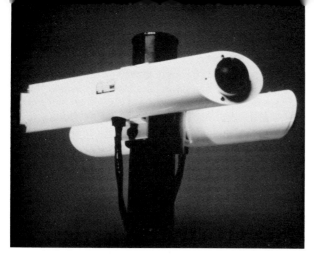

The shipboard installation of Matilda is quick and relatively simple. It consists of these three units: the detector horn, the alarm warning unit and the information processing package. (*MEL*)

On the one hand, it is argued that the cost of arming a merchant vessel would go a long way towards providing another escort, be it frigate, helicopter, or MR patrol aircraft. Furthermore, the merchant ship's armaments would need to be operated by naval crews who would be better employed elsewhere, or perhaps more to the point, might need to be drawn from existing units thus lowering the effectiveness of standing naval forces. Both these arguments have a large element of truth.

On the other hand, it is said that a container ship can be equipped with a complete range of modern weapons systems for about one third the cost of an equivalent naval unit (albeit that the container ship may be only one third as effective as the purpose-built naval vessel). Another point is that for the same capital outlay the armaments can be in three times as many places simultaneously in order to equate marginally better with the quantitive superiority of the aggressor.

In practice, however, armed merchant vessels could be extremely useful, as indeed they have been in the past. Obviously, the problem is one of finance: in an ideal world additional funds would be available for both extra escorts and merchant ship armaments. However, in an ideal world there would be no need for either. The answer therefore is one of equating the cost-effectiveness of arming merchant vessels with the cost-effectiveness of other systems upon which the same funds might be spent.

For aggressive purposes, the naval vessel will obviously score highest. There can be no doubt that the commercial designs of merchant ships do not lend themselves to hunter-killer operations. Likewise, the complexity of command and control equipment is such that it could not be rapidly fitted to a merchant ship in time of war. Furthermore, the usefulness of an armed merchant ship in dealing with a threatening surface action group is also neglibible – the merchant ship lacks reaction ability as the surface threat must be dealt with as far away from the merchant convoy as is possible. One could not, for example, divert an armed merchant ship up-threat from a convoy to provide an effective screen. Only the purpose-built naval vessel is suitable for this task, although armed merchant vessels such as the *Rawalpindi* and *Jervis Bay* have done precisely that in the past.

In practice therefore the field of convoy defence open to the merchant ship is thus limited to defence against incoming missiles, aircraft and torpedoes, and to acting as platforms for naval aircraft, be they fixed-wing or rotary.

The business end of MEL's small ship Matilda/Protean passive decoy system, is the launcher package which can fire either chaff or infra-red flares. (*MEL*)

Artist's impression of an RFA 'Fort' class supply ship fitted with BAe's containerised SeaWolf point-defence anti-missile system. (*BAe Dynamics*)

The next limitation imposed however is that of the merchant ship's need to carry commercial cargoes at economical rates during peace time. This dictates that the ship is built to commercial standards without expensive built-in features of naval orientation. As such, this imposes the requirement that any naval equipment must be quickly and easily retro-fitted and removed as necessary. By extension this once again limits the specific types of defensive equipment available. Nevertheless, the miniturisation and containerisation of certain weapons systems, coupled to the large merchant ship's useful role as a helicopter platform, does present us with a list of varied options.

Of the concepts presently envisaged, some require that the merchant ship is adapted during peace time (preferably when under construction) to accept weapons systems strategically stockpiled at various Western ports which are simply bolted-on when the tension rises. They would not, of course, carry these weapons during peace time, but would be adapted to allow speedy fitment when necessary.

The principals options envisaged in ascending scale of complexity are:

Level 1: *Purely passive measures.* This concept of self-defence includes the fitment of infra-red and Chaff decoy rockets such as the Plessey *Shield* system, and MEL's *MATILDA/PROTEAN* system to provide defence against incoming infra-red or radar-guided missiles. This effective form of defence has been tried and proven during the Falklands conflict. During 1983, 11 British RFA vessels have been newly fitted with the Plessey *Shield* derivative of this concept.

Also available under this level of defence are various towed decoys which transmit an underwater sound pattern upon which hostile torpedoes are invited to home, thus decoying them away from the ship itself. But the above systems also have the inherent advantage

in that being passive they do not promote the legal status of the merchant vessel to that of a warship, thus allowing the merchantman to enter foreign/neutral ports without fear of internment. They are thus politically quite acceptable. They are also (relatively) cheap to provide, and if manufactured in sufficient quantities could be an extremely cost-effective boost to the merchant fleet's survivability.

Level 2: *Deterrant armaments.* A low-level defensive armament concept, in which ships would be fitted with gun systems such as the 20/40 mm Oerlikon and Bofors types and/or various small-bore weapons. During the Falklands conflict several ships were so armed, and while no great level of aircraft losses were attributable to these weapons, there was a general concensus of opinion that such gunnery was instrumental to both the increased morale of the defenders and the decreased morale of the attackers, in some cases causing attacking aircraft to drop short or miss their targets entirely.

In the North Atlantic scenario this factor would probably be of lesser value, and while it could be useful to fit some vessels with guns on an as-available basis, there seems little justification in manufacturing weapons specifically for this purpose.

Level 3: *DEMS (Defensively Armed Merchant Ships).* A more costly but more effective alternative to Level 2, the DEMS concept envisages the fitment of containerised guided weapons systems to selected high-value targets such as container ships and the larger ro-ro vessels. Particular examples of this nature of armament are fairly numerous, although BAe Dynamics Seawolf anti-missile system is perhaps the most advanced. Other options which have been considered under this general outline include General

A Royal Navy SeaKing has a 'dunk' with her Dunking sonar. The SeaKing is probably the most cost-effective ASW asset the West possesses. (*RNAS Culdrose*)

171

A Wessex helicopter ferries stores to and from Cunard's *Atlantic Causeway* which acted in the ARAPAHO concept as an operating base for the ten SeaKings of No. 825 squadron during the Falklands conflict. (*Flag Officer Naval Air Command*)

Dynamics Vulcan/Phalanx radar-guided Gatling gun, Sea Dart area-defence missile system, containerised Rapier and Sea Sparrow point-defence missile systems, and other radar-guided gunnery systems such as Goalkeeper and Seaguard.

All these systems benefit from the fact that they can be mounted in standard ISO containers and are thus quickly fitted but nevertheless require a sophisticated set of surveillance and target-acquisition radars, magazines, control systems and provision for the necessary operating personnel who would, of necessity, be naval.

As stated, this is a costly concept but an effective one. It would require some peacetime alteration to the merchant vessels to be so fitted, but it would enhance their survivability to a considerable degree. There is every justification for adopting this level for high-value units, initially on the basis of adapting said vessels for possible future fitment if necessary. In addition, a large number of pre-sited weapons containers would then need to be provided. The costs of such systems would however be far lower than the replacement costs of a high-value ship and its cargo.

Level 4: *Aviation capability.* This level of adaption would be intended to provide a merchant vessel with an adequate platform for helicopter (AEW or ASW) operations. Tried and effectively proven to be of high military utility during the Falklands conflict, there can be no reason why many vessels could not be so adapted. A number of new constructions are already fitted with heli-decks for mercantile utility, and there can be little doubt that with governmental assistance at a relatively low level many commercial owners could be presuaded to include this facility in their new buildings. No great complications or costs are involved, and it would save considerable time to have heli-decks already available on a large number of Western merchant vessels.

Co-operation between owners, builders and navies would be required in the design stages, and a small level of governmental subsidy would be needed for this provision. This is an extremely cost-effective option.

Obviously, this factor alone would not alleviate the problem of numerical deficiencies in ASW helicopters. But with the helicopter's cost-effectiveness as an ASW weapon being beyond question, additional new constructions, retention of older units, and a conversion programme to adapt commercial variants during times of conflict, a drastically enhanced ASW effort could be provided freeing some specialist naval vessels to go on the offensive.

Level 5: *ARAPAHO.* Under the ARAPAHO project developed in the United States, suitable large merchant container ships and Con-ro vessels are adapted to operate as specialist ASW escort cruisers. With the required level of adaption necessary, such vessels would need identification and fairly major modifications sometime prior to the expected outbreak of hostilities. During 1983 the container ship *Astronomer* was chartered by the British MoD and converted for this role as the RFA *Reliant*. Trials were also undertaken on the US container ship *Export Leader*.

The concept of this operation is that suitable vessels are removed from commercial service, adapted, and then returned to their normal trades. In the event of conflict, these ships are then called up and hastily fitted with their pre-sited ARAPAHO equipment. Typically, it is envisaged that such ships would operate between six and ten Sea King helicopters, or equivalent types.

Much use of this general concept was made during the Falklands, where *Atlantic Causeway* embarked ten Sea Kings of the Royal Navy's 825 Squadron. Although not operating under the full ARAPAHO concept, these operations proved most effective nonetheless, and experience gained at that time has most certainly advanced this project to a considerable degree.

The ARAPAHO's ability to assist in ASW defence of convoys will be a welcome boost to the merchant fleet, although there are still problems as regards a general shortage of the requisite helicopters themselves.

Level 6: *Merchant Aircraft Carriers.* SCADS (Ship's Containerised Air Defence Systems), a British development along the earlier theme of the US ARAPAHO, takes the concept of Shipborne aviation one step further. The availability of the world's only effective operational vector thrust V/STOL aircraft allows the merchant ship to undertake many of the roles normally associated with the conventional aircraft carrier. Under the top-level of the SCADS concept, suitable merchant ships would be adapted either during construction or during a period of commercial idleness so that during time of conflict they would be readily adapted to their SCADS role with the addition of containerised anti-missile systems such as Seawolf, containerised radar and surveillance systems such as the Plessey AWS6 radar, containerised power generator modules, accommodation modules, magazine, fuel, and a variety of other supply modules and finally, a containerised version of Fairey Engineering's Medium Girder Bridge

(MGB) which would fold out across the tops of the ship's containers to provide a full 450-ft long flight deck and ski-jump from which both FRS-1 Sea Harriers/AV-8Bs and various AEW and ASW helicopters could operate. Beneath this flight deck and between the containers, would be provided a large hanger area with maintenance facilities for the aircraft. In short, such container ships would provide a comprehensive aviation support facility for operations in support of the convoys.

This top level system-concept is very expensive, but not so expensive as an aircraft carrier/ASW cruiser of the 'Invincible' class for example. Naturally, the SCADS ship would not be so capable or survivable either, but could cost-effectively supplement naval forces to a great degree. During a conflict, these vessels would likely be most cost-effective indeed, but during peace time the prospect of paying for them is a hard nut to swallow.

Politically however there is an attraction to the SCADS proposal. If suitable new constructions (for example the new Cunard/ACL G3 class *Atlantic Conveyor* replacement ship or the 12 new 4,000 TEU + United States Lines ships) are built with the necessary modifications to allow speedy retrofit of SCADS, governments can intervene in a manner which is beneficial not only for reasons of military utility, but beneficial also to the national operator/ owner and the nation's shipbuilding industry. Indeed, as regards the Cunard vessel, it was only government intervention with a subsidy for military utility that prevented the order for this ship going abroad. And

---

Cunard's *Atlantic Causeway* was rapidly converted and was returned to commercial service within a relatively short space of time, thus interrupting her profit-making activities by the smallest extent possible. (*FotoFlite, Ashford*)

The remarkable V/STOL operating envelope of the FRS-1 Sea Harrier makes it a natural subject to advocate the merchant aircraft carrier conversion. (*A J Ambrose*)

important not only from the commercial justification point of view, but also from the strategic asset angle too. Trawlers have considerable uses in the mine countermeasures and sweeping context, a subject not concentrated on in this article, but vitally important nevertheless.

The provision of decoy systems, the inclusion of heli-deck spaces in new constructions and the building up of helicopter reserves could be vital factors in the Western survival, and yet could be undertaken at proportionately low cost in relation to the drastic improvements in the merchant ship's survivability that would be obtained.

High speed in convoy escorts does not seem to be so important today, now that the ASW helicopter is available to negate some of the attacker's previous advantages. Concentration on cheaper escorts such as the Giles-Thornycroft S-90 design could therefore prove extremely useful in making the limited procurement assets go further. Nevertheless, it must be remembered that concentration on one area to the exclusion of others is also a fatal mistake as history has proven on numerous ocassions.

NATO's merchant and naval fleets can not be allowed to fall any further into a non-recoverable position of commercial and strategic inferiority to those of the Warsaw Pact. NATO needs her fleets far more than do the opposition. And while recent events have brought this subject to the fore and thus produced marked but slight improvements in some fields, we can never again allow ourselves the luxury of letting

although there has not, to date, been any official confirmation that the G3 will be a SCADS ship, as time progresses it seems more and more likely that this will be so.

To return to the point of political attraction, however, with the adoption of this process governments have covered the only long-lead items in SCADS procurement, and can therefore leave the expensive part – the ordering of the SCADS stockpile equipment and aircraft – to the next government, or, if they *are* the next government, they can effectively forget about it and hope that public opinion will too.

In this manner, we could well see the appearance of a lot of ships fitted for SCADS (and/or ARAPAHO) but not any new stockpile manufacturing of the requisite missile systems or aircraft, as the money for these would probably find other uses.

In conclusion

In the final analysis, anything that can help NATO to get more of the right type of merchant ships built, and anything that can help in their defence, is useful. This must however be channelled in the right direction so as to make the most effective use of the finite assets available. Particularly attention is needed on the rebuilding of the West's fishing fleets following the Soviet's massive onslaught in this field. This is

The ski-jump used for the SCADS concept conversions is, like the ski-jump idea itself, a relatively simple device which extends the Sea Harrier's operating envelope by a tremendous margin. Built by Fairey Engineering, it is simply the Army's Medium Girder Bridge lifted at one end. It can be folded up into standard ISO containers. (*Fairey Engineering*)

An ideal SCADS carrier is evident in OCL's 'Tokyo Bay' class container ships. With these vessels, Sea Harrier and helicopter operations are separated, and scissor lifts built into the original cargo spaces serve hanger areas below. (*Drawing: Michael J Ambrose*)

our merchant fleets fall under the illusive cloak of the virtual 'applied apathy' of previous years.

The rewards and luxury of security and commercial success do not come free in the maritime field, nor in any other. The ultimate way of winning this or any other conflict is not to allow it to take place in the first instance. To achieve that ultimate result, the West must present credible and *obviously* effective evidence that such conflict would be unacceptable to the opponent. By extension, this *must* mean that the Atlantic Bridge will not collapse under pressure, be it through shortage of ships, lack of defence, or lack of willpower.

To achieve such standing, the West must remove the decay and invest in its own fleets. In short, it must invest in its own future: as without the necessary investment, there can be no rewards to be reaped.

At the end of the day, if the European reinforcement does not arrive, then the Soviet armoured divisions will.

One item of equipment which has been put forward as a possible merchant ship defence weapon is the Rapier missile. During the Falklands conflict it was reported that they did not travel well although they proved most effective in action. The British MoD has been giving some consideration to proposals based on the Rapier and similar missile systems in 1983, with particular interest in their ability to be fitted to the smaller types of ship. (*MoD*)